Better Homes and Gardens®

Annual Recipes 2015

ROASTED GRAPE AND ROSEMARY SCONES
Recipe on page 92

from the editor

At *Better Homes and Gardens*® we combine a longstanding tradition of authority with an eye towards what's fresh and modern in the world of food.

Since I was a kid, we've had a joke in my family that as soon as we put down the fork at one meal, we are already discussing options for the next. So it's no surprise that when I began as the new editor in chief of *Better Homes and Gardens* this year, I gravitated toward the food department—not only for our editors' expertise but also for the wonderful food that flows from our Test Kitchen. It is the oldest media company test kitchen in the country—chopping, sautéing, cooking, and baking for nearly 90 years now. (The photo, right, is in its cookbook-lined library). In our food editors' research and travels throughout the year, they discover fresh ideas to bring to you—and it's the Test Kitchen that helps hone them. This bound collection of all the recipes that appeared in the 2015 issues of the magazine allows you to easily find just what you're looking for. For every recipe, for all the beautiful and delicious food you see on our pages, we are guided by these few principles.

Fresher, healthier ways of eating. The pendulum has shifted from processed foods. The growing number of farmers' markets, home gardens, and CSAs is proof that we want to eat lighter, with lots of fruits and vegetables. Take a look at Farro, Chickpeas and Greens (page 95) and Zucchini Ribbons, Pasta and Arugula (page 202)—both of which go together in 30 minutes or less.

Interesting flavors, accessible ingredients. We all want to broaden our palates with new cuisines, spices, cooking techniques, and flavors, and at the same time gather ingredients that are easy to find. Roasted Grape and Arugula Pizza (page 232) features a new way to use grapes, while Marinated Manchego and Oranges (page 106), combines oranges, tomatoes, olive oil, thyme, and black pepper with that sharp Spanish sheep's milk cheese for a truly enticing flavor combination.

Tried and true, fresh and new. Our roots are in the authority and tradition of the venerable "red plaid"—the *Better Homes and Gardens New Cookbook*, and we continue to look forward. The macaroni and cheese recipe in the 1950s edition of that book calls for cheddar. The recipe in the edition that came out last year—the 16th—calls for Gouda, cheddar, Swiss, and Parmesan, with truffled, squash, and blue cheese variations.

Keep it current, keep it simple. We bring you recipes that are fun, interesting, and on trend. Most importantly, we want you to take pleasure in cooking for family and friends—and to get perfect results every time. Our terrific team of editors and Test Kitchen experts make sure of that. Enjoy!

Stephen Orr, Editor in Chief
Better Homes and Gardens® magazine

Annual Recipes 2015

Test Kitchen

Our seal assures you that every recipe in *Better Homes and Gardens® Annual Recipes 2015* has been tested in the Better Homes and Gardens® Test Kitchen. This means that each recipe is practical and reliable, and it meets our high standards of taste appeal. We guarantee your satisfaction with this book for as long as you own it.

All of us at Meredith Consumer Marketing are dedicated to providing you with information and ideas to enhance your home. We welcome your comments and suggestions. Write to us at: Meredith Consumer Marketing, 1716 Locust St., Des Moines, IA 50309-3023.

Pictured on front cover:
Buttermilk Cardamom Pumpkin Pie, Salted Pecan Bourbon Pumpkin Pie, and Mexican Chocolate Pumpkin Pie recipes on page 279. Pumpkin Pie with Pomegranate Poached Pears, recipe on page 277.

MEREDITH CONSUMER MARKETING
Consumer Marketing Product Director: Heather Sorensen
Consumer Marketing Product Manager: Wendy Merical
Consumer Marketing Billing/Renewal Manager: Tami Beachem
Business Director: Ron Clingman
Senior Production Manager: Al Rodruck

WATERBURY PUBLICATIONS, INC.
Editorial Director: Lisa Kingsley
Associate Editor: Tricia Bergman
Creative Director: Ken Carlson
Associate Design Director: Doug Samuelson
Contributing Copy Editors: Terri Fredrickson, Peg Smith
Contributing Indexer: Mary Williams

BETTER HOMES AND GARDENS® MAGAZINE
Editor in Chief: Stephen Orr
Senior Deputy Editor: Nancy Wall Hopkins

MEREDITH NATIONAL MEDIA GROUP
President: Tom Harty

MEREDITH CORPORATION
Chairman and Chief Executive Officer: Stephen M. Lacy

In Memoriam: E.T. Meredith III (1933–2003)

**OVEN-TO-GRILL BABY
BACK RIBS**
Recipe on page 167

GRILLED CHERRY FLATBREAD
Recipe on page 149

food and fun go hand-in-hand As cooking and sharing meals become even more social, family and guests gather and participate in the kitchen, enthusiastic foodies instantly share photos of scrumptious dishes, and shoppers flock to local farmers markets to sample foods from reliable to unusual to exotic. Trend-setting restaurateurs, cookbook authors, and food bloggers dish out myriad recipes—calling for fresh ingredients, intriguing flavors, and cutting-edge techniques. Now, at your fingertips, *Better Homes and Gardens Annual Recipes 2015* invites you to sample a year's selection of delicious dishes. Whatever the event—weekend brunch, patio party, holiday celebration, or quick-to-the-table weeknight meal—we wish you happy and inspired cooking!

Look for

Monthly Features Let mouthwatering recipes and the stories behind the food inspire you. *Local Milk* blogger Beth Kirby, who adores cakes, shares her recipes for simply elegant confections. Tim Love, chef and owner of six Texas restaurants has a simple philosophy: Think fun, then food, then create a party around a menu. His recipe collection reflects his love of grilling. Sara Forte, *Sprouted Kitchen* author and blogger, reaps her inspiration from food in its purest form. Her goal, with produce-focused recipes, is to bridge the gap between eating well and entertaining. Add to that, what's old becomes new again—with reinvented classic pasta salads, hot pots, and Caesar salad.

Home Cooking Pros share expertise to guide you to success in cooking classes in your own kitchen. Matt Lewis and Renalto Poliafito, of NYC's Baked, tempt with gooey, fudgy brownies. Celebrity Chef Fabio Viviani offers delicious twists on Italian comfort food—juicy, tender meatballs. Lessons continue for making tender, bakery-worthy scones and rich, savory quiche.

New Ways Get creative juices flowing with this collection of recipes that feature a fresh approach using popular ingredients. Roasted grapes complement spicy arugula and creamy brie pizza; Indian-spiced cauliflower tops nachos; asparagus is a beautiful addition to falafel; and grapefruit earns its place as the center of dessert.

Weeknight Delicious At the heart of weeknights is the question "What's for dinner?" These recipes feature fresh produce, lean protein, and easy cooking techniques to get family-friendly dinners on the table pronto.

Recipe Icons Helpful recipe icons indicate whether a recipe is Fast (30 minutes or fewer), Kid Friendly, or Low Fat (see nutrition guidelines on page 335).

**FIRECRACKER
CHOCOLATE CHERRY
COBBLER**
Recipe on page 159

contents

110

228

239

**BOURBON
STRAWBERRY
SMASH**
Recipe on page 184

BOURBON CRANBERRY CHIPPERS
Recipe on page 285

SWEET AND SAVORY GREENS QUICHE

january

food reset Add new recipes to weeknight dinners and try updated classics. Then top off dinner with tangy, tart grapefruit desserts.

16

20

31

weeknight changeups

Rely on four basic one-dish recipes to increase your recipe repertoire by 16. It's easy to do—substitute spices, herbs, condiments, and vegetables to create fresh flavors and diversity to meals that please the whole family.

BASIL CHICKEN WITH SPROUTS, SQUASH, AND APPLES

This collection of recipes provides basics—with methods you can trust. Each chicken rub packs enough flavor to penetrate the surrounding veggies as they cook.

Basil Chicken with Sprouts, Squash, and Apples

PREP 25 min. ROAST 35 min.

- ¼ cup snipped fresh basil
- 1 tsp. finely shredded lemon peel
- ½ tsp. salt
- ¼ tsp. crushed red pepper
- 2½ to 3 lb. meaty chicken pieces (breast halves, cut if large, thighs, and drumsticks)
- 8 oz. Brussels sprouts, trimmed and halved
- 3 Tbsp. olive oil
- 1 lb. delicata squash, halved lengthwise, seeded, and cut into ½-inch slices
- 2 medium cooking apples (Fuji, Gala, or Cortland), cored and cut into 8 wedges each
- 1 lemon, sliced
- 1 tsp. fennel seeds, slightly crushed

1. Preheat oven to 450°F. Line a large shallow baking pan with foil. For rub, in a small bowl combine basil, lemon peel, salt, and crushed red pepper. Pat chicken dry with paper towels. Spread rub evenly over chicken. Arrange on prepared baking pan; add Brussels sprouts. Drizzle with 2 Tbsp. of the oil. Roast, uncovered, 20 minutes, stirring sprouts once.
2. Add squash, apples, lemon, and fennel seeds to pan. Drizzle with remaining oil; toss to coat. Roast 15 minutes more or until chicken is done (170°F for thighs and 165°F for breasts). Makes 4 to 6 servings.
EACH SERVING *619 cal, 39 g fat, 144 mg chol, 419 mg sodium, 33 g carb, 8 g fiber, 39 g pro.*

HONEY-MUSTARD CHICKEN WITH CAULIFLOWER For rub, combine 2 Tbsp. yellow mustard, 1 Tbsp. honey, 2 Tbsp. snipped fresh Italian parsley, ¼ tsp. salt, and ¼ tsp. pepper. Brush over chicken. Substitute 12 oz. cauliflower florets for the squash. Omit the apples, lemon, and fennel seeds.
EACH SERVING *580 cal, 39 g fat, 144 mg chol, 525 mg sodium, 21 g carb, 5 g fiber, 40 g pro.*

SMOKY CHICKEN WITH FINGERLINGS For rub, combine 1 Tbsp. chili powder, 1 Tbsp. packed brown sugar, 1 tsp. smoked paprika, and ½ tsp. salt. Substitute 1 lb. halved fingerling potatoes for squash. Omit lemon and fennel seeds.
EACH SERVING *664 cal, 39 g fat, 144 mg chol, 465 mg sodium, 40 g carb, 5 g fiber, 40 g pro.*

CILANTRO-LIME CHICKEN AND SWEET POTATOES For rub, combine ¼ cup snipped fresh cilantro, 1 tsp. finely shredded lime peel, 2 cloves minced garlic, ½ tsp. salt, and ¼ tsp. crushed red pepper. Substitute 1 lb. cut-up sweet potatoes for squash. Omit lemon and fennel seeds.
EACH SERVING *643 cal, 38 g fat, 144 mg chol, 460 mg sodium, 37 g carb, 7 g fiber, 40 g pro.*

HONEY-MUSTARD CHICKEN WITH CAULIFLOWER

SMOKY CHICKEN WITH FINGERLINGS

CILANTRO-LIME CHICKEN AND SWEET POTATOES

Build a main dish around any flavor of cooked chicken sausage and a rotating cast of greens, beans, and punchy vinegars.

BEANS AND GREENS WITH SAUSAGE AND PEAR

BLACK BEANS, ANDOUILLE, AND COLLARDS

BUTTER BEANS, ITALIAN SAUSAGE, AND CHARD

FAST

Greens, Cannellini Beans, and Andouille Sausage Pan Stew

START TO FINISH 30 min.

- 1 Tbsp. olive oil
- 4 3-oz. cooked chicken andouille sausage links, sliced or cut up
- 1 medium onion, cut into wedges (½ cup)
- 1 15- to 16-oz. can cannellini beans, rinsed and drained
- 2 Tbsp. fresh thyme leaves
- 2 cloves garlic, minced
- 1 14½-oz. can reduced-sodium chicken broth
- 12 cups chopped kale (about 7 oz.)
- 2 Tbsp. balsamic vinegar

1. In a very large skillet heat oil over medium heat. Add sausage and onion wedges; cook and stir 6 to 8 minutes or until browned. Remove from skillet and keep warm.
2. Add beans, thyme, and garlic to the skillet; cook for 1 minute or until heated through. Add broth; bring to boiling. Reduce heat. Boil gently, uncovered, 3 to 4 minutes or until reduced by about half. Gradually add kale, tossing until wilted before adding more. Cook and stir 2 to 3 minutes or until tender. Add sausage mixture and vinegar; heat through. Top with additional thyme. Makes 4 servings.
EACH SERVING *376 cal, 13 g fat, 65 mg chol, 1,012 mg sodium, 38 g carb, 10 g fiber, 31 g pro.*

BEANS AND GREENS WITH SAUSAGE AND PEAR Cook 1 firm medium pear, cored and cut into wedges, with onion and cooked chicken-apple sausage (in place of the andouille). Substitute cider vinegar for the balsamic vinegar and add 1 Tbsp. Dijon-style mustard.
EACH SERVING *330 cal, 15 g fat, 65 mg chol, 1,108 mg sodium, 36 g carb, 9 g fiber, 26 g pro.*

BLACK BEANS, ANDOUILLE, AND COLLARDS Substitute black beans for cannellini beans, cilantro for thyme, collard greens for kale, and lime juice for balsamic vinegar. Top with salted roasted pumpkin seeds (pepitas). Serve with lime wedges.
EACH SERVING *330 cal, 15 g fat, 65 mg chol, 1,072 mg sodium, 28 g carb, 9 g fiber, 26 g pro.*

BUTTER BEANS, ITALIAN SAUSAGE, AND CHARD Substitute sweet Italian chicken sausage for andouille, oregano for thyme, chopped Swiss chard for kale. Substitute butter beans for cannellini beans, adding them with the vinegar. Top with shaved Parmesan cheese.
EACH SERVING *314 cal, 12 g fat, 69 mg chol, 1,311 mg sodium, 24 g carb, 6 g fiber, 25 g pro.*

GREENS, CANNELLINI BEANS, AND ANDOUILLE SAUSAGE PAN STEW

CHEESEBURGER
SHEPHERD'S PIE

Shepherd's pie is a hearty comfort food however you mix it. These variations—plus your own twist—mean the dish will remain a favorite.

KID FRIENDLY

Cheeseburger Shepherd's Pie

PREP 30 min. BAKE 20 min.

- 1½ lb. russet potatoes, peeled and cut up
- ½ cup light sour cream
- ¼ cup milk
- ½ tsp. salt
- 4 oz. shredded cheddar cheese (1 cup)
- 1½ lb. lean ground beef
- ¾ cup chopped red sweet pepper
- ½ cup chopped onion
- 2 cloves garlic, minced
- 1½ cups frozen yellow corn
- 1 cup water
- 1 6-oz. can tomato paste
- ½ cup coarsely chopped dill pickles
- ¼ cup yellow mustard
- 1 tsp. dried oregano, crushed
  Shredded cheddar cheese
  Sliced green onions (optional)
  Crumbled cooked bacon (optional)

1. Preheat oven to 350°F. In a large saucepan cook potatoes in enough lightly salted boiling water to cover for 15 to 20 minutes or until tender; drain. Return potatoes to the saucepan. Mash with a potato masher or beat with an electric mixer on low speed just until light and fluffy. Gradually add sour cream, milk, and salt. Stir in ½ cup of the cheese.
2. Meanwhile, in a skillet cook beef, sweet pepper, onion, and garlic over medium heat until browned, stirring to break up meat. Drain off fat. Stir in corn, water, tomato paste, pickles, mustard, and oregano. Bring to boiling; reduce heat. Simmer, uncovered, 5 minutes. Stir in remaining cheese.

3. Spoon beef mixture into a 2½-qt. baking dish. Spoon mashed potatoes in mounds over filling. Sprinkle with additional cheddar cheese. Bake 20 minutes or until heated through and cheese is melted. If desired, top with sliced green onions and bacon. Makes 6 servings.
EACH SERVING *438 cal, 20 g fat, 101 mg chol, 875 mg sodium, 32 g carb, 4 g fiber, 34 g pro.*

BARBECUE SHEPHERD'S PIE
Substitute sweet potatoes for russet potatoes, and ground pork for ground beef. Eliminate the water and substitute one 14.5-oz. can diced tomatoes for tomato paste. Add 1 cup hot and spicy barbecue sauce to the pork mixture.
EACH SERVING *547 cal, 25 g fat, 98 mg chol, 1,372 mg sodium, 51 g carb, 6 g fiber, 29 g pro.*

CUMIN-SPIKED SHEPHERD'S PIE
Substitute Mexican blend shredded cheddar cheese for cheddar. Eliminate the water and substitute one 14.5-oz. can fire-roasted tomatoes for tomato paste, ½ cup chopped pickled jalapeño peppers for pickles, and stir in 1 Tbsp. ground cumin.
EACH SERVING *420 cal, 19 g fat, 99 mg chol, 823 mg sodium, 31 g carb, 3 g fiber, 32 g pro.*

HOT ITALIAN SHEPHERD'S PIE
Substitute bulk sweet or hot Italian sausage for ground beef, peas for corn, shredded provolone for cheddar. Eliminate the water and substitute ¼ cup chopped pepperoncini peppers for pickles. Top with snipped oil-packed dried tomatoes and/or basil leaves.
EACH SERVING *366 cal, 18 g fat, 50 mg chol, 1,301 mg sodium, 30 g carb, 5 g fiber, 27 g pro.*

BARBECUE SHEPHERD'S PIE

CUMIN-SPIKED SHEPHERD'S PIE

HOT ITALIAN SHEPHERD'S PIE

As parchment packets steam the veggies and shrimp, the food retains bright color and crisp texture. A bit of butter, right before baking, adds just enough richness for the flavors to meld.

SOUTHWESTERN SHRIMP

PROSCIUTTO AND BROCCOLINI SHRIMP

GINGER-SOY SHRIMP

Garden Veggie Shrimp

PREP 30 min.   BAKE 20 min.

- 8 oz. uncooked Israeli couscous
- 4 carrots, cut into thin strips
- 2 large yellow and/or red sweet peppers, cut into thin strips
- 4 green onions, trimmed and halved
- 4 cloves garlic, minced
- 1 lb. fresh or frozen peeled and deveined large shrimp, thawed
- ¼ cup olive oil
- ¼ cup white balsamic vinegar
  Salt and black pepper
- 4 sprigs fresh thyme
- 4 lemon wedges
- 2 Tbsp. butter

1. Cook couscous according to package directions. Preheat oven to 350°F. Spoon couscous on one side of four 15-inch squares of parchment. For each packet layer carrots, sweet peppers, green onions, and garlic next to couscous. Top vegetables with shrimp. Drizzle with oil and vinegar. Sprinkle with salt and black pepper to taste. Top with thyme, lemon wedges, and ½ Tbsp. butter.
2. Fold parchment over shrimp and vegetables; fold in open sides of parchment several times to secure, allowing space for steam to build. Place packets in a single layer on two 15×10×1-inch baking pans. Place pans on separate oven racks. Bake 20 minutes or until shrimp turn opaque. Transfer packets to dinner plates and open carefully. Makes 4 servings.
EACH SERVING *570 cal, 20 g fat, 198 mg chol, 379 mg sodium, 65 g carb, 6 g fiber, 31 g pro.*

SOUTHWESTERN SHRIMP Use 2 carrots and 1 large sweet pepper. Add 1 cup fresh or frozen corn kernels and 1 cup red and/or yellow cherry tomatoes. Substitute lime juice for vinegar, and add 2 tsp. chili powder. Use ¼ cup cilantro leaves in place of thyme. Serve with lime wedges in place of lemon wedges.
EACH SERVING *568 cal, 21 g fat, 198 mg chol, 398 mg sodium, 64 g carb, 7 g fiber, 32 g pro.*

PROSCIUTTO AND BROCCOLINI SHRIMP Substitute 8 oz. Broccolini for carrots and green onions. Increase garlic to 8 cloves. Use oregano in place of the thyme. Sprinkle with crisp-cooked prosciutto or pancetta. Omit lemon wedges.
EACH SERVING *600 cal, 23 g fat, 205 mg chol, 621 mg sodium, 64 g carb, 6 g fiber, 34 g pro.*

GINGER-SOY SHRIMP Use 2 carrots and 1 large sweet pepper. Add 1 cup cut-up bok choy and 1 cup frozen shelled edamame. Omit the oil, vinegar, thyme, and lemon. Add ¼ tsp. minced fresh ginger to each packet and drizzle with 2 Tbsp. reduced-sodium soy sauce and 1 Tbsp. honey.
EACH SERVING *540 cal, 9 g fat, 200 mg chol, 1,471 mg sodium, 78 g carb, 7 g fiber, 37 g pro.*

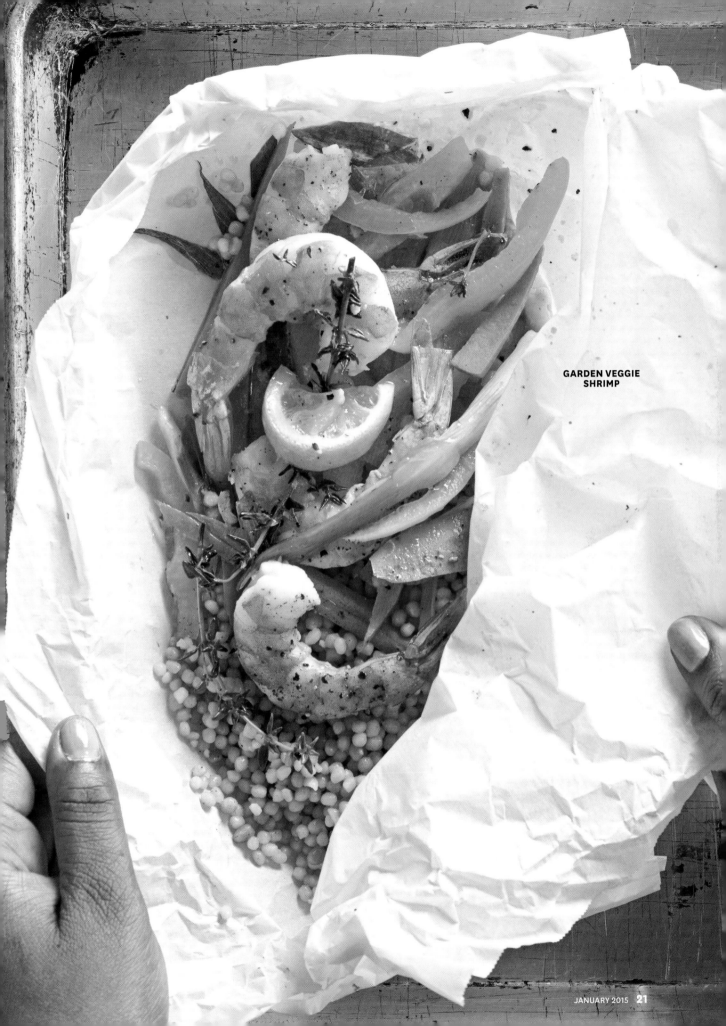

GARDEN VEGGIE SHRIMP

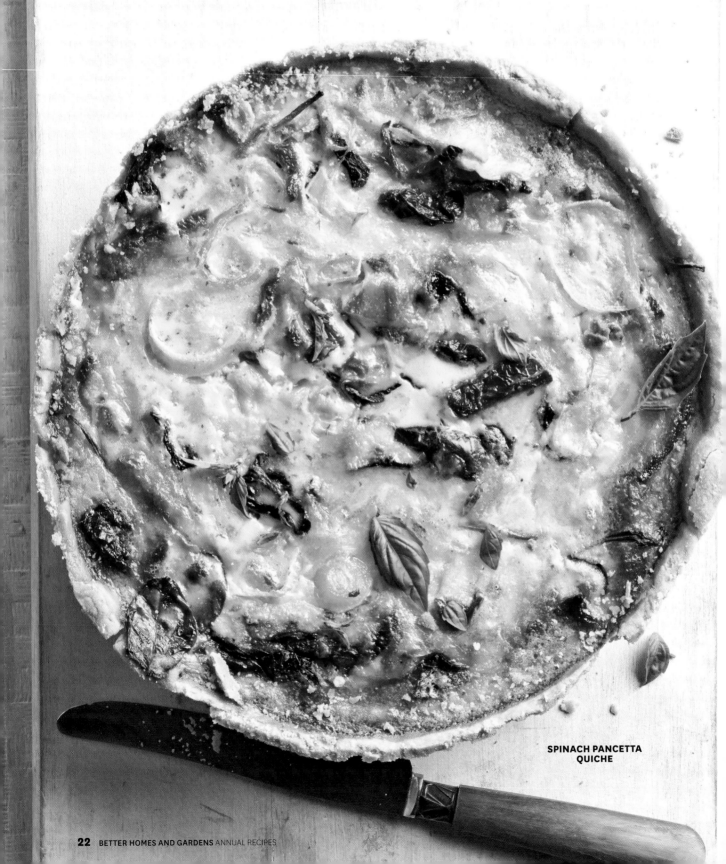

home cooking: *quiche*

Resolve to fall in love with this versatile savory pie all over again.

SPINACH PANCETTA QUICHE

Deep-Dish Pastry Shell

A springform pan is responsible for a seriously deep crust.

PREP 30 min. CHILL 30 min.
FREEZE 20 min. BAKE 30 min.

- 2 cups all-purpose flour
- 1 tsp. salt
- 8 Tbsp. cold unsalted butter, cut into small pieces
- 1 large egg
- ¼ cup cold water

1. In a food processor combine flour and salt. Pulse several times to combine. Add butter; pulse until mixture resembles coarse crumbs. In a small bowl combine egg and the water; add to food processor. Pulse until dough just begins to stick together. Transfer to plastic wrap; shape into a disk. Cover and chill at least 30 minutes.
2. Transfer dough to lightly floured surface. Roll into a 15-inch circle. Carefully roll dough around rolling pin; transfer to a 9×2½-inch springform pan. Gently press into pan. Trim overhanging dough to 1 inch and press firmly against the outer rim. Use trimmings to fill any cracks in pastry. Freeze shell 20 minutes.
3. Preheat oven to 400°F. Place springform pan on a baking sheet. Line pastry shell with a double thickness of foil long enough to extend over the sides. Bake 20 minutes, or until edge of the pastry is lightly browned. Remove foil. Bake 10 to 15 minutes more or until lightly browned on the bottom. Cool completely on baking sheet on a wire rack.

Spinach Pancetta Quiche

Extra light and healthful—thank you, Greek yogurt!—this modern take is a showstopper.

PREP 1 hr. BAKE 1 hr., 20 min.
COOL 40 min.

- 1 recipe Deep-Dish Pastry Shell (left)
- 8 oz. pancetta, diced
- 2 cups thinly sliced onions
- ½ tsp. dried thyme, crushed
- ½ cup oil-packed dried tomatoes, drained and chopped
- 4 cups baby spinach
- 8 oz. Havarti cheese, shredded
- 6 large eggs
- 2 cups plain fat-free Greek yogurt
- 1 cup 2% milk
- ½ tsp. salt
- ¼ tsp. white pepper
- ⅛ tsp. ground nutmeg
  Fresh basil leaves (optional)

1. Prepare Deep-Dish Pastry Shell; set on baking sheet. Preheat oven to 325°F.
2. In a large skillet cook pancetta over medium heat, stirring occasionally, until lightly browned, about 10 minutes. Using a slotted spoon, transfer pancetta to paper towels; drain.
3. Remove all but 2 Tbsp. drippings from skillet. Return to medium heat. Add onions and dried thyme; cook and stir until tender and golden brown, about 20 minutes. Stir in dried tomatoes; cook 1 minute. Add spinach; cook 2 minutes more. Remove from heat. Cool 10 minutes. Stir in pancetta and cheese.
4. For the custard, in a blender combine eggs, Greek yogurt, milk, salt, pepper, and nutmeg. Cover; blend until frothy.
5. Place onion mixture in prebaked pastry shell. Pour custard over. Bake 1 hour 20 minutes to 1½ hours or just until top is lightly browned and custard is set in the center (165°F). Cool in pan 40 minutes. Using a serrated knife, cut pastry shell flush with the top of the pan. Carefully remove springform pan ring. Cut into wedges. Sprinkle with fresh basil, if desired. Makes 10 to 12 servings.
EACH SERVING *455 cal, 27 g fat, 182 mg chol, 728 mg sodium, 28 g carb, 2 g fiber, 22 g pro.*

PRESS IN DOUGH A 1-inch overhang pressed around the top ring prevents shrinking. Use extra dough to fill interior cracks and to keep custard from spilling out of the pastry.

BLEND FILLING A blender makes quick work of the custard mixture and creates a light, fluffy texture. Greek yogurt is a healthful addition with a little tang too.

TRIM AND CUT Let the quiche cool at least 40 minutes for easy slicing. Use a serrated knife to cut away excess crust around the top of the pan.

Call it dinner. A hearty main-dish pie chock-full of chicken and cheddar with a touch of smokiness and heat.

CHIPOTLE CHICKEN QUICHE
Recipe on page 26

**SWEET AND SAVORY
GREENS QUICHE**
Recipe on page 26

KID FRIENDLY

Chipotle Chicken Quiche

Photo on page 24

Serve this flavorful dish with fresh salsa and sprinkle with green onions.
PREP 30 min. BAKE 1 hr., 20 min. COOL 40 min.

- 1 recipe Deep-Dish Pastry Shell (page 23)
- 6 large eggs
- 2 cups plain fat-free Greek yogurt
- 1 cup 2% milk
- 1 tsp. ground cumin
- 1 tsp. chili powder
- ½ tsp. ground chipotle pepper
- ½ tsp. salt
- 2 cups chopped cooked chicken (about 10 oz.)
- 1½ cups shredded cheddar cheese
  Fresh salsa and/or chopped green onions (optional)

1. Prepare Deep-Dish Pastry Shell; set on a baking sheet. Preheat oven to 325°F.
2. For the custard, in a blender combine eggs, yogurt, milk, cumin, chili powder, ground chipotle, and salt. Cover; blend until frothy.
3. Place chicken and cheese in prebaked pastry shell. Pour custard over chicken and cheese. Bake 1 hour 20 minutes to 1½ hours or just until top is lightly browned and custard is set in the center (165°F). Cool in pan on a wire rack 40 minutes. Using a serrated knife, cut the pastry shell flush with the top of the pan. Carefully remove springform pan ring. If desired, top with fresh salsa and/or green onions. Cut into wedges. Makes 10 to 12 servings.

EACH SERVING 385 cal, 21 g fat, 199 mg chol, 563 mg sodium, 23 g carb, 1 g fiber, 25 g pro.

Sweet and Savory Greens Quiche

Photo on page 25

PREP 40 min. BAKE 1 hr., 20 min. COOL 40 min.

- 1 recipe Deep-Dish Pastry Shell (page 23)
- 2 Tbsp. extra-virgin olive oil
- 8 cups Swiss chard, torn
- 1 cup chopped red onion
- 3 cloves garlic, minced
- ¼ cup finely chopped golden raisins
- 3 Tbsp. pine nuts
- 2 tsp. balsamic vinegar
- 6 large eggs
- 2 cups plain fat-free Greek yogurt
- 1 cup 2% milk
- ½ tsp. salt
- ¼ tsp. ground white pepper
- ⅛ tsp. ground nutmeg
- 1 cup shredded provolone cheese
  Snipped fresh herbs (optional)

1. Prepare Deep-Dish Pastry Shell; set on a baking sheet. Preheat oven to 325°F.
2. In a large skillet heat oil over medium-high heat. Add chard, onion, and garlic; cook and stir 4 to 6 minutes or just until chard is wilted. Add raisins and pine nuts; cook and stir 2 minutes. Add vinegar; toss to combine. Remove from heat. Cool 5 minutes.
3. For the custard, in a blender combine eggs, yogurt, milk, salt, pepper, and nutmeg. Cover; blend until frothy.
4. Place chard mixture in prebaked pastry shell. Sprinkle with cheese. Pour custard over. Bake 1 hour 20 minutes to 1½ hours or just until top is lightly browned and custard is set in center (165°F). Cool in pan 40 minutes. Using a serrated knife, cut pastry shell flush with top of pan. Remove pan ring. Cut into wedges. If desired, top with fresh herbs. Makes 10 to 12 servings.

EACH SERVING 369 cal, 21 g fat, 164 mg chol, 591 mg sodium, 29 g carb, 2 g fiber, 17 g pro.

Caramelized Pear and Blue Cheese Quiche

PREP 20 min. BAKE 1 hr., 20 min. COOL 40 min.

- 1 recipe Deep-Dish Pastry Shell (page 23)
- 3 medium firm pears, cored
- 2 Tbsp. unsalted butter, divided
- 1 Tbsp. sugar
- ½ cup crumbled blue cheese
- 6 large eggs
- 2 cups plain fat-free Greek yogurt
- 1 cup 2% milk
- ½ tsp. salt
- ¼ tsp. ground white pepper
- ⅛ tsp. ground nutmeg
  Crumbled blue cheese and/or fresh sage leaves (optional)

1. Prepare Deep-Dish Pastry Shell; set on a baking sheet. Preheat oven to 325°F.
2. Cut 2 of the pears into ½-inch cubes. Cut the remaining pear into thin slices.
3. In a large skillet melt 1 Tbsp. of the butter over medium-high heat. Add cubed pears and sugar. Cook, stirring occasionally, 7 minutes or until lightly browned. Transfer to prebaked pastry shell. Sprinkle with blue cheese. Melt remaining 1 Tbsp. butter in skillet. Add pear slices. Cook, stirring occasionally, 3 to 4 minutes or just until softened.
4. For the custard, in a blender combine eggs, yogurt, milk, salt, pepper, and nutmeg. Cover; blend until frothy.
5. Pour custard over filling in pastry shell. Arrange pear slices on top of custard. Bake 1 hour 20 minutes to 1½ hours or just until top is lightly browned and custard is set in center (165°F). Cool in pan on a wire rack for 40 minutes. Using a serrated knife, cut pastry shell flush with top of pan. Remove pan ring. Cut into wedges. If desired, sprinkle with additional blue cheese and fresh sage leaves. Makes 10 to 12 servings.

EACH SERVING 288 cal, 15 g fat, 141 mg chol, 457 mg sodium, 26 g carb, 2 g fiber, 12 g pro.

CARAMELIZED PEAR AND
BLUE CHEESE QUICHE

new ways with grapefruit

Updated classic desserts show off the sweet side of this winter citrus star.

KID FRIENDLY

Grapefruit and Pear Crumble

PREP 30 min. BAKE 30 min.

Nonstick cooking spray
1 pear, peeled, cored, and thinly sliced
1 Tbsp. all-purpose flour
4 grapefruit, peeled, pith removed, and sliced
2 Tbsp. chia seeds
½ cup packed brown sugar
½ cup quick-cooking rolled oats
¼ cup all-purpose flour
¼ cup flaxseed meal
¼ cup coarsely chopped roasted salted pumpkin seeds (pepitas)
½ cup butter
Sweetened whipped cream or yogurt (optional)

1. Preheat oven to 375°F. Lightly coat a 2-qt. baking dish with cooking spray. Toss pear slices with 1 Tbsp. flour and arrange in the prepared dish. Top pears with half the grapefruit slices and sprinkle with half the chia seeds. Repeat with remaining grapefruit and chia seeds.

2. For crumble, in a medium bowl combine the brown sugar, oats, ¼ cup flour, flaxseed meal, and pumpkin seeds. Cut in butter until mixture starts to cling together. Sprinkle fruit with crumble.

3. Bake 30 minutes or until filling is bubbly and crumble is lightly browned. If desired, serve with whipped cream or yogurt. Makes 6 servings.

PER SERVING *436 cal, 24 g fat, 41 mg chol, 166 mg sodium, 54 g carb, 8 g fiber, 8 g pro.*

Sparkling Grapefruit Sorbet Floats

PREP 20 min. FREEZE 2 hr., 40 min.

4 grapefruit, peeled, pith removed, quartered, and seeded
¾ cup sugar
Vanilla ice cream

Prosecco or sparkling cider, chilled
Grapefruit peel strips (optional)

1. In a blender combine the grapefruit and sugar; cover and blend until smooth. Strain through a fine-mesh sieve. Freeze in a 1½- to 2-qt. ice cream freezer according to manufacturer's directions. Transfer to a freezer container. Cover and freeze at least 2 hours.

2. Serve sorbet with scoops of vanilla ice cream and Prosecco. Top with peel, if desired. Makes 10 servings.

PER SERVING *208 cal, 4 g fat, 25 mg chol, 19 mg sodium, 34 g carb, 2 g fiber, 2 g pro.*

KID FRIENDLY

Upside-Down Grapefruit Cakes

PREP 30 min. BAKE 25 min.
COOL 10 min.

- 2 to 3 grapefruits
- ⅓ cup granulated sugar
- ¼ cup butter, melted
- 1¼ cups all-purpose flour
- 1 cup granulated sugar
- 1 tsp. baking powder
- ¼ tsp. salt
- ¾ cup unrefined coconut oil, melted
- 2 eggs, lightly beaten
- 1 tsp. vanilla bean paste or vanilla
  Mint leaves (optional)
  Powdered sugar (optional)

1. Preheat oven to 400°F. Lightly grease six 8-ounce ramekins or 6-ounce custard cups. Line a shallow baking pan with foil; arrange prepared dishes in pan; set aside. Peel and remove pith and seeds from 1 or 2 grapefruits and cut into ¼-inch slices (you need six slices). Place 1 grapefruit slice into the bottom of each prepared dish. Squeeze ½ cup of juice from the remaining grapefruit; set aside. In a small bowl stir together ⅓ cup sugar and melted butter until nearly smooth; spoon over slices in dishes.

2. In a large bowl combine flour, 1 cup sugar, baking powder, and salt; make a well in the center. In a medium bowl combine the reserved grapefruit juice, oil, eggs, and vanilla. Add juice mixture to flour mixture, stirring to combine. Divide batter among ramekins.

3. Bake 25 to 30 minutes or until a toothpick inserted in centers comes out clean. Cool in ramekins 10 minutes. Loosen sides and invert onto plates. Serve cakes warm, sprinkled with mint and powdered sugar, if desired. Makes 6 servings.

PER SERVING *631 cal, 37 g fat, 32 mg chol, 270 mg sodium, 74 g carb, 2 g fiber, 5 g pro.*

KID FRIENDLY

Tangy Grapefruit Tart

PREP 30 min. BAKE 5 min.
CHILL 4 hr.

1 graham cracker crumb pie shell
1 egg white, lightly beaten
¼ cup coconut, toasted
¾ cup sugar
3 Tbsp. cornstarch
1½ cups grapefruit juice
3 egg yolks
6 Tbsp. butter, cut up
1 drop red food coloring
2 Tbsp. chopped dry-roasted
    pistachio nuts

1. Preheat oven to 400°F. Lightly brush crust with egg white. Bake 5 minutes or until lightly browned; set aside. Spread coconut on a baking sheet; bake 5 to 7 minutes or until golden, stirring once.
2. Meanwhile, in a medium saucepan stir together the sugar and cornstarch. Add juice; cook and stir over medium heat until thickened and bubbly.

Gradually whisk half the mixture into the egg yolks; return to saucepan. Cook and stir constantly until mixture boils gently. Cook and stir for 2 minutes more. Remove from heat. Add butter and stir until melted. Stir in food coloring. Pour filling into crust. Cover loosely with plastic wrap; chill 4 to 6 hours or until set.
3. Sprinkle slices with coconut and pistachios. Makes 10 servings.
PER SERVING *262 cal, 14 g fat, 74 mg chol, 170 mg sodium, 34 g carb, 1 g fiber, 3 g pro.*

DEEP DARK CHOCOLATE BROWNIES

february

temptations Gooey, fudgy, foolproof brownies—worth every scrumptious calorie—and warming hot pots to keep winter at bay. Plus, dinner recipes to satisfy hungry appetites.

38

45

47

SWEET POTATO
PEANUT STEW

hot pots

Think of cold weather as an opportunity to cozy up to nourishing stew. Here are four satisfying one-pot wonders to savor.

LOW FAT

Sweet Potato Peanut Stew

This hearty vegetarian stew holds its own for dinner. Chunks of sweet potato and savory broth make it satisfying.

PREP 20 min. COOK 25 min.

     2 Tbsp. canola oil
 1½ cups chopped red sweet peppers
     1 cup chopped onion
     6 cloves garlic, minced
     2 Tbsp. grated ginger
     1 tsp. ground allspice
   ⅛ tsp. cayenne pepper (optional)
     2 lb. sweet potatoes, peeled and
       chopped
     4 cups vegetable broth
     1 6-oz. can tomato paste
     1 14-oz. can coconut milk
     1 cup peanut butter
       Mango slices (optional)
     1 recipe Toasted Peanut Butter
       Sandwich Bites (optional)

1. Heat canola oil in a 4- to 6-qt. Dutch oven over medium heat. Add red peppers and onion; cook and stir 5 minutes or until vegetables are tender. Add garlic, ginger, allspice and, if desired, cayenne pepper; cook 1 minute. Add potatoes, broth, and tomato paste; bring to boiling. Simmer, covered, 20 minutes.

2. Whisk together coconut milk and peanut butter until smooth. Stir into stew; simmer 5 minutes.

3. If desired, top with mango slices and Toasted Peanut Butter Sandwich Bites. Makes 8 servings.

EACH SERVING *457 cal, 28 g fat, 0 mg chol, 799 mg sodium, 43 g carb, 8 g fiber, 12 g pro.*

Toasted Peanut Butter Sandwich Bites Spread 2 slices of sandwich bread with peanut butter; top each with a slice. Brush both sides of bread with melted butter. Cook sandwiches in a skillet over medium heat until golden brown, turning once. Cut each sandwich into fourths.

Big Basil Shrimp Chowder

Photo on page 36

PREP 25 min. COOK 20 min.

     2 Tbsp. butter
     2 stalks celery, chopped
     1 red onion, chopped
   ½ green pepper, chopped
     2 Tbsp. flour
     2 cups water
   16 oz. clam juice
     2 tsp. Old Bay seasoning
     1 tsp. dried basil
 1½ lb. large shrimp in shells, peeled
   12 oz. frozen corn
     2 Tbsp. capers
     8 oz. mascarpone cheese
       Fresh basil leaves (optional)
     1 recipe Cheesy Polenta (optional)

1. Heat butter in a 4- to 6-qt. Dutch oven over medium heat. Add celery, onion, and green pepper; cook and stir 5 minutes or until tender. Stir in flour. Add the water, clam juice, seasoning, and basil. Bring to boiling; reduce heat.

2. Stir in shrimp, corn, and capers. Cook 2 to 5 minutes or until shrimp are bright pink. Remove from heat; stir in mascarpone.

3. Serve chowder with basil leaves and polenta, if desired. Makes 8 servings.

EACH SERVING *267 cal, 16 g fat, 167 mg chol, 449 mg sodium, 13 g carb, 12 g fiber, 8 g pro.*

Cheesy Polenta In a large saucepan bring 2½ cups water to boiling. In a medium bowl combine 1 cup white or yellow cornmeal, 1 cup cold water, and ½ tsp. salt. Slowly add cornmeal mixture to boiling water, stirring constantly. Cook and stir until boiling. Reduce heat to low. Cook, uncovered, 10 to 15 minutes or until polenta is very thick, stirring occasionally. Add 1 cup shredded sharp cheddar cheese and ½ cup milk; stir until cheese is melted. Stir in 1 Tbsp. snipped fresh basil.

Tender beef is the reward of long simmering. This stew borrows the flavors of a takeout favorite—crispy orange beef.

Orange Teriyaki Beef Stew

Photo on page 37

To cook this stew in a slow cooker, prepare as directed, placing ingredients in a 4-qt. slow cooker. Cover and cook on low for 8 to 9 hours or high for 4 to 4½ hours, then stir in the bok choy leaves.

PREP 30 min. COOK 45 min.

- 2 lb. beef chuck stew meat, cut into 1-inch pieces
- 1 Tbsp. Chinese five-spice powder Salt
- 1 Tbsp. canola oil
- 4 oz. shiitake mushrooms, sliced
- 12 oz. bok choy, sliced crosswise, stems and leaves separated
- 3 cloves garlic, minced
- 1 Tbsp. grated ginger
- ½ tsp. crushed red pepper
- 2 cups lower-sodium beef broth
- 1 cup orange juice
- ½ cup reduced-sodium teriyaki sauce
- 2 naval oranges, peeled and sliced Hot cooked rice (optional)

1. Toss beef with Chinese five-spice powder and salt. Heat canola oil in a 4- to 6-qt. Dutch oven over medium-high heat. Add beef in batches; sear until browned, about 5 minutes. Remove; set aside.
2. Add mushrooms, bok choy stems (reserve green leaves), garlic, ginger, and red pepper; cook and stir 2 minutes. Add broth, orange juice, and teriyaki sauce; bring to boiling, scraping up brown bits from bottom of pan. Return beef to pan. Simmer, covered, 45 minutes or until beef is tender. Add bok choy leaves the last 5 minutes of cooking.
3. Top with orange slices. If desired, serve with hot cooked rice. Makes 8 servings.
EACH SERVING *314 cal, 19 g fat, 99 mg chol, 665 mg sodium, 11 g carb, 1 g fiber, 25 g pro.*

FAST

Chicken Chorizo Gumbo

Everything you love about gumbo with a smoky whisper of paprika. Spanish chorizo replaces andouille, and crisp-tender rings of okra remain at its heart.

PREP 40 min. COOK 45 min.

- 8 oz. Spanish chorizo, thinly sliced
- 12 oz. okra, sliced, or 2 cups frozen cut okra
- 2 stalks celery, chopped
- 1 green pepper, chopped
- 1 onion, chopped
- 3 cloves garlic, minced
- ½ cup canola oil
- ½ cup all-purpose flour
- 4 cups reduced-sodium chicken broth
- 2 14½-oz. cans stewed tomatoes, undrained
- 12 oz. skinless, boneless chicken thighs
- 1 Tbsp. smoked paprika Orange Herbed Rice (optional)

1. In a 4- to 6-qt. Dutch oven cook chorizo over medium heat until bottom of the pan has a thin layer of fat, about 4 minutes. Transfer chorizo to a bowl; reserve drippings in pan.
2. Add okra, celery, green pepper, onion, and garlic to pan; cook 10 minutes or until vegetables are tender, stirring occasionally. Transfer to bowl with chorizo.
3. Add canola oil to pan. Gradually whisk in flour until mixture thickens and turns a medium brown, about 6 minutes. Whisk in broth. Stir in reserved vegetables and chorizo, undrained tomatoes, chicken, and paprika. Bring to boiling; reduce heat. Simmer, uncovered, for 45 minutes, stirring occasionally.
4. Remove chicken from gumbo. Shred with two forks; return to gumbo. Heat through. Serve over Orange-Herbed Rice, if desired. Makes 8 servings.
EACH SERVING *401 cal, 28 g fat, 280 mg chol, 897 sodium, 19 g carb, 4 g fiber, 20 g pro.*
Orange-Herbed Rice Stir 2 Tbsp. snipped fresh Italian parsley, 4 tsp. finely shredded orange peel, and ¼ tsp. cracked black pepper into 4 cups hot cooked white rice.

CHICKEN CHORIZO
GUMBO

home cooking: brownies

These ooey-gooey temptations from Matt Lewis and Renato Poliafito of NYC's Baked are worth every indulgent bite.

KID FRIENDLY

Sweet and Spicy Brownie Bites

Matt and Renato combine freshly grated ginger and fruity, smoky ancho chile powder to create subtle spiciness in this brownie.

PREP 25 min. BAKE 30 min.

1¼ cups all-purpose flour
  2 Tbsp. unsweetened cocoa powder
  4 tsp. ground ancho chile powder
  1 tsp. ground cinnamon
  ½ tsp. kosher salt
  ½ tsp. freshly grated ginger
  9 oz. quality dark chocolate (60% to 72% cacao), coarsely chopped
  1 cup unsalted butter, cut into 1-inch pieces
1¼ cups granulated sugar
  ½ cup packed light brown sugar
  5 eggs, room temperature
     Cocoa powder and ancho chile powder (optional)

1. Preheat oven to 350°F. Butter sides and bottom of a 3-qt. baking dish or 13×9×2-inch baking pan.
2. In a medium bowl whisk together flour, cocoa powder, chile powder, cinnamon, salt, and grated ginger; set aside.
3. Place chocolate and butter in a large heatproof bowl. Set over a pan of barely simmering water (bottom of bowl should not touch water). Heat and stir occasionally until chocolate and butter are melted and combined. Remove from heat, keeping bowl over water. Add sugars; whisk until completely combined. Remove bowl from water. Let cool to room temperature.
4. Add 3 eggs to chocolate mixture; whisk just until combined. Add remaining eggs; whisk until combined.
5. Sprinkle flour mixture over chocolate mixture. Using a spatula (not a whisk), fold just until a trace of flour mixture is visible.
6. Pour batter into prepared dish. Smooth top with spatula. Bake 30 minutes or until a toothpick inserted near center comes out with a few moist crumbs, rotating pan halfway through baking. Cool on a wire rack. Sprinkle with additional cocoa powder and ancho chile powder, if desired. Makes 48 brownies.

EACH BROWNIE *110 cal, 6 g fat, 30 mg chol, 29 mg sodium, 13 g carb, 1 g fiber, 1 g pro.*

Good-quality chocolate, dark cocoa powder, and a hint of coffee make humble brownies all the more rich and decadent.

KID FRIENDLY

Deep Dark Chocolate Brownies

PREP 25 min. BAKE 25 min.

- 1¼ cups all-purpose flour
- 2 Tbsp. unsweetened cocoa powder
- 1 tsp. kosher salt
- 11 oz. quality dark chocolate (60% to 72% cacao), coarsely chopped
- 1 cup unsalted butter, cut into 1-inch cubes
- 1 tsp. instant espresso coffee powder
- 1½ cups granulated sugar
- ½ cup packed light brown sugar
- 5 eggs, room temperature
- 2 tsp. vanilla
- 1 recipe Chocolate Ganache (optional)

1. Preheat oven to 350°F. Butter sides and bottom of a 3-qt. baking dish or 13×9×2-inch baking pan; set aside.

2. In a medium bowl whisk together flour, cocoa powder, and salt; set aside.

3. Place chocolate, butter, and espresso powder in a large heatproof bowl. Set over a pan of barely simmering water (bottom of bowl should not touch water). Heat and stir until chocolate and butter are melted and combined. Remove from heat, keeping bowl over water. Add sugars; whisk until completely combined. Remove bowl from water. Let cool to room temperature.

4. Add 3 eggs to chocolate mixture; whisk just until combined. Add remaining eggs; whisk just until combined. Add vanilla; stir until combined.

5. Sprinkle flour mixture over chocolate mixture. Using a spatula (not a whisk), fold just until a trace amount of flour mixture is visible.

6. Pour batter into prepared dish; smooth top with a spatula. Bake 25 to 30 minutes or until a toothpick inserted near center comes out with a few moist crumbs, rotating pan halfway through baking. Cool on a wire rack. Top with Chocolate Ganache, if desired. Makes 24 brownies.

EACH BROWNIE *240 cal, 14 g fat, 59 mg chol, 100 mg sodium, 30 g carb, 1 g fiber, 3 g pro.*

Chocolate Ganache Place 6 oz. coarsely chopped dark chocolate in a heatproof bowl. Heat ½ cup heavy cream in a saucepan over medium heat just until bubbles form around edge; pour over chocolate. Let stand 1 minute. Whisk until smooth. Pour over cooled brownies. Spread evenly. Let stand 10 minutes. Refrigerate 15 minutes to set.

**DEEP DARK
CHOCOLATE BROWNIES**

KID FRIENDLY

Raspberry Swirl Brownies

PREP 25 min. BAKE 25 min.

- 1 cup fresh raspberries
- 1¼ cups all-purpose flour
- 2 Tbsp. unsweetened cocoa powder
- 1 tsp. kosher salt
- 11 oz. quality dark chocolate (60% to 72% cacao), coarsely chopped
- 1 cup unsalted butter, cut into 1-inch cubes
- 1 cup granulated sugar
- ½ cup packed light brown sugar
- 5 eggs, room temperature
- 1½ tsp. vanilla

1. Preheat oven to 350°F. Butter sides and bottom of a 3-qt. baking dish or 13×9×2-inch baking pan.

2. Place raspberries in a food processor; blend until smooth. If desired, strain puree to remove seeds. Set puree aside. In a medium bowl whisk together flour, cocoa powder, and salt; set aside.

3. Place chocolate and butter in a large heatproof bowl. Set over a pan of barely simmering water (bottom of bowl should not touch water). Heat and stir occasionally until chocolate and butter are melted and combined. Remove from heat, keeping bowl over water. Add sugars; whisk until completely combined. Remove bowl from water. Let cool to room temperature.

4. Add 3 eggs to chocolate mixture; whisk just until combined. Add remaining eggs; whisk just until combined. Add vanilla; stir until combined.

5. Sprinkle flour mixture over chocolate mixture. Using a spatula, fold just until a trace amount of flour mixture is visible.

6. Pour batter into prepared pan. Smooth top with spatula. Drizzle raspberry puree over batter. Swirl in with a knife. Bake 25 to 30 minutes or until a toothpick inserted near center comes out with a few moist crumbs, rotating pan halfway through. Cool on wire rack. Makes 24 brownies.

EACH BROWNIE *224 cal, 12 g fat, 36 mg chol, 89 mg sodium, 29 g carb, 2 g fiber, 3 g pro.*

The secret to perfect brownies is a gentle touch—resist the urge to overstir, overbeat, or overbake.

SET UP A DOUBLE BOILER "It's really easy to burn chocolate," Matt says. "A double boiler uses indirect heat to gently melt the chocolate."

AVOID OVERBEATING If you overmix, the brownies will be tough. One of Renato's tricks: "Room-temp eggs are easier to incorporate." To quickly incorporate eggs without overstirring, use a whisk.

FOLD IN THE DRY "Your eyes and a spatula are your best tools," Renato says. "Stop when there's still a trace amount of flour and cocoa visible."

DON'T OVERBAKE "Insert a toothpick at a 45-degree angle and remove," Matt says. "A bit of clinging cooked batter is a good sign."

weeknight delicious

Fast and fresh solutions for dinner tonight.

LENTIL VEGGIE BURGERS

LOW FAT

Lentil Veggie Burgers

Prepare a big batch of lentils on the weekend, then use them throughout the week for soups, quick salads, and burgers—like these.

PREP **40 min.** BAKE **10 min.**

- ¾ cup dry lentils
- 1¾ cups water
  Nonstick cooking spray
- 8 oz. fresh cremini mushrooms, trimmed and chopped
- 1 cup sweet potato, peeled and chopped
- 4 cloves garlic, minced
- 1 cup arugula
- 2 Tbsp. reduced-sodium soy sauce
- 2 Tbsp. yellow cornmeal
- 2 Tbsp. olive oil
  Sandwich rounds, mixed greens, warmed red pepper jelly, and/or sautéed sliced sweet miniature peppers (optional)

1. In a saucepan combine lentils and the water. Bring to boiling; reduce heat. Simmer, covered, 30 minutes or until lentils are very soft. Drain.
2. Meanwhile, coat an extra-large skillet with nonstick cooking spray. Add mushrooms, sweet potato, and garlic; cook and stir over medium heat for 8 minutes or until potato chunks are tender. Remove from heat; cool slightly. In a food processor combine sweet potato mixture, 1 cup lentils, arugula, and soy sauce. Pulse just until smooth. Stir in remaining lentils. (Mixture will be soft.) Shape into four ½-inch-thick patties. Sprinkle both sides with cornmeal.
3. In the same skillet heat oil over medium heat. Cook patties for 10 minutes, turning once. If desired, serve on sandwich rounds with mixed greens and red pepper jelly. Top with sautéed sliced peppers, if desired. Makes 4 servings.
EACH SERVING *262 cal, 8 g fat, 0 mg chol, 301 mg sodium, 36 g carb, 13 g fiber, 13 g pro.*

ROSEMARY AND
RAVIOLI CHICKEN SOUP

KID FRIENDLY

Rosemary and Ravioli Chicken Soup

A vegetable broth base starts soup off with neutral flavor to give herbs—like rosemary and basil—a chance to show off.

START TO FINISH **35 min.**

- 1 32-oz. box vegetable broth
- 1 cup water
- 8 oz. red potatoes, coarsely chopped (1½ cups)
- 1 Tbsp. snipped fresh rosemary
- 1 9- to 12-oz. package refrigerated spinach or mushroom ravioli
- ½ rotisserie chicken, meat removed and cut up
- 8 oz. fresh green beans, trimmed and cut into 1-inch pieces (2 cups)
- 1 Tbsp. butter
  Cracked black pepper
  Snipped fresh basil

1. In a 4-qt. Dutch oven bring vegetable broth and the water to boiling over medium-high heat. Add potatoes and rosemary; cook 10 minutes. Add ravioli, chicken, and green beans. Bring to boiling. Reduce heat. Simmer, covered, 5 to 7 minutes or until pasta and potatoes are tender. Stir in butter. Top with freshly cracked black pepper and basil. Makes 4 servings.
EACH SERVING *362 cal, 13 g fat, 112 mg chol, 1,326 mg sodium, 38 g carb, 4 g fiber, 25 g pro.*

**BUTTERNUT SQUASH
AND CHICKPEA CURRY**

FAST

Butternut Squash and Chickpea Curry

Green curry paste is a quick ticket to major flavor. The blend of lemongrass, green chiles, and Thai ginger adds just enough heat to kick up dinner a notch.
START TO FINISH **30 min.**

1 Tbsp. coconut oil
1 large onion, chopped (1 cup)
2 cloves garlic, thinly sliced
1 14-oz. can coconut milk
¼ cup green curry paste
1 2-lb. butternut squash, peeled and cubed (6 cups)
1 15- to 16-oz. can chickpeas, rinsed and drained
⅓ cup chopped fresh cilantro

Cooked jasmine rice, snipped fresh cilantro, and/or lime wedges (optional)

1. In an extra-large skillet heat coconut oil over medium heat. Add onion and garlic; cook and stir over medium heat for 3 minutes. Add coconut milk and curry paste; bring to boiling, stirring constantly to combine.
2. Add squash; return to boiling. Reduce heat. Simmer, uncovered, 10 to 12 minutes or until squash is tender. Stir in chickpeas and cilantro; heat through. Serve with rice. If desired, top with additional fresh cilantro and a squeeze of lime. Makes 4 servings.
EACH SERVING *402 cal, 22 g fat, 0 mg chol, 1,061 mg sodium, 46 g carb, 12 g fiber, 7 g pro.*

LOW FAT   FAST

Zesty Salmon Pasta Salad

Asian sweet chili sauce—a thickened mixture of chiles, rice vinegar, sugar, garlic, and fish sauce—adds flavor to this knife-and-fork salad.
START TO FINISH **25 min.**

4 5- to 6-oz. fresh or frozen skinless salmon fillets, thawed
½ cup Asian sweet chili sauce
¼ cup reduced-sodium soy sauce
4 dried lasagna noodles, broken in half
4 medium carrots, peeled and thinly sliced lengthwise
1 5-oz. package mixed salad greens or baby spinach
¼ cup rice vinegar

1. Rinse and pat salmon dry. In a shallow dish combine chili sauce and soy sauce. Add salmon and turn once; set aside for 10 minutes.
2. Meanwhile, cook lasagna according to package directions, adding carrots the last 5 minutes. Drain. Divide noodles, carrots, and greens among four plates.
3. Add salmon and marinade to a large nonstick skillet. Bring to boiling; reduce heat. Cover and cook 8 to 10 minutes, turning once, or until salmon flakes easily when tested with a fork. Transfer salmon to plates, reserving marinade in skillet. Stir in vinegar; remove from heat. Drizzle dressing over salmon, noodles, and vegetables. Makes 4 servings.
EACH SERVING *425 cal, 10 g fat, 0 mg chol, 963 mg sodium, 40 g carb, 3 g fiber, 33 g pro.*

ZESTY SALMON
PASTA SALAD

RICOTTA
MEATBALLS

march

anticipation Awaiting the first bite of a new recipe—
luscious spring cakes, tender meatballs, savory soups,
or crunchy salads—is delightfully rewarding.

58

67

72

cake walk

The latest cake fashions on parade for your choosing. Beth Kirby of the blog *Local Milk* shares recipes for cakes that look as luscious as they taste!

KID FRIENDLY

Dark Chocolate Cake with Fresh Strawberry Buttercream

Fudgy chocolate takes a fanciful turn stacked tall and filled with fluffy strawberry frosting. Brownie fans will adore the texture; strawberry fans will beg for another slice.

PREP 1 hr., 30 min. BAKE 30 min.
COOL 10 min. CHILL 1 hr.

- 1½ cups water
- 3 cups granulated sugar (567 g)
- 2¼ cups all-purpose flour (281 g)
- 1½ cups unsweetened cocoa powder
- 2¼ tsp. baking soda
- 1¼ tsp. kosher salt
- 1¼ tsp. baking powder
- 3 large eggs, room temperature
- 1½ cups buttermilk, room temperature
- ¾ cup canola oil or olive oil
- 1 recipe Fresh Strawberry Buttercream
  Fresh halved strawberries (optional)
  Fresh basil leaves (optional)

1. Preheat oven to 350°F. Grease three 8×2-inch round cake pans. Line bottoms of pans with parchment. Grease; set aside. Bring the water to boiling.
2. In a very large bowl whisk together sugar, flour, cocoa, baking soda, salt, and baking powder. In a large bowl whisk together eggs, buttermilk, and oil. Add egg mixture to dry ingredients. Using a rubber spatula, stir to combine, scraping down to bottom of bowl to thoroughly combine. Add boiling water; stir just until combined.
3. Divide batter among prepared pans, filling each with 3 cups batter (half full). Bake about 30 minutes or until a toothpick inserted near centers comes out clean. Cool in pans on a wire rack for 10 minutes. Remove from pans; cool completely. Wrap layers in plastic wrap; chill for 1 hour.
4. Place a cake layer on a serving plate. Spread with 2 cups Fresh Strawberry Buttercream. Repeat with remaining cake layers and frosting. If desired, top with halved strawberries and fresh basil leaves. Makes 16 servings.

Fresh Strawberry Buttercream In a very large heatproof bowl set over a pan of simmering water, whisk together 8 egg whites (room temperature), 1½ cups sugar (300 grams), ½ tsp. cream of tartar, and ¼ tsp. salt until sugar is dissolved and mixture is 160°F. Remove from heat. Beat with a mixer on high speed until stiff peaks form. Add 6 sticks (1½ lb.) room temperature butter, 1 Tbsp. at a time, until mixture thickens and becomes smooth. (If it begins to curdle, continue to beat, adding another piece of butter until smooth.) Stir in beans from 1 split vanilla bean and 2 tsp. vanilla. In a food processor or blender puree 1½ cups strawberries, halved. Strain through a fine-mesh sieve (should have ¾ cup puree). Stir into the frosting. Makes 6 cups.
EACH SERVING *739 cal, 47 g fat, 128 mg chol, 478 mg sodium, 77 g carb, 3 g fiber, 8 g pro.*

BETH KIRBY
Beth is the creator of the food and lifestyle blog *Local Milk*. "Being Southern, I adore cakes and cake walks—both fine Southern traditions," she says. Beth updates her recipes with lavender, thyme, and olive and coconut oils. When Beth isn't dreaming up recipes for her blog (localmilkblog.com), she hosts workshops and freelances as a photographer.

DARK CHOCOLATE CAKE WITH FRESH STRAWBERRY BUTTERCREAM
Recipe on page 53

LEMON OLIVE OIL CAKE WITH LEMON CREAM
Recipe on page 56

LAVENDER THYME FLUTED CAKE WITH VANILLA CRÈME GLAZE
Recipe on page 56

"When I bake a cake, I like to tweak it and make it my own," Beth says. "You don't have to reinvent the wheel when you bake. Just learn the classics and bake a cake like your grandmother did, then play with different flavors."

YELLOW CAKE WITH SALTED CHOCOLATE GANACHE
Recipe on page 58

CARROT CAKE WITH CREAM CHEESE MASCARPONE FROSTING
Recipe on page 61

LEMON OLIVE OIL CAKE
WITH LEMON CREAM

Lemon Olive Oil Cake with Lemon Cream

This cake is elegant and simple. Bright, firm-textured layers and a swipe of citrusy cream have a sweet-tart pucker that lingers.

PREP 30 min. BAKE 20 min.
COOL 10 min.

2 eggs
1 cup sugar (189 g)
2 cups all-purpose flour (250 g)
1 tsp. kosher salt
1 tsp. baking powder
1 tsp. baking soda
⅔ cup olive oil
4 tsp. finely shredded lemon peel
½ cup lemon juice
½ cup buttermilk
1 tsp. vanilla
1 recipe Lemon Cream
1 recipe Sugared Meyer Lemon Peel (optional)

1. Preheat oven to 350°F. Grease three 6×2-inch round cake pans. Line bottoms of pans with parchment; grease the paper. Set aside.
2. In a large mixing bowl beat the eggs and sugar with an electric mixer on medium speed about 5 minutes or until pale and thick ribbons form.
3. In another large bowl whisk together flour, salt, baking powder, and baking soda. In a medium bowl combine olive oil, lemon peel, lemon juice, and buttermilk.
4. Beat vanilla into egg mixture on low speed. Add dry and wet ingredients in three additions, starting with dry and ending with wet. After last addition, turn off mixer and whisk until combined.
5. Divide batter among prepared pans, filling each with 1⅔ cups batter (half full). Bake 20 to 25 minutes or until a toothpick inserted near centers comes out clean and cakes are golden and pull away from sides. Cool in pans on wire rack 10 minutes. Remove from pans. Cool completely.
6. To assemble, place one cake layer on a serving plate. Spread top of cake with ½ cup Lemon Cream. Repeat layers twice. Spread ½ cup Lemon Cream over sides of cake as a thin crumb coat. Top with Sugared Meyer Lemon Peel. Makes 12 servings.
Lemon Cream In a bowl beat 1 cup cold whipping cream, 2 Tbsp. powdered sugar, 1 Tbsp. lemon zest, and 2 tsp. lemon juice until soft peaks form. Makes 2 cups.
EACH SERVING *343 cal, 21 g fat, 59 mg chol, 371 mg sodium, 36 g carb, 1 g fiber, 4 g pro.*
Sugared Meyer Lemon Peel Remove peel from 1 to 2 meyer lemons using a vegetable peeler; cut into thin strips. Place in a small bowl. Sprinkle with 1 to 2 Tbsp. sugar; toss to coat. Let stand for 1 to 4 hours, tossing occasionally.

Lavender Thyme Fluted Cake with Vanilla Crème Glaze

In one fell swoop, get intoxicating herbal flavor and an eye-catching shape. Pour the creamy glaze onto the ridges for a beautiful finish.

PREP 20 min. BAKE 30 min.
COOL 10 min.

3 cups all-purpose flour (375 g)
2 cups sugar (378 g)
1 Tbsp. chopped fresh thyme
1½ tsp. dried lavender buds, ground*
1½ tsp. kosher salt
1½ tsp. baking powder
½ tsp. baking soda
3 eggs, room temperature
1 cup coconut oil, melted
1 cup whole milk, room temperature
1 Tbsp. apple cider vinegar
1 recipe Vanilla Crème Glaze
Snipped fresh thyme

1. Preheat oven to 350°F. Grease a 10-inch fluted tube pan; set aside. In a large bowl whisk together flour, sugar, thyme, lavender, salt, baking powder, and baking soda. In another bowl whisk together eggs, oil, milk, and vinegar. Add wet ingredients to dry ingredients; stir to combine (batter may appear curdled). Spoon into prepared pan.
2. Bake 30 to 40 minutes or until golden brown and a toothpick inserted near center is clean. Cool in pan on a wire rack for 10 minutes. Remove from pan; cool completely on wire rack. Drizzle with Vanilla Crème Glaze. Sprinkle with snipped fresh thyme. Makes 16 to 20 servings.
Vanilla Crème Glaze In a medium bowl whisk together 8 oz. crème fraîche, 5 Tbsp. powdered sugar, and 1 tsp. vanilla. If necessary, add whole milk, 1 tsp. at a time, until glaze is desired consistency.
*Crush lavender buds with a mortar and pestle or clean spice grinder.
EACH SERVING *377 cal, 21 g fat, 57 mg chol, 329 mg sodium, 45 g carb, 1 g fiber, 4 g pro.*

LAVENDER THYME
FLUTED CAKE WITH
VANILLA CRÈME GLAZE

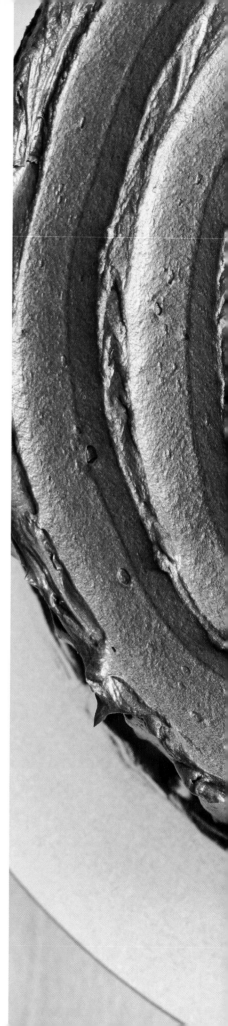

Grab a ruler and double-check the depth of your cake pans. For best results, they should be at least 2 inches deep.

Yellow Cake with Salted Chocolate Ganache

This is your classic yellow cake dressed for any occasion. Two buttermilk-infused layers are sandwiched together with dark chocolate frosting and showered with flakes of crunchy sea salt.
PREP **50 min.** BAKE **35 min.**
COOL **10 min.**

- 3 cups all-purpose flour (375 g)
- 2½ tsp. baking powder
- 1 tsp. kosher salt
- 2 cups sugar (380 g)
- 1 cup butter, room temperature
- 4 eggs plus 2 egg yolks, room temperature
- 1 tsp. vanilla
- 1 cup buttermilk, room temperature
- 1 recipe Salted Chocolate Ganache
  Large food-safe peony (optional)

1. Preheat oven to 350°F. Grease and flour two 9×2-inch round baking pans; set aside. In a medium bowl sift together flour, baking powder, and salt. In a very large bowl beat sugar and butter with an electric mixer on medium speed for 6 to 8 minutes or until very light and fluffy. Add eggs and yolks, one at a time, beating until combined after each addition. Beat in vanilla. Add flour mixture to beaten mixture in three additions, alternating with buttermilk. (Batter will be thick.)

2. Divide batter between prepared pans, filling with about 3¼ cups each (about half full). Bake about 35 minutes or until a toothpick inserted near centers comes out clean. Cool in pans on a wire rack for 10 minutes. Remove from pans and cool completely.

3. Spread Salted Chocolate Ganache over top of each layer; stack layers on plate. Frost sides. If desired, use an offset spatula to drag frosting vertically. If desired, add a large edible peony (grown without pesticides or chemicals). Sprinkle with sea salt. Makes 16 servings.

Salted Chocolate Ganache Place 16 oz. chopped dark chocolate in a large heatproof bowl. In a saucepan bring 2 cups whipping cream just to boiling; pour over chocolate. Let stand 2 minutes without stirring. Stir in ¼ tsp. kosher salt. Set bowl in a larger bowl with ice for 15 to 20 minutes or until cool, stirring occasionally. Beat with an electric mixer for 2 minutes or until light and fluffy.

EACH SERVING *565 cal, 36 g fat, 143 mg chol, 369 mg sodium, 61 g carb, 3 g fiber, 7 g pro.*

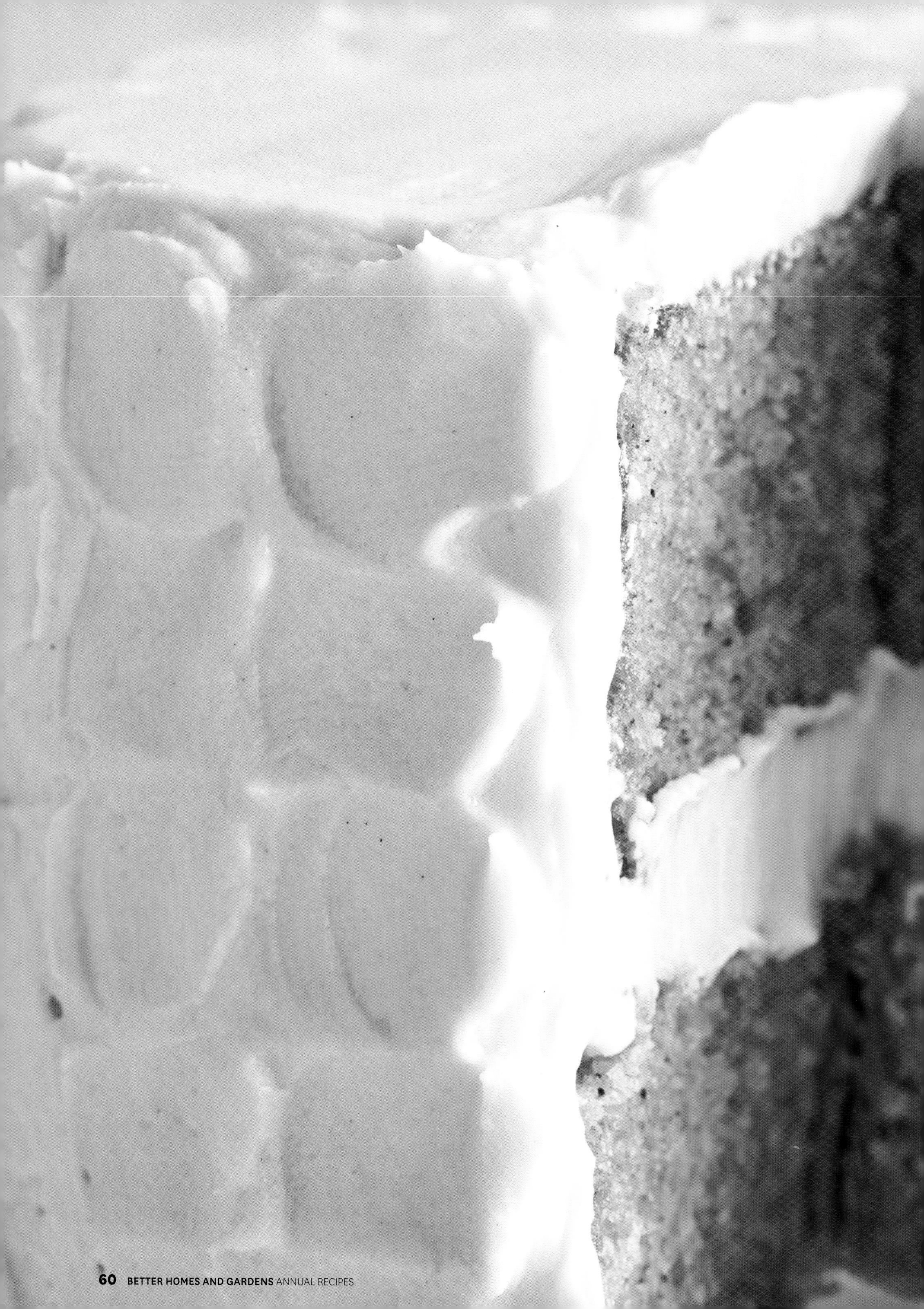

Beth measures ingredients by weight to ensure accuracy. Don't hesitate to pull out your kitchen scale for these recipes.

KID FRIENDLY

Carrot Cake with Cream Cheese Mascarpone Frosting

If there ever was a spring dessert, carrot cake is it. This deliciously simple version is accessorized with aromatic cardamom and paired with crowd-pleasing cream cheese frosting.

PREP 45 min. BAKE 30 min. COOL 10 min.

  4 large carrots, peeled
2½ cups all-purpose flour (313 g)
  2 tsp. ground cinnamon
  1 tsp. baking soda
  ½ tsp. kosher salt
  ½ tsp. ground cardamom
  ¼ tsp. freshly grated nutmeg
  1 cup unsalted butter, room temperature
  2 cups sugar (378 g)
  1 tsp. vanilla
  5 eggs, separated, room temperature
  ¾ cup buttermilk
  1 recipe Cream Cheese Mascarpone Frosting

1. Preheat oven to 350°F. Grease and flour two 9×2-inch round cake pans; set aside. Finely shred 3 carrots. Coarsely shred 1 carrot. In a medium bowl whisk together flour, cinnamon, baking soda, salt, cardamom, and nutmeg; set aside.
2. In a large mixing bowl beat butter with an electric mixer on medium speed for 30 seconds. Gradually beat in the sugar until combined. Beat in carrots and vanilla until combined. Beat in egg yolks, one at a time, just until combined after each addition. Alternately add flour mixture and buttermilk to butter mixture.
3. Thoroughly wash beaters. In a clean large bowl beat egg whites until stiff peaks form. Fold into batter. Divide batter between prepared pans, filling each with 3 cups batter (about one-third full). Bake 30 minutes or until a toothpick inserted near centers comes out clean. Cool in pans on wire rack for 10 minutes. Remove from pans and cool completely.
4. Spread Cream Cheese Mascarpone Frosting over top of each layer; stack layers on a cake plate. Frost sides. Makes 16 servings.

Cream Cheese Mascarpone Frosting In a very large bowl beat 3 sticks (¾ lb.) softened unsalted butter, 8 oz. softened cream cheese, and 8 oz. softened mascarpone cheese until light and fluffy. Beat in 1 lb. powdered sugar, ¼ tsp. kosher salt, ¼ tsp. ground cardamom, and 1 tsp. vanilla until smooth. Makes about 6 cups.
EACH SERVING *682 cal, 42 g fat, 171 mg chol, 292 mg sodium, 72 g carb, 1 g fiber, 6 g pro.*

FOUR-LAYER CARROT CAKE
Prepare recipe as directed and bake in two 9-inch layer pans. Prepare carrot cake recipe again, using two 6×2-inch round cake pans, adding 1 cup batter to each pan. Bake 25 to 30 minutes as directed. (Bake remaining batter as cupcakes.) To assemble the cake, double the frosting recipe; frost and stack cake layers. Make short horizontal pulls in frosting with an offset spatula to create ripple texture on the cake sides.

home cooking: meatballs

Celebrity chef Fabio Viviani shares his tricks for juicy, tender meatballs, plus he offers modern twists on this Italian favorite.

LOW FAT   KID FRIENDLY

Ricotta Meatballs

"When you finish the meatballs in marinara sauce, any excess juices that escape from the meatballs simply flavor the sauce even more," Fabio says.

PREP **40 min.**   BAKE **22 min.**

  1 large yellow onion, minced (1 cup)
  ¼ cup minced garlic
  3 Tbsp. olive oil
  2 eggs, lightly beaten
2½ lb. 80% lean ground beef
  1 cup grana Padano cheese, grated
  1 15-oz. carton whole milk ricotta cheese
  1 cup panko bread crumbs
  ½ cup fresh Italian parsley, chopped
  ½ cup fresh basil, chopped
  ½ tsp. salt
  ¼ tsp. black pepper
  2 25-oz. jars marinara sauce, warmed (optional)

1. Preheat oven to 350°F. Line two shallow baking pans with parchment; set aside.
2. In a large skillet cook onion and garlic in 1 Tbsp. of the olive oil for 8 minutes or until translucent. Let cool.
3. In a large bowl combine cooled onion mixture, eggs, ground beef, grana Padano, ricotta, panko, parsley, basil, salt, and pepper. Using your hands, mix to combine. Shape one 2-inch meatball. If it's too watery, add more bread crumbs or ground beef. If it's too dry, add more ricotta (should have 65 to 70 meatballs). Place on prepared pans.
4. Brush meatballs with remaining 2 Tbsp. olive oil. Bake 22 minutes or until 165°F.*
5. If desired, serve with marina sauce. Makes 12 servings.
***Tip** Freeze baked meatballs up to 1 month. When ready to use, simmer frozen meatballs in marinara sauce for 10 minutes or until heated through.

EACH MEATBALL *71 cal, 5 g fat, 22 mg chol, 59 mg sodium, 1 g carb, 0 g fiber, 5 g pro.*

START WITH THE MIX "I start by cooking the onion and garlic to caramelize the sugars in the onion and mellow the garlic flavor," Fabio says. "Also, some meatballs call for bread soaked in milk for moisture. In this version I add ricotta cheese, which is also a foolproof way to avoid a dry meatball."

USE YOUR HANDS "I'm an old-school guy, so I prefer to mix with my hands whenever I can," Fabio says. "I like that you can really feel the texture as everything comes together. But a stand mixer fitted with a paddle attachment works great too."

TEST ONE OUT "Before rolling the entire mixture into balls, I bake a test one," Fabio says. "It takes a little extra time, but it's helpful because the consistency of ricotta can vary greatly. If the ricotta is too watery and the meatball falls apart, add more bread crumbs or ground beef. If the meatball is too dry, add more ricotta."

BRUSH WITH OIL "Brush the meatballs with a little olive oil or rub your hands with a little olive oil before rolling them into balls," Fabio says. "The oil makes them glisten and prevents moisture from escaping from the meatballs so they stay juicy and tender."

"The perfect meatball is soft and moist and super juicy. When done right, it's the ultimate comfort." Fabio Viviani

Serve these meatballs on an antipasti platter with a little bowl of Mango Salsa—talk about a crowd-pleaser.

LOW FAT   KID FRIENDLY

Sweet and Spicy Meatballs with Mango Salsa

The flavor of marinated Calabrian peppers takes Fabio back to his childhood growing up in Italy. These peppers can be hard to find; if they're not available at your supermarket, substitute crushed red pepper.
PREP 30 min.   BAKE 22 min.

⅓ cup whole milk
⅓ cup fine dry bread crumbs
8 slices bacon, chopped
1 medium onion, finely chopped
2 Tbsp. minced garlic
1 Tbsp. Worcestershire sauce
1 tsp. ground cumin
2 Tbsp. minced marinated Calabrian peppers or 2 tsp. crushed red pepper
½ tsp. dried thyme, crushed
½ tsp. salt
¼ tsp. black pepper
1½ lb. 80% lean ground beef
1 lb. ground pork
2 eggs
¼ cup snipped fresh Italian parsley
2 Tbsp. olive oil
1 recipe Mango Salsa (optional)

1. Preheat oven to 350°F. Line a 15×10×1-inch baking pan with parchment; set aside.
2. In a large bowl combine milk and bread crumbs; set aside. In a large skillet cook bacon over medium heat until crisp. Transfer to paper towels, reserving 2 Tbsp. drippings in skillet.
3. Add onion and garlic to skillet. Cook and stir 2 minutes. Add Worcestershire sauce; deglaze pan by scraping up browned bits from the bottom.
4. Add cumin, Calabrian peppers, thyme, salt, and black pepper; cook 1 minute more. Add onion mixture to soaked bread crumbs; mix thoroughly.
5. Add beef, pork, reserved bacon, eggs, and parsley to bread crumb mixture. Using your hands, mix to combine. Shape into 2-inch meatballs. Brush with olive oil. Place on prepared pan.
6. Bake 22 to 25 minutes or until meatballs are cooked through (160°F). If desired, serve with Mango Salsa. Makes 24 meatballs.
EACH MEATBALL *163 cal, 12 g fat, 52 mg chol, 128 mg sodium, 2 g carb, 0 g fiber, 10 g pro.*
Mango Salsa In a medium bowl combine ¾ cup chopped fresh mango and/or papaya, ¼ cup chopped red sweet pepper, 3 sliced green onions, 2 Tbsp. olive oil, and 1 Tbsp. minced shallot. Season to taste with salt and black pepper.

FABIO VIVIANI
FROM ITALY, WITH LOVE
Born and raised in Florence, Fabio has made his mark on the United States in the past few years as a chef, restaurateur, and media personality. He is the executive chef of four restaurants in Los Angeles, Chicago, and Miami, as well as the "Fan Favorite" from *Top Chef Season 5*. His newest venture, the Fabio Viviani Wine Collection (available at fabiovivianiwines.com), launched in November 2014. His third cookbook, *Fabio's American Home Kitchen* (Hachette, $30) features Fabio's Italian spin on American favorites such as Italian Fried Missouri-Style Ravioli and Chicken Potpies.

LOW FAT **KID FRIENDLY**

Chicken Meatballs with Sun-Dried Tomatoes

Chicken meatballs get a burst of flavor from a mix of fresh and dried herbs. Use equal parts ground chicken breast and thighs for the most tender results.
PREP **25 min.** BAKE **16 min.**

3½ oz. oil-packed sun-dried tomatoes, blotted dry (¾ cup)
 3 cloves garlic
 ¼ tsp. salt
 ⅛ tsp. black pepper
 ¼ cup seasoned fine dry bread crumbs
1½ lb. ground chicken
 ½ cup whole milk ricotta cheese
 2 eggs, lightly beaten
 1 Tbsp. whole milk
 1 Tbsp. chopped fresh Italian parsley
 2 tsp. dried thyme, crushed
 1 tsp. dried oregano, crushed
 1 tsp. dried marjoram, crushed
 2 Tbsp. olive oil
 1 recipe White Sauce (optional)

1. Preheat oven to 350°F. Line a 15×10×1-inch baking pan with parchment. In a food processor pulse tomatoes, garlic, salt, and pepper. Add bread crumbs and pulse to combine.
2. Transfer mixture to a large bowl. Add chicken, ricotta, eggs, milk, parsley, thyme, oregano, and marjoram. Using your hands, mix to combine. Shape into 1½-inch balls. Brush with olive oil. Place on prepared pan.
3. Bake 16 minutes or until cooked through (165°F). If desired, serve with White Sauce. Makes 40 meatballs.
EACH MEATBALL *47 cal, 3 g fat, 26 mg chol, 46 mg sodium, 1 g carb, 0 g fiber, 4 g pro.*
White Sauce In a medium saucepan combine 3 Tbsp. flour and 2 Tbsp. butter over medium-high heat. Cook and stir 2 minutes or just until roux is golden. Add 1 cup chicken broth, 1 cup heavy cream, 1 Tbsp. white balsamic vinegar, 1 tsp. Worcestershire sauce, 1 tsp. dried thyme, ¼ tsp. salt, and ⅛ tsp. pepper. Cook and stir until thickened and bubbly. Cook 1 minute more. Stir in 2 Tbsp. chopped parsley.

dinner on a dollar

Enliven weeknights with Asian-inspired tacos that deliver tang, crunch, and spice with each bite.

LOW FAT FAST

Sesame Garlic Beef Tacos

Try something new for taco night. Season fillings with Asian cuisine flavors. Sesame oil, soy sauce, and rice vinegar give these tacos distinctive flavor, while pickled cucumbers and cabbage add crunch.

START TO FINISH **30 min.**

- 8 white or yellow corn tortillas
- 1 lb. ground beef
- 2 Tbsp. toasted sesame oil
- 2 cloves garlic, minced
- ¼ cup reduced-sodium soy sauce
- 3 Tbsp. packed brown sugar
- 3 Tbsp. rice vinegar
- 1 Tbsp. water
- ¼ tsp. crushed red pepper
- 1 recipe Quick Pickled Cucumbers and Slaw
   Lime wedges
   Asian chile sauce (Sriracha)

1. Preheat oven to 350°F. Stack tortillas and wrap in foil. Heat in oven for 10 minutes.
2. Meanwhile, in a large skillet brown ground beef over medium-high heat. Drain off fat; set aside.
3. Add sesame oil to skillet. Add garlic; cook 30 seconds over medium heat or until lightly browned. Stir in soy sauce, brown sugar, rice vinegar, the water, and crushed red pepper. Bring to boiling; reduce heat. Simmer, uncovered, for 5 minutes, stirring occasionally. Return beef to skillet; heat through.

4. Spoon beef onto tortillas. Using a slotted spoon, top with Quick Pickled Cucumbers and Slaw. Serve with lime wedges and chile sauce. Makes 4 servings.
Quick Pickled Cucumbers and Slaw In a medium bowl whisk together ¼ cup vinegar, 2 Tbsp. sugar, and ½ tsp. salt. Add 1 cup very thinly sliced cucumber and 1 cup shredded red cabbage. Let stand 15 minutes or up to 6 hours.
EACH TACO *250 cal, 12 g fat, 38 mg chol, 531 mg sodium, 23 g carb, 2 g fiber, 13 g pro.*

weeknight delicious

Fast and fresh solutions for dinner tonight.

**TEX-MEX
CHOPPED SALAD**

FRESH BASIL AND NAVY BEAN SOUP

FAST

FAST

Tex-Mex Chopped Salad

A generous amount of refreshing cilantro, chopped crisp vegetables, creamy avocado, and protein-filled black beans turns this salad into a dinner-worthy entrée.

START TO FINISH **30 min.**

- ⅓ cup lime juice
- ⅓ cup olive oil
- 1 tsp. sugar
- ½ tsp. kosher salt
- ¼ tsp. crushed red pepper
- 1 15- to 16-oz. can black beans, rinsed and drained
- 10 oz. frozen whole kernel corn, thawed
- 2 cups lightly packed cilantro, chopped
- 2 cups grape or cherry tomatoes, halved
- 1 avocado, halved, pitted, and chopped
- 1 green sweet pepper, chopped
- 6 green onions, thinly sliced
  Crushed tortilla chips (optional)

1. In a screw-top jar combine lime juice, oil, sugar, salt, and crushed red pepper. Shake well to combine.

2. Arrange black beans, corn, cilantro, tomatoes, avocado, sweet pepper, and green onions on plates. Drizzle with dressing. If desired, top each salad with crushed tortilla chips. Makes 4 servings.

EACH SERVING *400 cal, 24 g fat, 0 mg chol, 646 mg sodium, 44 g carb, 11 g fiber, 10 g pro.*

LOW FAT

Fresh Basil and Navy Bean Soup

START TO FINISH **40 min.**

- 4 cups reduced-sodium chicken broth
- 4 oz. dried medium shell pasta
- 1 14.5-oz. can diced tomatoes, undrained
- ¼ tsp. crushed red pepper (optional)
- 1 15- to 16-oz. can navy beans, rinsed and drained
- 1 cup chopped cooked chicken breast
- 1 cup fresh arugula
- ½ cup chopped fresh basil
- 1 Tbsp. extra-virgin olive oil
- ⅓ cup pitted Kalamata olives, coarsely chopped
  Salt and black pepper to taste
- ½ cup shaved Parmesan cheese

1. In a 4-qt. Dutch oven bring broth to boiling. Add pasta, undrained tomatoes, and crushed red pepper, if desired. Return to boiling; reduce heat. Cover and cook for 10 minutes or just until pasta is tender. Remove from heat.

2. Stir in remaining ingredients except cheese. Cover; let stand 5 minutes. Top with Parmesan cheese and, if desired, additional chopped olives and basil.

EACH SERVING *293 cal, 5 g fat, 30 mg chol, 1,114 mg sodium, 39 g carb, 7 g fiber, 23 g pro.*

RAVIOLI ZUCCHINI AND BROWN BUTTER

Three-Herb Chicken and Mushrooms

Adding herbs to the chicken and pan sauce makes this recipe extra-delicious. Parsley, rosemary, and thyme are a nice trio, but use other herbs that you have on hand.

START TO FINISH **35 min.**

- 8 chicken thighs, skin on
- ¼ tsp. kosher salt
- ⅛ tsp. black pepper
- 2 Tbsp. snipped fresh rosemary
- 2 Tbsp. snipped fresh thyme
- 1 Tbsp. extra-virgin olive oil
- 8 oz. cremini or button mushrooms, quartered or halved
- 1 Tbsp. all-purpose flour
- 1 cup chicken broth
- ½ cup dry white wine
- 2 Tbsp. Dijon mustard
- 1 Tbsp. snipped fresh Italian parsley

1. Preheat oven to 400°F. Season chicken on both sides with salt, pepper, 1 Tbsp. of the rosemary, and 1 Tbsp. of the thyme. In a large cast-iron or other oven-going skillet heat olive oil over medium heat. Add chicken, skin sides down; cook 5 to 7 minutes until browned on one side. Turn chicken pieces over and place skillet in the oven. Bake 15 to 20 minutes or until done (170°F.)

2. Remove chicken from skillet; set aside and cover to keep warm. In the same skillet cook and stir mushrooms over medium-high heat for 4 minutes. Add flour to skillet, stirring to coat. Stir in chicken broth, wine, and mustard. Cook and stir until thickened and bubbly; cook and stir 1 minute more. Remove skillet from heat. Add remaining rosemary, thyme, and the parsley. Serve mushrooms and sauce over chicken. Makes 4 servings.

EACH SERVING *246 cal, 9 g fat, 131 mg chol, 647 mg sodium, 5 g carb, 1 g fiber, 29 g pro.*

Ravioli Zucchini and Brown Butter

This pasta toss doesn't need to be piping hot—it's delicious at any temperature.

START TO FINISH **30 min.**

- 2 tsp. extra-virgin olive oil
- 1 lb. zucchini, halved lengthwise and thinly sliced
- 1 9-oz. package four-cheese ravioli
- ¼ cup butter
- ½ tsp. kosher salt
- ½ cup toasted almonds, chopped
- 2 to 4 Tbsp. balsamic vinegar
- 2 Tbsp. snipped mint

1. In an extra-large nonstick skillet heat olive oil over medium-high heat. Add zucchini; cook and stir 4 minutes or until tender. Transfer zucchini to a bowl; set aside.

2. Prepare ravioli according to package instructions; drain and keep warm. In the same skillet heat butter and salt over medium heat about 3 minutes or until butter is browned, stirring occasionally. Add almonds; cook and stir 2 minutes or until toasted. Add zucchini; toss to coat. Gently stir in ravioli, balsamic vinegar, and mint. Makes 4 servings.

EACH SERVING *428 cal, 30 g fat, 67 mg chol, 683 mg sodium, 35 g carb, 5 g fiber, 13 g pro.*

BROWN BUTTER BASICS Opt for a light color pan when you make brown butter. Watch carefully—butter can quickly change from brown to burned.

**THREE-HERB
CHICKEN AND
MUSHROOMS**

new ways with carrots

Carrots add color, crunch, sweetness, and healthful nutrients to main dishes.

Vietnamese-Style Carrot Salad

PREP 30 min. STAND 2 hr.

- 1 medium seedless cucumber, halved lengthwise and thinly sliced (about 8 ounces)
- 1 fresh serrano pepper, thinly sliced (tip, page 96)
- 1 cup rice vinegar
- 2 Tbsp. packed brown sugar
- ½ tsp. kosher salt
- 1 lb. carrots, peeled and very thinly sliced (3 cups)
- ¼ cup olive oil
- 6 cups coarsely shredded Napa cabbage
- 12 oz. cooked pork loin, thinly sliced
- 1 cup cilantro leaves
- ⅓ cup peanuts, chopped
  Toasted bread (optional)

1. In a medium heatproof bowl combine the cucumber and serrano pepper; set aside. In a medium saucepan combine rice vinegar, sugar, and salt. Bring vinegar mixture to boiling, stirring to dissolve sugar. Add carrots; return to boiling. Reduce heat. Cook, covered, for 1 minute. Pour carrot mixture over cucumber mixture; stir to combine. Cover and let stand 2 hours, stirring occasionally.

2. Drain vegetables, reserving ¼ cup of the pickling liquid. In a large bowl combine reserved liquid with the olive oil; add cabbage and toss to coat. Top cabbage with pork, pickled vegetables, cilantro, peanuts, and toasted bread, if desired. Makes 6 servings.

PER SERVING *327 cal, 23 g fat, 47 mg chol, 187 mg sodium, 14 g carb, 4 g fiber, 18 g pro.*

LOW FAT

Spicy Carrot Chicken Sandwich

PREP 15 min. ROAST 20 min.

- 1 lb. carrots, peeled and chopped (3 cups)
- 1 Tbsp. olive oil
- ¼ cup sliced almonds, toasted
- 1 6-oz. carton plain Greek yogurt
- 2 Tbsp. lemon juice
- 1 Tbsp. snipped fresh thyme
- 1 Tbsp. water

- 1 Tbsp. harissa paste
- ½ tsp. kosher salt
- 2 cups chopped cooked chicken
- 2 stalks celery, thinly sliced (1 cup)
- ¼ cup golden raisins
- 16 slices wheat sandwich bread, toasted
- 8 leaves butterhead lettuce

1. Preheat oven to 375°F. Line a 15×10×1-inch baking pan with foil. Add carrots to pan, drizzle with olive oil and toss to coat. Roast, uncovered, 20 minutes or until tender; set aside.

2. Meanwhile, in a dry skillet toast almonds over medium heat for 2 minutes or until golden, stirring frequently. In a large bowl stir together yogurt, lemon juice, thyme, the water, harissa paste, and salt. Add the carrots, chicken, celery, almonds, and raisins; stir to combine.

3. Serve chicken salad on toasted bread with lettuce. Makes 8 servings.

PER SERVING *291 cal., 8 g fat, 32 mg chol, 481 mg sodium, 37 g carb, 5 g fiber, 19 g pro.*

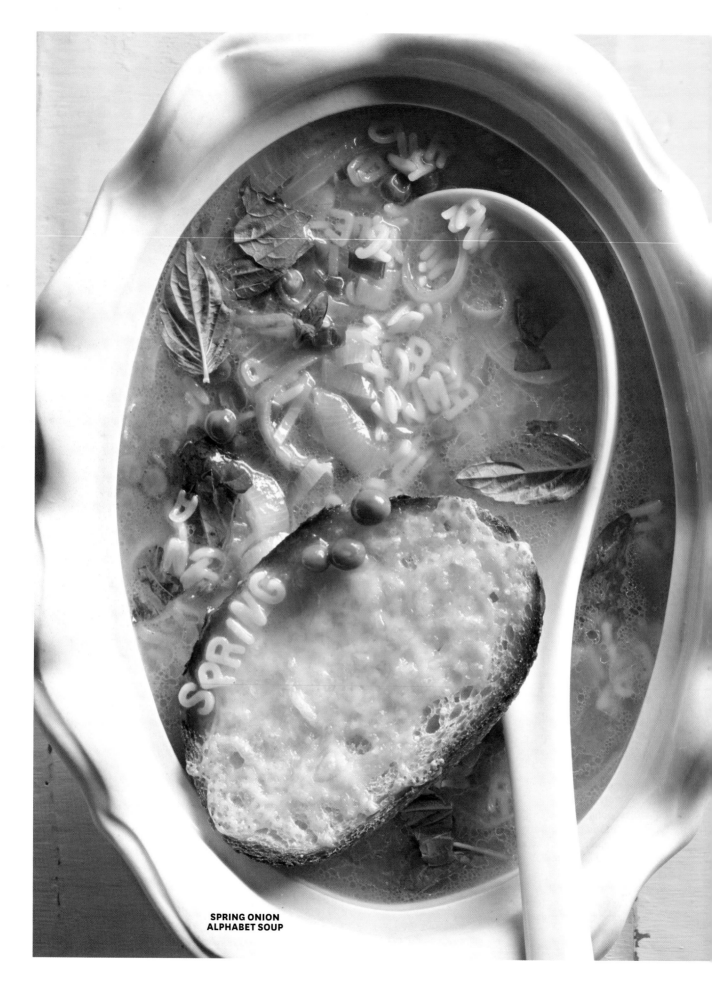

**SPRING ONION
ALPHABET SOUP**

spring days With more sunshine comes a yearning for new takes on classic fare: Updated pasta, herb-kissed scones, Passover mainstays, and healthful meals.

89

96

99

**BAGEL AND LOX
RIGATONI SALAD**

pasta's new day

With pumped-up flavors and fresh techniques, these pasta recipes will put a little spring in your step.

FAST

Bagel and Lox Rigatoni Salad

START TO FINISH 30 min.

- 8 oz. dried rigatoni pasta
- 8 oz. fresh green beans, trimmed and halved
- 1 "everything" bagel or your choice, cut into 1-inch pieces
- 1 Tbsp. olive oil
- ½ cup white balsamic vinegar
- 1 tsp. Dijon mustard
- ¼ tsp. kosher salt
- ¾ cup olive oil
- 1 cup finely chopped red onion
- ¼ cup drained capers
- 2 cups chopped romaine lettuce
- 8 oz. bite-size fresh mozzarella balls
- 6 to 8 oz. sliced smoked salmon (lox-style), coarsely chopped
  Cracked black pepper

1. Preheat oven to 400°F. Cook pasta according to package directions, adding green beans during the last 5 minutes. Drain; rinse with cold water.
2. Meanwhile, for croutons, toss bagel pieces with the 1 tbsp. oil. Transfer to a baking pan. Bake for 8 to 10 minutes or until golden, stirring once. Cool on a wire rack.
3. For vinaigrette, in a saucepan whisk together vinegar, mustard, and salt. Slowly whisk in the ¾ cup oil. Heat over medium-low just until warm, whisking constantly. Remove. Stir in onion and capers.
5. In an extra-large bowl drizzle pasta and beans, lettuce, mozzarella, salmon, and croutons with vinaigrette; gently toss. Drizzle with vinaigrette; gently toss. Sprinkle with cracked black pepper. Makes 6 servings.
EACH SERVING *622 cal, 38 g fat, 33 mg chol, 49 g carb, 1,019 mg sodium, 3 g fiber, 19 g pro.*

With smoked salmon and warm caper dressing, this pasta salad is a veggie-packed riff on a brunch classic.

LOW FAT   FAST

Carrot Orzotto

Photo on page 80

Fast-cooking orzo and a savory chicken-carrot juice blend ensures the creamy goodness of risotto yet in a fraction of the time of the classic version.

START TO FINISH 30 min.

- 2 cups carrot juice
- 1 14½-oz. can chicken broth (1¾ cups)
- 1 Tbsp. olive oil
- 2 Tbsp. butter
- 10 oz. orzo pasta
- 1 cup purchased shredded carrots
- ½ cup water
- ¼ tsp. kosher salt
- ½ lemon, zested and juiced
- ½ cup crumbled feta cheese
  Black pepper
  Fresh mint leaves (optional)

1. In a medium saucepan heat carrot juice and chicken broth over medium heat; cover to keep warm.
2. Meanwhile, in a large skillet heat oil and butter until melted. Add orzo; cook and stir 3 to 5 minutes or until orzo is golden brown; stir in carrots. Add 1 cup warm broth mixture to orzo. Stir until absorbed. Continue adding broth mixture, 1 cup at a time, stirring just until absorbed. Cook until orzo is tender; remove from heat. Slowly stir in the water until creamy. Stir in salt, lemon zest, and lemon juice. Top with feta, black pepper and, if desired, mint leaves. Makes 6 servings.
EACH SERVING *302 cal, 10 g fat, 23 mg chol, 45 g carb, 555 mg sodium, 3 g fiber, 9 g pro.*

CARROT ORZOTTO
Recipe on page 79

This cozy and compact nest of bacon, eggs, and bucatini is one reason to add pasta to morning meals.

Eggs and Bacon Bucatini Nest

PREP 25 min. BAKE 30 min.
STAND 2 min.

- 8 oz. bucatini pasta
- 8 slices bacon, halved and sliced lengthwise
- 2 cloves garlic, smashed
- 2 Tbsp. olive oil
- 7 eggs
- ¼ tsp. kosher salt
- ½ tsp. cracked black pepper
- ¾ cup white cheddar cheese, shredded
  Snipped fresh Italian parsley

1. Preheat oven to 400°F. Grease six 10-oz. ramekins or custard cups. Set aside. Cook pasta according to package directions. Drain; set aside.
2. In a large skillet cook bacon until lightly browned yet still limp. Transfer to paper towels; drain.
3. In a saucepan cook garlic in hot oil over low heat for 2 minutes or until fragrant. Remove from heat and discard garlic. In a bowl whisk together the garlic-flavor oil, 1 egg, salt, and pepper. Add pasta and bacon; toss until coated.
4. Place about 1 cup pasta mixture in each ramekin and twirl with a fork. Create an indent in the center. Bake 5 minutes. Divide cheese among ramekins. Crack 1 egg into center of each ramekin. Return to oven.
5. Bake 25 minutes or until egg whites are firmly set and yolks are thickened. Remove from oven; let stand 2 minutes. Remove from ramekins. Sprinkle with parsley and additional kosher salt and cracked pepper. Makes 6 servings.
EACH SERVING *373 cal, 19 g fat, 242 mg chol, 29 g carb, 465 mg sodium, 1 g fiber, 20 g pro.*

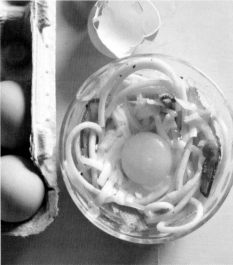

ASPARAGUS RAVIOLI PIE
Recipe on page 86

**HOT HONEY PASTA
AND BEETS**
Recipe on page 86

The first crops of spring—tender asparagus, baby beets, and bright green peas—are celebrated in light pasta dishes.

Asparagus Ravioli Pie

Photo on page 84

PREP 40 min. BAKE 20 min.

Nonstick cooking spray
12 oz. refrigerated chicken-filled ravioli
12 oz. asparagus spears, trimmed and shaved
3 cloves garlic, minced
3 Tbsp. butter
3 Tbsp. all-purpose flour
2½ cups milk
3 Tbsp. grated Parmesan cheese
1 Tbsp. snipped fresh tarragon
1 Tbsp. finely shredded lemon peel
½ tsp. salt
Shaved asparagus and/or shredded lemon peel (optional)

1. Preheat oven to 375°F. Coat a 9-inch pie plate with nonstick cooking spray. Cook ravioli according to package directions. Using a slotted spoon remove ravioli from cooking water and place on a baking sheet lined with parchment paper to drain. Add asparagus to cooking water for 1 minute. Drain; rinse with cold water.
2. In a medium saucepan cook garlic in butter over medium heat for 1 minute. Stir in flour. Stir in milk all at once; cook and stir until thickened and bubbly. Remove from heat. Stir in cheese, tarragon, lemon peel, and salt.
3. Spread ½ cup sauce in prepared pie plate. Arrange half the ravioli on sauce. Spoon half the remaining sauce over ravioli. Top with asparagus. Add remaining ravioli and sauce.
4. Bake, uncovered, 20 to 25 minutes or until bubbly. Cool 10 minutes on a wire rack. If desired, top with shaved asparagus and lemon peel. Makes 6 servings.

EACH SERVING 296 cal, 15 g fat, 64 mg chol, 24 g carb, 598 mg sodium, 1 g fiber, 14 g pro.

Hot Honey Pasta and Beets

Photo on page 85

PREP 30 min. BAKE 7 min.

1 cup walnut halves
2 tsp. olive oil
½ tsp. kosher salt
1½ lb. small golden beets, peeled and quartered
12 oz. orecchiette pasta
2 Tbsp. olive oil
1 medium red onion, cut into thin wedges
3 cloves garlic, sliced
3 Tbsp. lemon juice
2 Tbsp. honey
½ tsp. crushed red pepper
¼ cup chopped fresh dill

1. Preheat oven to 350°F. In a bowl combine walnuts, the 2 tsp. olive oil, and salt. Transfer to shallow baking pan. Bake 7 minutes or until walnuts are lightly browned; set aside.
2. Meanwhile, bring a large pot of salted water to boiling. Add beets; return to boiling. Add pasta and cook according to package directions. Reserve ½ cup pasta water. Drain pasta and beets.
3. In an extra-large skillet heat the 2 Tbsp. olive oil over low heat. Add onion and garlic; cook and stir until fragrant. Add lemon juice, honey, and crushed red pepper. Increase heat to medium. Add pasta; toss until coated, adding pasta water as needed if pasta seems dry. Season to taste with salt. Remove from heat. Toss with walnuts and dill. Makes 6 servings.

EACH SERVING 443 cal, 18 g fat, 0 g chol, 73 g carb, 252 mg sodium, 6 g fiber, 10 g pro.

Spring Onion Alphabet Soup

PREP 20 min. COOK 30 min.

¼ cup butter
1 Tbsp. olive oil
1 cup thinly sliced Vidalia onion
1 large leek, white part thinly sliced
1 bunch green onions, thinly sliced
2 cups fresh or frozen shelled peas
4 cups reduced-sodium chicken broth
4 cups water
1 cup small pasta (alphabet-shape or acini di pepe)
1 tsp. kosher salt
3 Tbsp. fresh lemon juice
1 cup torn basil leaves
1 recipe Lemon Sour Cream
1 recipe Fontina Toast (optional)

1. In a 4-qt. Dutch oven heat butter and olive oil over medium-low heat until butter is melted. Add Vidalia onion; stir until coated. Cook, covered, for 15 minutes or until translucent, stirring occasionally. Add leek and green onions. Cook, covered, 10 minutes. Stir in peas. Add chicken broth, the water, pasta, and salt. Bring to boiling. Reduce heat. Simmer, uncovered, 5 minutes. Stir in lemon juice and basil.
2. Serve with Lemon Sour Cream and, if desired, Fontina Toast. Makes 6 servings.

Lemon Sour Cream In a bowl combine ½ cup sour cream, ¼ cup mayonnaise, ¼ cup chopped chives, 1 Tbsp. lemon juice, and dash of garlic powder. Season with salt and pepper.

EACH SERVING 352 cal, 19 g fat, 37 mg chol, 34 g carb, 715 mg sodium, 4 g fiber, 11 g pro.

Fontina Toast Top 6 slices of sourdough bread with 6 slices fontina cheese. Arrange on a baking sheet. Broil 3 to 4 inches from the heat for 1 to 2 minutes or until cheese is melted.

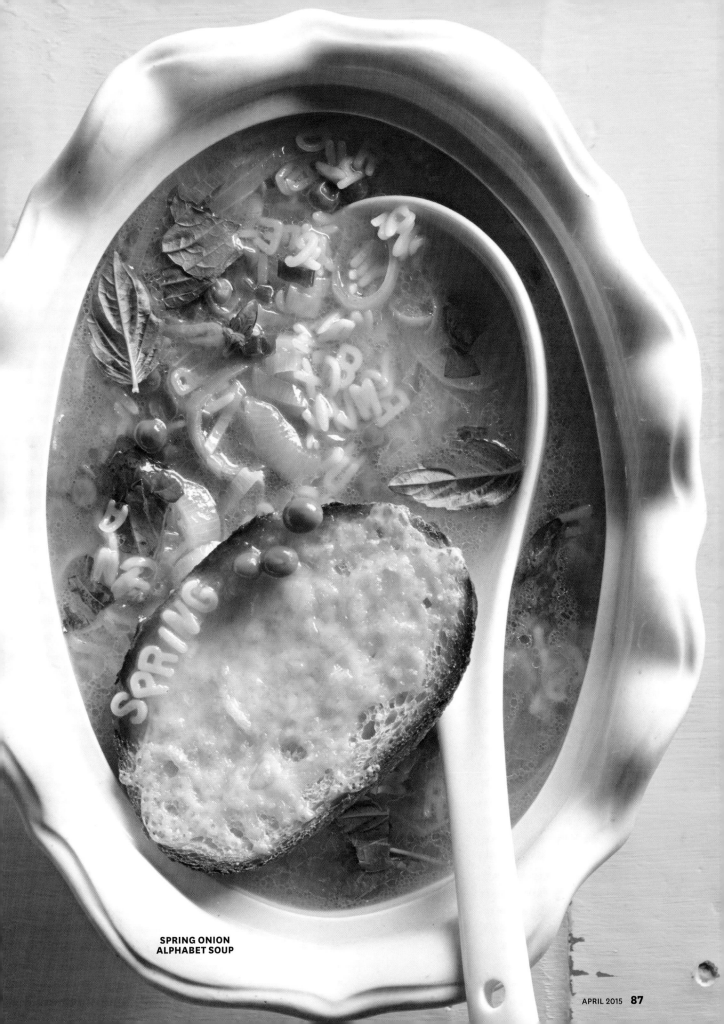

SPRING ONION
ALPHABET SOUP

home cooking: scones

Dress them up for brunch or nibble them in afternoon tea—four delicious takes and our best tips for perfecting these humble pastries.

Lavender-Honey Scones

Dried lavender buds steeped in warm cream impart delightfully light floral essence. Let the cream cool completely before adding it to the flour mixture to prevent melting the cut-in butter.

PREP 20 min. CHILL 30 min.
BAKE 13 min.

MAKE A WELL The biggest fail when making scones is overmixing. That's where the well helps. When you pour the cream mixture in the center—as opposed to all over—it's quicker to stir together the liquid and dry ingredients.

> ¾ cup whipping cream
> 2 Tbsp. honey
> 1 Tbsp. dried lavender buds
> 2½ cups all-purpose flour
> 1 Tbsp. baking powder
> ¼ tsp. salt
> 6 Tbsp. butter
> 1 egg, lightly beaten

1. Preheat oven to 400°F. In a small saucepan combine whipping cream, honey, and lavender. Warm over medium heat until mixture begins to steam, about 10 minutes. Chill about 30 minutes or until completely cooled.
2. Meanwhile, in a large bowl combine flour, baking powder, and salt. Using a pastry blender, cut in butter until mixture resembles coarse crumbs. Make a well in the center of flour mixture; set aside.
3. Whisk egg into cooled cream mixture. Add egg mixture all at once to flour mixture. Using a fork, stir just until moistened.
4. Turn dough out onto a lightly floured surface. Knead dough by folding and gently pressing 10 to 12 strokes or until dough is nearly smooth. Pat dough into a 10×4-inch rectangle. Cut in half lengthwise and in sixths crosswise to make 12 rectangles.
5. Place rectangles 2 inches apart on an ungreased baking sheet. Brush with additional whipping cream. Bake 13 to 15 minutes or until golden brown. Drizzle with additional honey, if desired. Serve warm. Makes 12 scones.
EACH SCONE *224 cal, 13 g fat, 55 mg chol, 181 mg sodium, 24 g carb, 1 g fiber, 4 g pro.*

STIR LIGHTLY A fork works best for cutting through the wet and dry ingredients. A spoon or spatula tends to create clumps as you stir. Combine just until moistened and a few dry spots remain. Don't overmix.

KNEAD GENTLY A light touch is key. Unlike yeast breads, which call for several minutes of kneading to develop gluten, knead scone dough just until it holds together. Over-kneading creates a tough crust and flat scone.

The perfect scone is light, flaky, tender, slightly sweet, and best eaten warm right out of the oven.

STRAWBERRY SHORTCAKE SCONES
Recipe on page 92

**ROASTED GRAPE AND
ROSEMARY SCONES**
Recipe on page 92

KID FRIENDLY

Strawberry Shortcake Scones

Photo on page 90

Creamy ricotta makes these scones extra-tender.

PREP 20 min. BAKE 15 min.

- 1 cup chopped fresh strawberries
- 1 Tbsp. all-purpose flour
- 2½ cups all-purpose flour
- 3 Tbsp. sugar
- 1 Tbsp. baking powder
- ¼ tsp. salt
- 6 Tbsp. butter
- 1 egg, lightly beaten
- ¾ cup whole milk ricotta cheese
- ¼ cup whipping cream

1. Preheat oven to 400°F. In a small bowl toss together strawberries and the 1 Tbsp. flour. In a large bowl combine the 2½ cups flour, sugar, baking powder, and salt. Using a pastry blender, cut in butter until mixture resembles coarse crumbs. Make a well in center of flour mixture.
2. In a medium bowl combine egg, ricotta, and whipping cream. Add egg mixture all at once to flour mixture. Add strawberries. Using a fork, stir just until moistened.
3. Turn dough out onto a lightly floured surface. Knead dough by folding and gently pressing 10 to 12 strokes or until nearly smooth. Pat dough into a 10×4-inch rectangle. Cut in half lengthwise and in sixths crosswise to make 12 rectangles.
4. Place rectangles 2 inches apart on an ungreased baking sheet. Brush with additional whipping cream. Sprinkle with coarse sugar. Bake 15 to 18 minutes or until golden brown. Serve warm. Makes 12 scones.
EACH SCONE *227 cal, 11 g fat, 49 mg chol, 238 mg sodium, 27 g carb, 1 g fiber, 5 g pro.*

Roasted Grape and Rosemary Scones

Photo on page 91

Roasting grapes caramelizes their sugars—like raisins that are fresher, juicier, and bursting with sweetness. They are paired with rosemary for this recipe and are equally delicious with thyme or basil.

PREP 25 min. ROAST 20 min. BAKE 13 min.

- 1½ cups seedless green grapes
- 2½ cups all-purpose flour
- 2 Tbsp. sugar
- 1 Tbsp. baking powder
- ¼ tsp. salt
- 6 Tbsp. butter
- 1 egg, lightly beaten
- 1 8-oz. carton crème fraîche
- ¼ cup whipping cream
- 1 Tbsp. chopped fresh rosemary

1. Preheat oven to 400°F. Place grapes on an ungreased baking sheet. Roast 20 to 25 minutes or until browned and starting to burst; set aside.
2. In a large bowl combine flour, sugar, baking powder, and salt. Using a pastry blender, cut in butter until mixture resembles coarse crumbs. Make a well in center of flour mixture; set aside.
3. In a medium bowl combine egg, crème fraîche, and whipping cream. Add egg mixture all at once to flour mixture. Sprinkle with roasted grapes and rosemary. Using a fork, stir just until moistened.
4. Turn dough out onto a lightly floured surface. Knead dough by folding and gently pressing 10 to 12 strokes or until dough is nearly smooth. Pat dough into a 10×4-inch rectangle. Cut in half lengthwise and in sixths crosswise to make 12 rectangles.
5. Place rectangles 2 inches apart on an ungreased baking sheet. Brush with additional whipping cream. Bake 13 to 15 minutes or until golden brown. Serve warm. Makes 12 scones.
EACH SCONE *267 cal, 17 g fat, 68 mg chol, 232 mg sodium, 26 g carb, 1 g fiber, 4 g pro.*

KID FRIENDLY

Toasted Coconut and Chocolate Chip Scones

Toasted coconut is ground fine for subtle flavor and sweetness that begs to be dunked in a cup of coffee.

PREP 20 min. BAKE 13 min.

- 1 cup shredded unsweetened coconut
- 2¼ cups all-purpose flour
- 1 Tbsp. sugar
- 1 Tbsp. baking powder
- ¼ tsp. salt
- 6 Tbsp. cold butter
- 1 egg, lightly beaten
- ¾ cup whipping cream
- 1 cup semisweet chocolate pieces

1. Preheat oven to 400°F. Spread coconut on a baking sheet; bake 5 to 7 minutes or until golden brown, stirring once. Cool slightly. Transfer to a food processor. Process until finely ground.
2. In a large bowl combine flour, sugar, baking powder, and salt. Using a pastry blender, cut in butter until mixture resembles coarse crumbs. Make a well in center of flour mixture.
3. In a medium bowl combine egg and whipping cream. Add egg mixture all at once to flour mixture. Add toasted coconut and chocolate pieces. Using a fork, stir just until moistened.
4. Turn dough out onto a lightly floured surface. Knead dough by folding and gently pressing 10 to 12 strokes or until dough is nearly smooth. Pat dough into a 10×4-inch rectangle. Cut in half lengthwise and in sixths crosswise to make 12 rectangles.
5. Place rectangles 2 inches apart on an ungreased baking sheet. Brush with additional whipping cream. Bake 13 to 15 minutes or until golden brown. If desired, top scones with additional shredded coconut the last 5 minutes of baking. Serve warm. Makes 12 scones.
EACH SCONE *305 cal, 19 g fat, 55 mg chol, 248 mg sodium, 32 g carb, 2 g fiber, 4 g pro.*

**TOASTED COCONUT
AND CHOCOLATE
CHIP SCONES**

weeknight delicious

Fast and fresh solutions for dinner tonight.

PORK AND POTATOES WITH MINTED YOGURT

Pork and Potatoes with Minted Yogurt

Cumin, chili, and garlic add a savory boost to meat. Try this rub on chicken or seafood, or stir into tomato soup.

PREP 25 min. ROAST 25 min. STAND 3 min.

- 2 tsp. ground cumin
- 2 tsp. chili powder
- 1 tsp. salt
- ½ tsp. garlic powder
- 1 1-lb. pork tenderloin
- 2 Tbsp. canola oil
- 1 lb. tiny yellow new potatoes, cut into 1-inch chunks

Minted Yogurt
- 1 cup plain Greek yogurt
- ½ cup chopped cucumber
- ½ cup chopped fresh mint
- 1 tsp. shredded lemon peel
- 1 tsp. fresh lemon juice

1. Preheat oven to 425°F. Line a shallow baking pan with foil; set aside.
2. For spice rub, in a small bowl combine cumin, chili powder, salt, and garlic powder. Set aside 1 tsp. rub. Place pork tenderloin on prepared baking pan. Brush pork with 1 Tbsp. of the oil. Rub pork with remaining rub. Arrange potatoes around pork. Drizzle potatoes with remaining 1 Tbsp. oil and sprinkle with reserved 1 tsp. rub; toss to coat.
3. Roast 25 to 30 minutes or until pork is done (145°F) and potatoes are tender. Cover; let stand 3 minutes.
4. Meanwhile, for Minted Yogurt, in a small bowl stir together yogurt, cucumber, mint, lemon peel, and juice. Season to taste with salt and black pepper. Serve with sliced pork and potatoes. Makes 4 servings.

EACH SERVING *321 cal, 11 g fat, 77 mg chol, 736 mg sodium, 23 g carb, 4 g fiber, 32 g pro.*

FARRO, CHICKPEAS, AND GREENS

Farro, Chickpeas, and Greens

With nutty flavor and chewy texture, farro is a sturdy companion to hearty greens like kale and chard.

START TO FINISH 30 min.

- 1 cup uncooked farro
- 1 15- to 16-oz. can chickpeas (garbanzo beans)
- 2 cups loosely packed fresh hearty greens (such as mustard, chard, or kale), coarsely chopped
- 1 cup grape tomatoes, halved
- ¼ cup extra-virgin olive oil
- 2 Tbsp. lemon juice
- 1 clove garlic, minced
- 4 oz. feta cheese, crumbled
  Salt and coarse black pepper

1. Cook farro according to package directions. Place chickpeas in a colander. Drain farro over chickpeas; rinse with cold water. Drain well.
2. In a bowl combine farro-chickpea mixture with greens, tomatoes, oil, lemon juice, and garlic. Top with cheese. Season to taste with salt and pepper. Makes 4 servings.

EACH SERVING *461 cal, 21 g fat, 25 mg chol, 419 mg sodium, 51 g carb, 8 g fiber, 16 g pro.*

CREAMY TUNA-NOODLE TOSS

In less than 30 minutes whip up healthful weeknight meals that are big on flavor.

LOW FAT   FAST   KID FRIENDLY

Chicken Sausages with Pineapple Relish

The fiery part of a pepper isn't the seeds but the membrane they're attached to. Start with one pepper and taste. You can add heat if you choose, but you can't take it away.
START TO FINISH **25 min.**

- ½ cup finely chopped fresh pineapple
- 1 jalapeño pepper, seeded and finely chopped*
- 2 Tbsp. finely chopped red onion
- 1 tsp. grated fresh ginger
- 1 tsp. cider vinegar
- 4 cooked chicken apple sausage links
- 4 hot dog buns, split and toasted

1. For Pineapple Relish, in a small bowl combine pineapple, jalapeño, onion, ginger, and vinegar.
2. Grill sausages on a grill rack or in a grill pan over medium-low heat for 7 to 9 minutes or until heated through.
3. Serve sausages in buns. Top with relish. Makes 4 servings.
EACH SERVING *293 cal, 9 g fat, 60 mg chol, 696 mg sodium, 35 g carb, 1 g fiber, 18 g pro.*
*Tip Chile peppers contain oils that can irritate skin and eyes. Wear plastic or rubber gloves when working with them.

FAST   KID FRIENDLY

Creamy Tuna-Noodle Toss

This stovetop version of tuna-noodle casserole gets a spritz of lemon and a generous addition of seasonal fresh peas (frozen peas work well too).
START TO FINISH **30 min.**

- 6 oz. wide egg noodles
- 1½ cups fresh or frozen peas
- 3 Tbsp. butter
- 1 small red onion, quartered and sliced
- 2 cloves garlic, minced
- ¼ tsp. freshly ground black pepper
- 2 Tbsp. all-purpose flour
- 1¼ cups milk
- 1 5-oz. can solid white tuna, drained and broken in chunks
- ½ cup grated Parmesan cheese
- 1 Tbsp. fresh lemon juice

1. Cook noodles according to package directions, adding peas during the last 2 minutes of cooking. Drain; return to pan.
2. Meanwhile, in a medium saucepan melt butter. Add onion, garlic, and black pepper; cook and stir over medium heat about 3 minutes or just until onion is tender. Stir in flour until blended. Add milk all at once. Cook and stir until thickened and bubbly. Remove from heat. Add tuna and ¼ cup of the cheese.
3. Pour tuna mixture over noodles and peas in pan. Toss gently to combine. Add additional milk, 1 Tbsp. at a time, until desired consistency. Season to taste with salt. Drizzle with lemon juice. Sprinkle with remaining cheese. Makes 4 servings.
EACH SERVING *438 cal, 16 g fat, 89 mg chol, 614 mg sodium, 48 g carb, 4 g fiber, 25 g pro.*

CHICKEN SAUSAGES WITH PINEAPPLE RELISH

new passover classics

Chef Todd Gray and Ellen Kassoff Gray of Equinox restaurant in Washington, D.C., take a fresh look at two traditional favorites.

KID FRIENDLY

Todd's Modern-Day Brisket

This pressed, red wine-braised brisket is infused with layers of flavor reminiscent of beef Bourguignon.

PREP **45 min.** BAKE **3 hr.**
REFRIGERATE **Overnight**

- 1 Tbsp. salt
- 1 Tbsp. smoked paprika
- 1 Tbsp. mustard seed
- 1 tsp. black pepper
- 1 3-lb. beef brisket, trimmed
- 2 Tbsp. canola oil
- 2 sprigs fresh rosemary
- 2 sprigs fresh thyme
- 3 garlic cloves, crushed
- 1 carrot, chopped
- 2 celery ribs, chopped
- 1 small onion, chopped
- 4 cups veal or beef stock
- 2 cups dry red wine (such as Cabernet Sauvignon)
- ½ cup balsamic vinegar
  Fresh Italian parsley sprigs (optional)

1. Preheat oven to 325°F. In a small bowl combine salt, paprika, mustard seed, and black pepper. Rub over brisket. In a large skillet heat oil over medium-high heat. Add brisket; brown on both sides, turning once, about 5 to 7 minutes per side.
2. Transfer brisket to a 4-qt. Dutch oven. Add rosemary, thyme, and garlic. Add vegetables; pour in stock, wine, and vinegar. Cover with heavy-duty aluminum foil.
3. Bake 3 to 4 hours or until brisket is fork-tender. Transfer brisket to a plate. Strain liquid through a fine-mesh strainer into a small saucepan (discard herbs, vegetables, and garlic). Wash and dry baking dish.
4. Return brisket to the baking dish. Place another heavy dish on top of the meat (ideal weight is 2½ lb.). Wrap foil over weights and baking dish; refrigerate overnight and until shortly before ready to serve.

5. Meanwhile, for sauce, bring the strained braising liquid to boiling over medium heat. Reduce heat; simmer, uncovered, until reduced to about 2½ cups and has a glazelike consistency (20 to 45 minutes). Season to taste with additional salt and black pepper. Refrigerate until it is ready to reheat the brisket.
6. Shortly before serving, remove sauce and brisket from refrigerator and place brisket on a cutting board. Cut brisket into 2- to 3-inch cubes. (Cubes don't need to be exactly this size or perfect along the edges.) Place brisket in a single layer in a 4-qt. Dutch oven. Pour enough sauce over to just cover brisket (add a little stock or water if needed). Heat over low heat for 10 minutes or until warmed through. Spoon brisket onto a serving platter. Pour remaining sauce over brisket. Sprinkle with fresh parsley, if desired. Makes 6 to 8 servings.
EACH SERVING *431 cal, 13 g fat, 147 mg chol, 1,659 mg sodium, 7 g carb, 0 g fiber, 52 g pro.*

THE NEW JEWISH TABLE
In their debut cookbook, Todd and Ellen share seasonal recipes, helpful tips, menus for all occasions, and the story of Equinox restaurant (celebrating its 15th anniversary). Rooted in tradition with a fresh, modern approach, this is food for every table.

Bring comfort and elegance to the Passover table with decadent brisket and golden matzo ball soup.

Matzo Ball Soup

Todd often serves this soup with kosher pappardelle noodles for the Passover menu at Equinox.

PREP 1 hr. CHILL 1 hr.
COOK 1 hr., 30 min.

- 3 large eggs
- 2 Tbsp. unsalted butter, melted (or 2 Tbsp. vegetable oil to keep it kosher)
- ¼ cup club soda
- 1 cup matzo meal
- ½ cup chopped Caramelized Onions
- 1 tsp. salt
- ⅛ tsp. black pepper
- 1 3-lb. whole chicken
- 1 large yellow onion, chopped
- 2 celery ribs, chopped
- 2 small carrots, chopped
- 1 medium turnip, peeled and chopped
- 3 garlic cloves, crushed
- ½ cup snipped fresh Italian parsley
- 1 bay leaf
- 2 Tbsp. snipped fresh thyme
- 12 black peppercorns
- 1 Tbsp. salt
  Sliced green onions (optional)
  Cracked black pepper (optional)

1. For matzo balls, in a large bowl whisk together eggs and butter. Whisk in club soda then matzo meal, Caramelized Onions, salt, and black pepper. As batter thickens, tap excess from whisk and continue mixing with a wooden spoon. Cover and refrigerate for 1 hour.
2. Meanwhile, for soup, remove gizzard and liver from chicken. Wash chicken under cold water; cut into eight pieces and place in a large stockpot. Add onion, celery, carrots, turnip, garlic, parsley, bay leaf, thyme, peppercorns, and the 1 Tbsp. salt. Add water to cover chicken. Bring soup to a simmer over high heat. Reduce to medium-low; simmer 1½ hours.
3. For the matzo balls, about an hour before serving, bring a large pot of lightly salted water to boiling. Spoon two or three ladles of soup into the pot for flavor. Shape matzo dough into balls about 1½ inches in diameter, rolling them between your palms (moisten hands with water). Add matzo balls to boiling water. Simmer, covered, for 30 to 40 minutes or until cooked. Use a slotted spoon transfer matzo balls to a paper towel-lined plate to drain; keep warm.

4. Remove and discard the bay leaf from the soup. Transfer chicken to a cutting board. Cool until you can shred it by hand into bite-size pieces. Pour broth through a fine-mesh sieve into a bowl; discard vegetables, if desired. Return broth and vegetables (if using) to pot. Add shredded chicken and matzo balls.
5. If desired, sprinkle soup with green onions and cracked black pepper. Makes 6 to 8 servings.
Caramelized Onions Thinly slice 2 medium onions (3 cups). Heat ¼ cup canola oil in a large skillet over medium heat. Stir in onions and ¼ tsp. salt; cook 4 minutes. Reduce to low; cook and stir onions for 20 to 30 minutes or until amber color. Drain in a colander. Makes about 2 cups. Refrigerate up to 4 days.

EACH SERVING *608 cal, 38 g fat, 218 mg chol, 1,813 mg sodium, 30 g carb, 4 g fiber, 36 g pro.*

**FISH TACOS WITH
ROASTED TOMATO
SALSA**

may

party time May is filled with celebrations. Take your pick of salads and finger foods to tote, plus count on quick-to-the-table fare to serve on busy nights.

110

124

126

rock the potluck

The season for gathering is here—from Mother's Day and graduations to block parties. These big-batch recipes will feed a hungry crowd.

Summer Spaghetti Salad

Spaghetti, string cheese, and swirls of squash "noodles" get the freshest tomato topping.
START TO FINISH **50 min.**

- ½ cup olive oil
- 3 cloves garlic, sliced
- 1 12-oz. package spaghetti, broken in half
- 3 cups reduced-sodium chicken broth
- 1 medium zucchini, ends trimmed
- 1 medium yellow summer squash, ends trimmed
- 6 sticks string cheese
- 4 cups cherry tomatoes, halved
- 1 large onion, finely chopped (1 cup)
- 1 cup chopped fresh Italian parsley
- ¾ tsp. kosher salt
- ½ tsp. black pepper
- ¼ cup red wine vinegar
- 1 recipe Salted Toasted Walnuts (optional)

1. Heat 2 Tbsp. of the oil in an extra-large skillet over medium heat. Add garlic and stir 1 minute. Add pasta; toss to combine. Add broth and simmer, uncovered, over medium heat for 10 minutes or until liquid is nearly absorbed, stirring occasionally. Remove from heat and cool 10 minutes. Transfer to a large bowl.

2. Meanwhile, using a spiral vegetable slicer, cut zucchini and yellow squash into long strands; snip into shorter lengths, if desired. Add to skillet; let cool completely. Pull cheese into thin strands; chill until ready to serve.

3. In a medium bowl toss together tomatoes, onion, parsley, salt, black pepper, remaining oil, and vinegar. Add cheese to spaghetti mixture. Top with tomatoes and, if desired, Salted Toasted Walnuts. Makes 10 to 12 servings.

Salted Toasted Walnuts In a shallow baking pan toss together ½ cup walnuts, 1 tsp. olive oil, and ¼ tsp. kosher salt. Bake in a 350°F oven for 5 to 10 minutes or until lightly browned.

EACH ½-CUP SERVING *335 cal, 19 g fat, 9 mg chol, 443 mg sodium, 33 g carb, 2 g fiber, 12 g pro.*

These fresh and colorful recipes attract second looks—plus invite second helpings.

Marinated Manchego and Oranges

Spain's most famous cheese, Manchego, is a semihard sheep's milk cheese, aged three months to one year, depending upon the desired texture (moist to crumbly) and flavor (nutty and mild to complex and sharp).
PREP 5 min.   MARINATE 4 hr.
STAND 1 hr.

- 8 to 10 oz. Manchego cheese, cut into wedges
- 1 orange, thinly sliced
- 4 to 5 sprigs fresh thyme
- ½ tsp. fresh cracked black pepper
- 1 cup olive oil
- 3 to 4 small assorted tomatoes, sliced
- ½ cup almonds, toasted* and chopped

1. Place cheese, orange slices, thyme, and pepper in a wide-mouth pint jar. Add olive oil to cover. Cover; chill 4 hours or up to 3 days. Let stand at room temperature 1 hour before serving.
2. To serve, arrange cheese and oranges on a platter. Top with tomatoes, additional fresh thyme, and almonds. Drizzle with remaining olive oil. Makes 10 servings.
EACH SERVING *206 cal, 18 g fat, 22 mg chol, 196 mg sodium, 5 g carb, 2 g fiber, 8 g pro.*
*Tip To toast whole nuts or large pieces, spread them in a shallow pan. Bake in a 350°F oven for 5 to 10 minutes, shaking the pan once or twice. Toast coconut in the same way, watching it closely to avoid burning. Toast finely chopped or ground nuts, or seeds in a dry skillet over medium heat for 2 minutes or until golden brown, stirring often.

FAST
Sweet Potato Deviled Eggs

Mexican crema is a thinner, tangier version of sour cream found in most Mexican markets and larger grocery stores. If you have trouble locating it, substitute sour cream thinned with a bit of milk.
START TO FINISH 30 min.

- 1 cup peeled, shredded sweet potato
- ½ cup Mexican crema
- ½ tsp. bottled hot pepper sauce
- 2 green onions, sliced
- 1 jalapeño pepper, stemmed, seeded, and finely chopped (tip, page 96)
- ½ tsp. salt
- ⅛ tsp. freshly ground black pepper
- 6 hard-cooked eggs, halved

1. Place potato in a small microwave-safe bowl; add 1 Tbsp. water. Cover with waxed paper. Microwave on high for 3 minutes or until tender. Let cool.
2. In a medium bowl combine crema and hot pepper sauce; set aside 1 Tbsp. Add potato, onions, jalapeño, salt, and a pinch of pepper to remaining crema mixture. For deviled filling, remove yolks from eggs; add to potato mixture. Mash with a fork; spoon filling into egg white halves. Drizzle with reserved crema mixture. Top with additional green onions. Makes 12 servings.
EACH SERVING *69 cal, 5 g fat, 102 mg chol, 147 mg sodium, 3 g carb, 0 g fiber, 4 g pro.*

FAST
Triple-Ruby Relish

The season's go-with-everything condiment is a balsamic-scented medley of watermelon, strawberries, radishes, and mint.
START TO FINISH 30 min.

- 16 oz. strawberries, hulled and chopped
- 6 radishes, cut into strips
- ½ cup chopped watermelon
- 3 Tbsp. white balsamic vinegar
- 1 to 2 Tbsp. snipped fresh mint

1. In a large bowl combine strawberries, radishes, and watermelon. Add vinegar. Let stand 10 minutes. Drain. Sprinkle with mint. Makes 3 cups.
EACH ¼-CUP SERVING *22 cal, 0 g fat, 0 mg chol, 1 mg sodium, 5 g carb, 1 g fiber, 0 g pro.*

**MARINATED
MANCHEGO AND
ORANGES**

**TRIPLE-
RUBY
RELISH**

**SWEET POTATO
DEVILED EGGS**

Can a recipe make you look good? You bet!
With party-size flavor, these big-batch
dishes are as pretty as they are delicious.

LOW FAT

Grilled Polenta and Arugula-Raspberry Salad

This savory cake is grilled until crisp then topped with a peppery arugula, sweet raspberry, and cool mint salad. A sprinkle of salty feta cheese brings it all together.

PREP 55 min. STAND 30 min.
CHILL 1 hr. GRILL 15 min.

- 1 cup yellow cornmeal
- 1 tsp. kosher salt
- 1 tsp. cumin
- ¼ cup bulgur
- ¼ cup finely chopped green onions
- 4 Tbsp. olive oil
- 3 Tbsp. lemon juice
  Salt and cracked black pepper
- 1 cup arugula
- 1 cup fresh raspberries
- ½ medium cucumber, sliced
- ½ cup chopped fresh Italian parsley
- ½ cup chopped fresh mint
- ¼ cup crumbled feta cheese

1. For polenta, in a medium saucepan bring 2½ cups water to boiling. Meanwhile, in a bowl stir together cornmeal, ¾ cup cold water, salt, and cumin. Slowly add cornmeal mixture to boiling water, stirring constantly. Reduce heat to medium; cook 15 minutes or until very thick, stirring occasionally. Remove from heat; stir in bulgur and green onions.
2. Spread polenta into a plastic wrap-lined 9-inch round cake pan. Let stand, uncovered, 30 minutes. Cover; chill at least 1 hour or until firm.
3. Heat a charcoal or gas grill to medium. Remove polenta from pan; pat dry. Brush both sides with 1 Tbsp. of the olive oil. Place directly on greased grill rack. Grill, covered, for 15 minutes or until heated through, turning once using a flat baking sheet. Transfer to a serving platter.

4. In a large bowl whisk together remaining oil and lemon juice. Season to taste with salt and cracked black pepper. Add arugula, raspberries, cucumber, parsley, and mint; place on polenta cake. Sprinkle with feta. Makes 10 servings.
EACH SERVING *136 cal, 7 g fat, 3 mg chol, 240 mg sodium, 17 g carb, 2 g fiber, 3 g pro.*

Choose a refreshing make-and-take salad: crunchy, sweet, and salty, or light and tangy with a bit of heat.

Confetti Corn Salad

This quick-to-the-table corn and melon salad will be a crowd favorite: fresh and crunchy vegetables and nuts with a silky coconut milk dressing.

START TO FINISH 30 min.

- 1 cup canned light coconut milk
- ¼ cup lime juice
- ½ tsp. kosher salt
- 1 tsp. ground turmeric
- 6 ears fresh corn, kernels removed
- 2 red sweet peppers, finely chopped
- 1 green onion, thinly sliced
- 1 cup chopped cantaloupe
- 1 cup dry-roasted, salted cashews
- ¼ cup unsweetened coconut flakes, toasted
- ½ cup plain corn nuts

1. In a large bowl whisk together coconut milk, lime juice, salt, and turmeric. Add fresh corn, peppers, green onion, cantaloupe, and cashews; toss to coat. Sprinkle with coconut and corn nuts. Serve immediately. Makes 10 servings.

EACH ½-CUP SERVING *177 cal, 11 g fat, 0 mg chol, 204 mg sodium, 20 g carb, 3 g fiber, 5 g pro.*

Avocado and Caramelized Pineapple

A delicious ode to the crisp, cool, sweet, and spicy flavors of summer.

START TO FINISH 40 min.

- 2 Tbsp. sugar
- ½ tsp. hot chili powder
- 1 3-lb. pineapple, peeled, cored, and cut into 1-inch slices
- ⅓ cup olive oil
- ⅓ cup white wine vinegar
- ⅓ cup orange juice
- ¼ cup snipped fresh cilantro leaves
- 2 cloves garlic, minced
- 1 tsp. sea salt or kosher salt
- ¼ tsp. freshly ground black pepper
- 1 medium red onion, coarsely chopped
- 1 large yellow or red sweet pepper, cut into 1-inch pieces
- 3 avocados, halved, seeded, peeled, and cut into 1-inch pieces
- 1 cup ripe blackberries, rinsed
- 2 hearts of romaine lettuce, chopped (about 2 cups)

1. In a small bowl combine sugar and chili powder; sprinkle evenly over pineapple. In an extra-large nonstick skillet cook pineapple for 10 minutes over medium heat, turning once, until sugar is caramelized and pineapple is golden brown. Remove pineapple from heat; cool 10 minutes. Cut into 1-inch pieces.

2. In a large bowl whisk together oil, vinegar, orange juice, cilantro, garlic, salt, and black pepper. Add pineapple, onion, sweet pepper, avocados, and blackberries; toss gently to combine. Add lettuce; toss gently to coat. Makes 12 servings.

EACH 1¼-CUP SERVING *162 cal, 11 g fat, 0 mg chol, 194 mg sodium, 15 g carb, 4 g fiber, 2 g pro.*

CONFETTI CORN
SALAD

AVOCADO AND
CARAMELIZED
PINEAPPLE

**ZESTY GREEN
BEAN SLAW**

**BASIL AND OLIVE
POTATOES**

Zesty Green Bean Slaw

This napa cabbage and green bean slaw gets sweet and salty flavor from a tangy dressing and a handful of salted peanuts.

PREP 20 min. CHILL 1 hr.

 1 lb. thin green beans, trimmed and cut up
 6 Tbsp. lime juice
 ¼ cup fish sauce
 ¼ cup sugar
 2 cloves garlic, minced
 8 cups shredded napa cabbage
 1 cup cilantro leaves and stems, chopped
 1 cup coarsely chopped salted peanuts
 1 fresh Fresno or Thai chile pepper, thinly sliced (tip, page 96)

1. In a medium saucepan cook beans in lightly salted water for 2 minutes. Drain. Plunge into ice water; set aside.
2. For dressing, in a screw-top jar combine lime juice, fish sauce, sugar, and garlic. Cover; shake well.
3. Drain beans. Transfer to a large bowl. Add cabbage and cilantro. Add dressing; toss gently to coat. Cover; chill up to 1 hour. Top with peanuts and pepper just before serving. Makes 10 servings.

EACH ½-CUP SERVING *126 cal, 7 g fat, 0 mg chol, 629 mg sodium, 13 g carb, 3 g fiber, 5 g pro.*

Basil and Olive Potatoes

Chunky potatoes and peppers are bathed in a warm basil dressing and tossed with olives.

START TO FINISH 40 min.

 2 lb. small new potatoes, quartered
 ⅓ cup canola oil
 1½ cups basil leaves
 3 cloves garlic, minced
 ⅓ cup white wine vinegar
 2 Tbsp. lemon juice
 2 Tbsp. mayonnaise
 ½ tsp. salt
 ½ tsp. black pepper
 2 large yellow sweet peppers
 1 cup Castelvetrano olives or other green olives, pitted

1. Add potatoes to a large pot of salted water; bring to boiling. Reduce heat. Cook, covered, for 10 minutes or just until tender. Drain. Transfer to a serving bowl.
2. Meanwhile, for dressing, in a saucepan warm oil, ½ cup of the basil, and garlic over low heat. Remove from heat; discard basil. Transfer oil and garlic to a blender. Add vinegar, lemon juice, mayonnaise, salt, and black pepper; blend until smooth. Pour dressing over potatoes.
3. Heat a gas or charcoal grill to medium heat. Add peppers to grill rack. Grill, covered, for 7 minutes or until charred, turning occasionally. Remove from heat; let cool. Halve peppers; remove stems and seeds. Cut into large pieces; add to potatoes along with olives. Toss in remaining basil. Serve at room temperature. Makes 10 servings.

EACH ½-CUP SERVING *180 cal, 11 g fat, 1 mg chol, 305 mg sodium, 19 g carb, 3 g fiber, 2 g pro.*

Farro and Fruit Salad

Photo on page 114

This hearty salad is pretty too! Nutty farro, juicy blueberries, earthy spinach, and a handful of salty pistachios sprinkled with goat cheese and tossed with a lemon vinaigrette. What's not to love?

START TO FINISH 45 min.

 1 Tbsp. extra-virgin olive oil
 3 shallots, finely chopped
 2 cups pearled farro
 4 cups reduced-sodium chicken broth
 ½ cup extra-virgin olive oil
 1 tsp. finely shredded lemon peel
 ¼ cup lemon juice
 1 Tbsp. chopped fresh oregano
 ½ tsp. salt
 ¼ tsp. black pepper
 4 cups baby spinach leaves
 2 cups blueberries
 1 fennel bulb, cored and thinly sliced
 1 bunch green onions, sliced
 1 cup roasted, salted pistachios, chopped
 8 oz. goat cheese, crumbled

1. In a large saucepan heat 1 Tbsp. of the oil over medium heat. Add 2 shallots; cook and stir 3 minutes. Add farro; cook and stir 1 minute more. Add broth; bring to boiling. Reduce heat. Simmer, covered, for 15 minutes or until soft. Rinse; drain. Let cool.
2. For dressing, in a screw-top jar add remaining shallot, the ½ cup oil, lemon peel and juice, oregano, salt, and pepper. Shake to combine. Toss half the dressing with farro. Chill dressing.
3. In a very large bowl toss farro, spinach, blueberries, fennel, green onions, pistachios, and goat cheese. Cover; chill up to 24 hours. Pour dressing over; toss to coat. Makes 10 servings.

EACH ½-CUP SERVING *442 cal, 26 g fat, 18 mg chol, 458 mg sodium, 41 g carb, 8 g fiber, 16 g pro.*

FARRO AND FRUIT SALAD
Recipe on page 113

**SWEET AND SPICY
PARTY WINGS**
Recipe on page 116

Take something new to a party—from a zesty batch of wings to an updated take on baked beans.

Sweet and Spicy Party Wings

Photo on page 115
Honey and hot pepper glaze on ultracrispy oven-baked wings is a crowd-pleaser.
PREP 35 min. BAKE 30 min.

6 lb. chicken wings (about 24), tips discarded and wings split
4 cloves garlic, thinly sliced
½ cup unsalted butter, melted
½ cup honey
¼ cup green hot pepper sauce
3 Tbsp. grated ginger
1 tsp. kosher salt
4 jalapeño peppers, seeded and chopped (tip, page 96)

1. Preheat oven to 450°F. Line two 15×10×1-inch baking pans with nonstick foil; set aside.
2. Bring a large pot of salted water to boiling. Add chicken and garlic. Simmer 8 minutes; drain. Pat wings dry. Transfer to prepared pans. Bake 30 minutes, rotating pans halfway through.
3. Meanwhile, for sauce, in a small saucepan stir together butter, honey, hot pepper sauce, ginger, and salt. Bring mixture to boiling. Reduce heat. Simmer, uncovered, 4 minutes or just until sauce is thickened.
4. Place wings in a large bowl. Add wing sauce; toss to coat. Sprinkle jalapeños on top. Serve immediately. Makes 10 servings.
EACH SERVING *375 cal, 25 g fat, 164 mg chol, 380 mg sodium, 15 g carb, 0 g fiber, 22 g pro.*

Deep and Smoky Baked Beans

Everything you love about baked beans, plus shredded pork and molasses sauce.
PREP 1 hr., 25 min.
BAKE 3 hr., 30 min.

1 lb. dry navy beans, rinsed
2 slices fresh ginger
2 Tbsp. canola oil
1 lb. boneless pork shoulder, trimmed of fat and cut into 1-inch pieces
1 cup diced white onion
⅓ cup tomato paste
⅓ cup dark molasses
3 Tbsp. soy sauce
2 Tbsp. rice vinegar
1 to 2 tsp. crushed red pepper
2 tsp. smoked paprika
8 cloves garlic, minced
Chopped kimchi (optional)

1. In a 4-qt. Dutch oven combine beans, ginger, and 8 cups water. Bring to boiling; reduce heat. Simmer, uncovered, 10 minutes. Remove from heat. Cover; let stand 1 hour. Drain beans, discarding ginger. Set aside.

2. Preheat oven to 325°F. In the same Dutch oven heat oil over medium heat. Add pork and onion. Cook and stir until browned, about 5 minutes.
3. Stir in drained beans, 4 cups water, tomato paste, molasses, soy sauce, rice vinegar, crushed red pepper, smoked paprika, and garlic.
4. Cover. Bake 2 hours. Uncover and stir; bake 1½ hours more or until desired consistency, stirring occasionally. Top with kimchi, if desired. Makes 10 servings.
EACH ½-CUP SERVING *289 cal, 6 g fat, 27 mg chol, 406 mg sodium, 40 g carb, 8 g fiber, 20 g pro.*
Canned Bean Variation Prepare as above, except omit dry navy beans, sliced ginger, and Step 1. Stir four 15-oz. cans navy beans, rinsed and drained, and 2 tsp. grated fresh ginger into pork mixture in Step 3. Reduce water to 3½ cups. Bake as directed.
Make Ahead Prepare as directed. Refrigerate overnight. Cover; cook over medium heat until heated through, about 20 minutes, stirring occasionally.

**DEEP AND SMOKY
BAKED BEANS**

fish tacos

Making this food truck fare is simpler than you think. Chef Marc Murphy grills up two fresh takes on the classic.

KID FRIENDLY

Fish Tacos with Roasted Tomato Salsa

PREP 45 min.

Roasted Tomato Salsa

- 2 medium tomatoes, cut into wedges
- ½ large red onion, cut into wedges
- ¼ cup olive oil
- ¼ tsp. salt
- ½ cup packed cilantro leaves
- 1 to 2 tsp. chipotle pepper in adobo sauce

Tacos

- 1 lb. fresh or frozen firm skinless whitefish fillets, such as cod, halibut, or sea bass
- 1 Tbsp. olive oil or vegetable oil
- 1 tsp. ground cumin or chili powder
- ½ tsp. salt
- ¼ tsp. black pepper
- 8 6-inch flour or corn tortillas
- ¼ cup sour cream
  Radish slices and/or snipped fresh cilantro

1. For Roasted Tomato Salsa, preheat oven to 450°F. Place tomatoes and onion in a shallow foil-lined baking pan. Drizzle with 1 Tbsp. of the oil. Sprinkle with salt; toss to coat. Roast 20 to 30 minutes or until browned. Cool slightly. In a food processor place roasted vegetables and cilantro. Process until smooth, gradually adding remaining oil with motor running. Add chipotle to taste.

2. Preheat grill pan or charcoal or gas grill. Brush fish with oil. Season with cumin, salt, and black pepper. Grill in a grill pan or grill rack over medium heat for 4 to 6 minutes per ½-inch thickness or until fish flakes easily when tested with a fork, turning once.

3. Warm tortillas in the pan or on the grill rack about 30 seconds on each side or until grill marks appear. Serve fish in tortillas with sour cream, Roasted Tomato Salsa, radish slices, and cilantro. Makes 4 servings.

EACH SERVING *359 cal, 17 g fat, 53 mg chol, 795 mg sodium, 27 g carb, 1 g fiber, 25 g pro.*

MARC MURPHY
OFF THE CHOPPING BLOCK

Marc is owner of four popular New York City restaurants, including the widely acclaimed Landmarc. You'll probably recognize him as a judge on Food Network's *Chopped*, where he's appeared since 2009. His first cookbook, *Season with Authority: Confident Home Cooking* ($30, Houghton Mifflin Harcourt), helps home cooks take comfort food to the next level. Think Deviled Eggs with Fried Oysters or Smoked Mozzarella and Ricotta Fritters, among others.

Citrus-Marinated Fish Tacos

START TO FINISH 35 min.

- 1 lb. fresh or frozen firm skinless whitefish fillets, such as cod, halibut, or sea bass
- ½ cup orange juice
- 1 Tbsp. honey
- 1 jalapeño chile pepper, chopped (tip, page 96)
- 1 clove garlic, minced
- 1 6-oz. container plain Greek yogurt
- 1 Tbsp. lemon juice
- ½ English cucumber, chopped (1 cup)
- ½ tsp. salt
- 8 6-inch flour or corn tortillas, warmed
  Shredded lettuce, jalapeño slices (tip, page 96), and/or orange zest

1. Cut fish into eight equal portions. In a shallow dish combine orange juice, honey, jalapeño, and garlic. Add fish; turn to coat. Cover; let stand 15 minutes, turning once.
2. Meanwhile, for yogurt-cucumber sauce, in a small bowl stir together yogurt, lemon juice, cucumber, and ¼ tsp. of the salt. Set aside.
3. Preheat a grill pan or gas or charcoal grill. Drain fish, discarding marinade. Sprinkle with the remaining ¼ tsp. salt. Place fish on the grill pan or greased grill rack over medium heat. Cover and grill 4 to 6 minutes per ½-inch thickness or until fish flakes easily when tested with a fork, turning once.
4. Place a piece of fish on each tortilla. If desired, top with shredded lettuce and jalapeño slices, and/or orange zest. Top with yogurt-cucumber sauce. Makes 4 servings.

EACH SERVING *301 cal, 9 g fat, 70 mg chol, 370 mg sodium, 27 g carb, 3 g fiber, 28 g pro.*

It's all about the fish. Here's what you need to know to get it right.

THE CUT Start with any flaky whitefish—cod, halibut, and sea bass work well. If you can find red snapper, that's great too. Choose a cut that's firm enough to grill.

DRY Use paper towels to dry the fish before seasoning or marinating. Even when you think it's dry, dry it some more. Excess water prevents the seasoning from really sinking in and will cause the fish to steam rather than get a deliciously crisp char.

OIL Seasoned fish should be lightly oiled. Marinated fish should be gently shaken to release excess. You don't want fish sticking to the grill, but too much oil can cause flareups.

FLIP When the edges turn up slightly, it's ready to flip. A flat metal spatula, sometimes called a fish spatula, works best.
FLAKE Press a fork into the flesh of the fish and twist gently. If it flakes easily, it's done.

weeknight delicious

Fast and fresh solutions for dinner tonight.

CHICKEN AND AVOCADO MASH WRAPS

Chicken and Avocado Mash Wraps

Sturdy romaine lettuce hearts hold a hearty filling of seared chicken, avocado, and tortilla chips for a summer-style taco salad.

START TO FINISH 30 min.

Nonstick cooking spray
1 lb. skinless, boneless chicken breast halves, flattened to ½-inch thickness
Salt and black pepper
2 avocados, halved, pitted, peeled, and coarsely mashed
½ cup chopped fresh cilantro
2 limes
8 romaine leaves
½ cup sour cream
½ cup thinly sliced green onions
1 cup grape tomatoes, halved
Tortilla chips, coarsely crushed (optional)

1. Heat a grill pan coated with nonstick cooking spray over medium-high heat. Season chicken with salt and pepper. Cook chicken for 8 to 10 minutes or until done (165°F), turning once. Place on a cutting board. Cover; let stand for 3 minutes before thinly slicing.
2. Meanwhile, in a bowl combine avocados, cilantro, and juice from 1 lime. Spoon avocado along the center of each lettuce leaf. Top with chicken. Halve the remaining lime; squeeze over chicken. Top with sour cream, green onions, tomatoes and, if desired, tortilla chips. Makes 4 servings.
EACH SERVING *316 cal, 18 g fat, 95 mg chol, 353 mg sodium, 12 g carb, 7 g fiber, 29 g pro.*

GNOCCHI AND SAUSAGE

Gnocchi and Sausage

Gnocchi, Italian for dumpling, are usually shaped into little balls, cooked in boiling water, and served as a side dish. Here, combined with sausage, peppers, and tomatoes the dumplings are part of an easy main dish.

START TO FINISH 30 min.

1 16- to 17.6-oz. package shelf-stable potato gnocchi
1 14- to 16-oz. package uncooked sweet Italian-flavor chicken sausage links, cut in ½-inch slices
1 medium yellow sweet pepper, seeded and chopped
½ cup onion, cut into slivers
2 cloves garlic, minced
2 roma tomatoes, sliced
1 cup arugula

1. Cook gnocchi according to package directions. Drain, reserving ⅓ cup cooking water. Set aside.
2. In a large skillet cook and stir sausage slices, sweet pepper, onion, and garlic over medium-high heat for 3 minutes. Add gnocchi, tomatoes, arugula, and reserved cooking water to skillet. Heat through, gently stirring occasionally. Makes 4 servings.
EACH SERVING *368 cal, 9 g fat, 76 mg chol, 911 mg sodium, 50 g carb, 5 g fiber, 22 g pro.*

LEMON BAKED FISH WITH DILL PANKO

KID FRIENDLY

Grilled Sirloin and Pepper Pasta Salad

Steak, peppers, blue cheese, and pasta—the gang's all here. Fire up the grill for this crowd-pleasing summer dinner salad.

PREP 25 min. GRILL 13 min.

- 6 oz. dried multigrain rotini pasta
- 8 oz. fresh asparagus spears, trimmed and cut into 2-inch pieces
  Nonstick cooking spray
- 1 lb. boneless beef sirloin steak
- ½ 16-oz. package miniature sweet peppers (about 10 peppers)
- ⅓ cup canola oil
- 3 Tbsp. balsamic vinegar
- 1 Tbsp. Dijon-style mustard
- 2 tsp. honey
- ½ tsp. salt
- ¼ tsp. black pepper
- 2 oz. blue cheese, crumbled

1. Cook pasta according to package directions, adding asparagus during the last 2 minutes of cooking. Drain and rinse with cold water; drain again.
2. Meanwhile, heat a grill or grill pan coated with cooking spray over medium-high heat. Add beef; grill 8 to 10 minutes or to desired doneness, turning halfway through. Transfer to a cutting board. Cover with foil.
3. Coat peppers with nonstick cooking spray. Grill 5 to 7 minutes or until lightly charred, turning frequently.
4. In a large bowl whisk together oil, vinegar, mustard, honey, salt, and black pepper. Thinly slice steak; add to bowl. Add pasta mixture to bowl; toss gently to coat. Sprinkle with cheese. Makes 4 servings.

EACH SERVING *618 cal, 36 g fat, 94 mg chol, 598 mg sodium, 39 g carb, 5 g fiber, 35 g pro.*

LOW FAT

Lemon Baked Fish with Dill Panko

Baking fish on a bed of lemon slices results in fresh citrus flavor with every bite.

PREP 20 min. BAKE 15 min.

- 1 lemon
  Nonstick cooking spray
- 4 6-oz. cod or tilapia fillets, rinsed and patted dry
- 2 Tbsp. extra-virgin olive oil
  Salt and black pepper
- 1 Tbsp. butter
- ½ cup panko bread crumbs
- 2 Tbsp. chopped fresh dill

1. Preheat oven to 425°F. Finely shred peel from lemon; set aside. Halve lemon. Thinly slice 1 lemon half. Coat a shallow baking pan with cooking spray. Arrange lemon slices in a single layer in prepared pan. Arrange fish on lemon slices. Brush with 1 Tbsp. of the oil. Season with salt and pepper. Bake 15 to 18 minutes or until fish flakes easily with a fork.
2. Meanwhile, melt butter in a large skillet over medium heat. Add panko; cook 1 to 2 minutes or until golden brown, stirring constantly. Remove from heat. Add remaining 1 Tbsp. oil, dill, and reserved lemon peel; toss together. Transfer fish to a serving platter; discard lemon slices. Squeeze remaining lemon over fish. Top with Dill Panko. Makes 4 servings.

EACH SERVING *253 cal, 11 g fat, 81 mg chol, 283 mg sodium, 6 g carb, 0 g fiber, 31 g pro.*

**GRILLED SIRLOIN
AND PEPPER
PASTA SALAD**

new ways with asparagus

Succulent and tender asparagus spears arrive with spring.

LOW FAT   FAST

Orange Asparagus and Calamari

START TO FINISH 25 min.

  2 oranges
  1 lb. asparagus, trimmed and chopped
  ½ lb. calamari, sliced ¼ inch thick
  2 tsp. coriander seeds, toasted and crushed
  ½ tsp. kosher salt
  2 Tbsp. extra-virgin olive oil
  ⅓ cup panko bread crumbs, toasted*

Snipped fresh Italian parsley and/or crushed red pepper (optional)

1. Using a vegetable peeler, remove three 4-inch long strips of orange peel from 1 orange; set aside. Using a paring knife, peel and segment oranges over a bowl to catch juices. Set aside.
2. In a very large nonstick skillet cook asparagus, calamari, coriander, reserved orange peel, and salt in hot oil over high heat, stirring frequently, for 4 minutes or until asparagus and calamari are tender. Remove from heat. Stir in orange segments and reserved juice. Sprinkle with toasted bread crumbs and, if desired, parsley and/or crushed red pepper. Makes 4 servings.
* To toast panko, in a bowl combine ⅓ cup panko bread crumbs with 1½ tsp. olive oil. Transfer to a skillet and toast over medium-high heat for 3 minutes or until golden brown.
PER SERVING 169 cal, 8 g fat, 132 mg chol, 289 mg sodium, 14 g carb, 4 g fiber, 12 g pro.

Asparagus Falafel

START TO FINISH **35 min.**

6 oz. fresh asparagus spears, trimmed and cut up
1 15-oz. can chickpeas (garbanzo beans), rinsed and drained
2 Tbsp. all-purpose flour
2 Tbsp. snipped fresh Italian parsley
3 Tbsp. olive oil
3 cloves garlic, halved
1 tsp. ground cumin
¼ tsp. salt
⅛ tsp. black pepper

Fresh asparagus tips (optional)
3 Tbsp. red wine vinegar
1 5.2-oz. container semi-soft cheese with fines herbs
4 cups mixed salad greens

1. In a food processor combine cut-up asparagus, chickpeas, flour, parsley, 1 Tbsp. olive oil, garlic, cumin, salt, and black pepper. Cover and process until finely chopped and mixture holds together (some visible pieces of chickpeas and asparagus).
2. Shape mixture into 12 patties. If desired, press asparagus tips into tops of patties. Heat remaining 2 Tbsp. oil in a large skillet over medium-high heat. Add patties. Cook 2 to 3 minutes per side or until browned and heated through.
3. For dressing, in a small bowl slowly whisk vinegar into half of the semi-soft cheese. Toss dressing with mixed greens. Serve asparagus patties with greens and remaining cheese. Makes 4 servings.

EACH SERVING *359 cal, 27 g fat, 38 mg chol, 506 mg sodium, 21 g carb, 5 g fiber, 9 g pro.*

Loaded Asparagus Hash Browns

START TO FINISH 35 min.

- 1 lb. asparagus, trimmed
- 3 cups frozen shredded hash brown potatoes
- ¼ tsp. kosher salt
- 3 Tbsp. extra-virgin olive oil
- 2 American cheese slices
- 6 oz. cooked Andouille sausage, sliced
- 1 red or yellow sweet pepper, cut in bite-size strips
- ½ cup chopped onion
- ¼ cup sliced pickled jalapeño peppers (optional)

1. Cut half the asparagus into matchstick-size strips. Bias-cut the remaining asparagus into 1-inch pieces.
2. In a large bowl combine matchstick-cut asparagus, hash browns, and salt. In a very large nonstick skillet heat 2 Tbsp. of the olive oil over medium-high heat. Add hash brown mixture to skillet and press down with a spatula. Cook hash browns for 5 to 7 minutes without stirring. Invert onto a baking sheet and return to skillet, adding more oil as needed. Cook 4 to 6 minutes or until crispy and browned. Transfer hash browns to a platter and top with American cheese; set aside.
3. In the same skillet heat remaining 1 Tbsp. olive oil over medium-high heat. Cook remaining asparagus, sausage, sweet pepper, and onion for 5 minutes or until vegetables are tender, stirring occasionally. Remove from heat and stir in jalapeños, if desired. Cut hash browns into wedges. Top with sausage stir-fry. Makes 4 servings.
PER SERVING *359 cal, 27 g fat, 36 mg chol, 804 mg sodium, 19 g carb, 5 g fiber, 12 g pro.*

FAST
Asparagus-White Bean Gratin

START TO FINISH 25 min.

- 1 cup half-and-half or light cream
- 2 cloves minced garlic
- 1 Tbsp. finely shredded lemon peel
- ¼ tsp. kosher salt
- 2 15- to 19-oz. cans cannellini beans, rinsed and drained
- ¾ cup finely shredded Parmesan cheese
- 1 lb. fresh asparagus spears, trimmed
- 3 to 4 oz. thinly sliced prosciutto

1. Preheat broiler. In a very large broiler-proof skillet stir together the half-and-half, garlic, lemon peel, and salt. Stir in beans and ½ cup Parmesan cheese. Bring to boiling, reduce heat, and simmer, uncovered, for 3 to 5 minutes or until slightly thickened. Meanwhile, wrap asparagus spears in bundles of 5 or 6 with prosciutto slices. Place bundles on bean mixture. Sprinkle with remaining cheese. Broil 4 to 6 inches from heat for 8 to 10 minutes or until browned and asparagus is tender. Makes 4 servings.

PER SERVING *368 cal, 14 g fat, 55 mg chol, 1,351 mg sodium, 33 g carb, 10 g fiber, 25 g pro.*

CARAMELIZED
BANANA
CREAM PIE

summer fun Warm days and long light call to outdoors. Meet family and friends for easy barbecues, refreshing cocktails, and succulent seasonal produce.

149

151

155

loving summer

Chef and TV personality Tim Love shares all the fixings for a backyard feast new Texas-style.

LOW FAT

Zucchini Pizza Tacos

Grilled pizza crust forms the shell of Tim's tacos, loaded with zucchini, squash blossoms, and ricotta. "This is a riff on the way kids eat pizza— folding it over like a taco," Tim says.
PREP 30 min. RISE 1 hr.

- 1 recipe Ranchero Sauce
- 2⅔ cups warm water (105°F)
- 2 Tbsp. granulated sugar
- 4½ tsp. active dry yeast
- 7½ cups all-purpose flour
- 6 Tbsp. extra-virgin olive oil
- 1 Tbsp. kosher salt
- 2 8-oz. balls fresh mozzarella cheese, sliced
- 3 lb. zucchini, quartered, grilled, and sliced
- 1 small red onion, thinly sliced
  Squash blossoms (optional)
- 15 oz. ricotta cheese, strained
  Snipped fresh chives and crushed red pepper

1. Prepare Ranchero Sauce. For dough, in a large bowl stir together warm water and sugar. Sprinkle yeast over top. Let stand 10 minutes or until foamy.
2. In a separate bowl whisk together flour, oil, and salt. Make a well in center; pour in yeast mixture. Stir with a wooden spoon until a dough ball forms. Transfer to a floured surface. Knead until smooth, about 5 minutes.
3. Divide dough into thirty 2-inch balls, about 2 oz. each. Arrange on an oiled baking sheet; brush with oil. Cover with plastic wrap. Let stand in a warm area 1 hour or until doubled in size.
4. Return dough balls to floured surface. Roll each to a 6-inch circle. Poke all over with a fork. Brush with additional oil. Season with salt and pepper. Place on grill rack. Cover and grill over medium heat for 1 to 3 minutes per side or until browned.
5. To assemble, spread each with 1 to 2 Tbsp. Ranchero Sauce. Add a few pieces of mozzarella, zucchini, red onion, and a squash blossom, if desired. Top with ricotta, chives, and crushed red pepper. Makes 30 tacos.

Ranchero Sauce In large saucepan heat 1 Tbsp. vegetable oil over medium heat. Add 2 chopped red sweet peppers, 2½ cups chopped tomatoes, 1 chopped medium white onion, and 2 chopped chile peppers in adobo sauce; cook until tender. Season with salt and pepper. Add ½ cup water; bring to boiling. Reduce heat; simmer, uncovered, 10 minutes. Remove from heat. Add ¼ cup honey. Transfer to blender. Puree until smooth.
EACH TACO *253 cal, 8 g fat, 18 mg chol, 349 mg sodium, 31 g carb, 2 g fiber, 9 g pro.*

THE LOVE EFFECT
Tim Love is a co-host on CNBC's *Restaurant Startup* and chef/owner of six Texas restaurants, including two locations of Lonesome Dove Western Bistro in Fort Worth and Austin. He also has a selection of products, including custom spice blends and his all-in-one grill, The Love Box.

Tim Love has a simple philosophy when it comes to entertaining.

"Fun first, then I think about the food," he says. "I've found that if I'm cooking in the kitchen, I feel left out of the party. But if I'm grilling, everyone congregates around the coals, we have a cocktail, and the party unfolds around the food." Tim cooks most of his no-fuss menu right on the grill, from fresh vegetable sides to the main course. "I obviously love cooking for people," says Tim, who helms six popular Texas restaurants, including Lonesome Dove Western Bistro in downtown Austin. "But to me, there's no greater moment than right before the meal, when everyone finds a place around the table, when the food is ready, and there's that feeling that a feast awaits. That sweet moment of anticipation gets me every time."

LOVE BOX

"A relaxed table means relaxed guests. If you're having fun, it's much more likely your guests will be too."

JALAPEÑO-CUCUMBER
MARGARITA

FAST

Jalapeño-Cucumber Margarita

"This is the best version of a margarita I know," Tim says. "The coolness of the cucumber and the spice of the jalapeño bring new flavor to this classic cocktail."

START TO FINISH 15 min.

- 1 lime, cut to wedges
- ½ tsp. kosher salt
- ½ medium English cucumber, sliced
- 1 jalapeño pepper, stemmed, seeded, and sliced (tip, page 96)
- 3 cups margarita mix
- 1½ cups gold tequila
- ¾ cup Patrón Citrónge or orange liqueur

1. Rub rims of 10 glasses with lime wedge; dip in kosher salt to coat.
2. In a large pitcher muddle cucumber and jalapeño with salt. Add margarita mix, tequila, and liqueur. Serve over ice. Makes 10 servings.

EACH SERVING *188 cal, 0 g fat, 0 mg chol, 99 mg sodium, 22 g carb, 0 g fiber, 0 g pro.*

FAST

Grilled Okra and Tomatoes

Photo on page 138

"Don't slow-cook okra or it gets slimy." Tim says. "Cook it fast and hot, and the texture is perfect."

PREP 25 min. GRILL 3 min.

- 1½ lb. fresh okra
- 1 lb. cherry tomatoes
- ¼ cup extra-virgin olive oil
- 12 cloves garlic, coarsely chopped
- ½ tsp. salt
- ¼ tsp. black pepper
- 1 cup mayonnaise
- 2 Tbsp. balsamic vinegar
- ½ Tbsp. lemon juice
- 1 cup walnut halves, toasted (tip, page 106) (optional)

1. In a large bowl combine okra, tomatoes, oil, garlic, salt, and pepper. Transfer to grill basket. Grill, covered, over high heat for 1 to 2 minutes for tomatoes and 3 minutes for okra or until charred and okra is crisp-tender, turning occasionally.
2. For balsamic aïoli, whisk together mayonnaise, vinegar, and lemon juice. Serve vegetables with aïoli and, if desired, walnuts. Makes 10 servings.

EACH SERVING *302 cal, 29 g fat, 9 mg chol, 265 mg sodium, 10 g carb, 3 g fiber, 4 g pro*

KID FRIENDLY

Char-Grilled Baby Carrots

Photo on page 139

"Kids love this dish," Tim says. "The carrots get irresistibly sweet, and they're fun to dip in creamy yogurt sauce."

PREP 20 min. GRILL 20 min.

- 3 lb. tricolor small carrots, tops trimmed
  Extra-virgin olive oil
- 2 cups plain Greek yogurt
- ¼ cup sour cream
- 1 Tbsp. steak rub
- ¼ tsp. kosher salt
- ½ cup roasted, salted pistachios, chopped

1. Wash and scrub carrots thoroughly under cold running water. Do not peel. Place in a large bowl. Toss with oil; sprinkle with salt and pepper. Place on a grill rack. Grill, covered, over medium heat for 20 to 25 minutes or until tender, occasionally rolling carrots up and down rack.
2. For yogurt sauce, stir together yogurt, sour cream, rub, and salt. Transfer carrots to a serving platter; top with pistachios. Serve with yogurt sauce. Makes 10 servings.

EACH SERVING *165 cal, 9 g fat, 5 mg chol, 510 mg sodium, 15 g carb, 4 g fiber, 7 g pro.*

**GRILLED OKRA
AND TOMATOES**
Recipe on page 137

**CHAR-GRILLED
BABY CARROTS**
Recipe on page 137

"Big flavor, big fun—that's the way we entertain in Texas," says Tim. "Bring the food out family-style and keep it coming off the grill."

STEAK ON THE COALS
WITH PICKLED PEPPERS

KID FRIENDLY

Steak on the Coals with Pickled Peppers

Tim lays skirt steak directly on the white-hot coals for intense smoky flavor. This technique delivers the ultimate heat for easy searing—a trick straight from the pros.

PREP **30 min.** COOL **1 hr.**
CHILL **up to 4 hr.** GRILL **3 min.**

- 2 lb. assorted peppers (miniature sweet, banana, or Anaheim), seeded and cut into rings
- 4 cups red wine vinegar
- 4 cups water
- ½ cup granulated sugar
- ¼ cup pickling spice
- ¼ cup kosher salt
- 4 lb. loin skirt or flank steak
   Canola oil
   Salt and black pepper
   Natural hardwood charcoal

1. For Pickled Peppers, add the peppers to a large heatproof container; set aside. In a large pot combine vinegar, water, sugar, pickling spice, and salt. Bring to boiling; stir until dissolved. Pour over peppers; stir. Cover with plastic wrap. Let stand 1 hour to cool. Transfer to an airtight container. Chill up to 4 hours. Drain; discard liquid.
2. Rub meat with canola oil. Sprinkle with salt and black pepper. Heat charcoal until white-hot. Spread coals in an even layer.
3. Place meat directly on coals. Grill 3 minutes for skirt steak or 5 minutes for flank steak, turning once. Remove; wrap in foil. Let stand 5 minutes. To serve, thinly slice meat across grain. Serve with Pickled Peppers.
EACH SERVING *307 cal, 16 g fat, 108 mg chol, 844 mg sodium, 5 g carb, 2 g fiber, 37 g pro.*

Fish and Veggie Wrap-Ups

The fish and veggies steam in parchment envelopes.
PREP **30 min.** BAKE **20 min.**

- 12 12×15-inch squares parchment paper
- 12 6-oz. skinless sea bass, halibut, or cod fillets, 1 inch thick
    Salt and black pepper
- 2 red/yellow sweet peppers, sliced into thin strips
- 1 Anaheim pepper, thinly sliced (tip, page 96)
- 1 bunch Broccolini (about 9 oz.)
- 1 small red onion, sliced
- 12 cloves garlic, sliced
- 3 Tbsp. extra-virgin olive oil
    Fresh mint leaves and lime wedges

1. Preheat oven to 375°F. For each packet place parchment on a flat surface. Place fillet in center. Season with salt and pepper. Stack a few slices of vegetables on fish. Drizzle with oil and top with some garlic. Fold parchment up and over fish. Fold in ends of parchment over fish. Roll packet over once. Fold in corners of top edge toward center to form a point (like an envelope). Tuck pointed end into the folded edge of the pouch.
2. Arrange packets on a very large baking sheet. Bake 20 to 25 minutes. Transfer to platter. To serve, carefully open each packet. Serve with additional oil, fresh mint leaves, and lime wedges. Makes 12 servings.
EACH SERVING *307 cal, 16 g fat, 102 mg chol, 484 mg sodium, 7 g carb, 2 g fiber, 34 g pro.*

FISH AND VEGGIE WRAP-UPS

Coffee with a kick: Tim spikes after-dinner iced espresso with coffee-infused tequila, a splash of milk, and a sprinkle of sugar. The chilled drink is a nice complement to the rich cream pies.

KID FRIENDLY

Caramelized Banana Cream Pie

"A great pie is my go-to summer dessert," says Tim, who serves mini banana cream, caramel, and chocolate pies at home. "I make them ahead of time, so there's nothing to do after dinner but sit back and enjoy dessert." He prefers them small, so guests can eat them without a fork.

PREP 2 hr. BAKE 12 minutes
COOL 1 hr. CHILL 1 hr.

- 1 recipe Cookie Tart Shells
- 2 cups packed light brown sugar
- 1 cup half-and-half or light cream
- ½ cup unsalted butter, cubed
- 1 Tbsp. kosher salt
- 2 Tbsp. vanilla
- 8 oz. white baking chocolate, chopped
- 3 egg yolks
- 3 Tbsp. granulated sugar
- 2 cups whipping cream
- 2½ lb. bananas, sliced ¼ inch thick
- 1 lemon, juiced
  Shaved chocolate

1. Prepare Cookie Tart Shells. For caramel sauce, in a large saucepan combine brown sugar, half-and-half, butter, and salt over medium-low heat. Cook 5 to 7 minutes or until bubbly around the edges, whisking gently. Add vanilla; cook 1 to 2 minutes or until slightly thickened. Transfer to a bowl; cover and chill up to 2 days. Let stand at room temperature for 1 to 2 hours before using.

2. For white chocolate cream, place white chocolate in a medium bowl. Set aside. In a separate bowl whisk egg yolks and sugar for 2 minutes or until pale in color. In a saucepan bring ½ cup of the whipping cream to a simmer over medium heat. Slowly whisk into yolk mixture. Return to saucepan; stir with a spoon until mixture coats the back of a spoon. Pour through a fine-mesh sieve placed over the bowl of white chocolate. Let stand 5 minutes. Stir until nearly smooth. Cool 1 hour.

3. In a separate bowl whip remaining cream to almost stiff peaks. Fold half into white chocolate mixture to lighten, then fold in remaining whipped cream. Cover and chill 1 hour or until set.

4. To assemble, in a medium bowl combine ¼ cup caramel sauce, bananas, and lemon juice. Fill each shell with ½ cup banana mixture. Top with white chocolate cream and shaved chocolate. Drizzle with caramel. Makes 12 servings.

Cookie Tart Shells In a large bowl knead two 16½-oz. rolls refrigerated sugar cookie dough and ½ cup all-purpose flour until combined. On a lightly floured surface roll dough, half at a time, to ¼-inch thickness. Using a 4½-inch fluted or round cutter, cut 12 rounds. Press rounds into 4-inch pie or tart pans. Bake in a 350°F oven for 12 to 15 minutes or until edges are golden brown (dough will puff in pans but fall during cooling). Cool completely on wire racks. Use a small sharp knife to loosen edges from pans. Set aside until ready to use or store in airtight containers up to 2 days.

EACH PIE *911 cal, 48 g fat, 140 mg chol, 737 mg sodium, 117 g carb, 3 g fiber, 8 g pro.*

sweet sizzle

Fresh seasonal fruit meet grill. Introduce these two to make delicious summer magic.

KID FRIENDLY

Skillet Dulce de Leche Peach Pie

PREP 30 min.   GRILL 45 min.
COOL 2 hr.

3½ lb. peaches, halved and pitted
 1 Tbsp. canola oil
 ½ cup granulated sugar
 3 Tbsp. cornstarch
 1 Tbsp. lemon juice
 1 14.1-oz. package rolled refrigerated unbaked piecrust (2 crusts)
 ¼ cup dulce de leche
 ½ tsp. kosher salt
 1 egg, lightly beaten
    Coarse sugar
    Vanilla ice cream and/or fresh mint leaves (optional)

1. Brush cut sides of peaches with oil. Arrange a charcoal or gas grill for indirect grilling. Place peach halves, cut sides down, on rack over medium heat. Grill peaches directly over heated side of grill, covered, for 3 minutes. Remove from grill and cut into ½-inch slices. Transfer to an extra-large bowl. Toss with sugar, cornstarch, and lemon juice.
2. Grease a 9- or 10-inch cast-iron skillet and line with 1 piecrust. Spoon peaches into crust-lined skillet. Spoon dulce de leche in mounds over filling. Sprinkle with salt. Cut slits in second crust; place over filling. Tuck dough in sides of skillet. Crimp edge as desired. Brush pastry edges with egg. Sprinkle with coarse sugar.
3. Place skillet on rack over unlit side of grill. Grill, covered, 45 to 50 minutes or until crust is golden brown, rotating once halfway through. Cool on a wire rack at least 2 hours. If desired, serve with ice cream and sprinkle with mint leaves. Makes 8 servings.
EACH SERVING *410 cal, 17 g fat, 31 mg chol, 352 mg sodium, 65 g carb, 3 g fiber, 4 g pro.*

Charcoal vs. gas? A charcoal grill imparts deep, smoky flavor, while gas lends a more mild flavor. Either is delicious!

**GRILLED FRUIT
COUSCOUS SALAD**
Recipe on page 149

Grilling unleashes the full potential flavor
of fruit and heightens sweetness.

**GRILLED CHERRY
FLATBREAD**
Recipe on page 149

FAST

Grilled Fruit Couscous Salad

Photo on page 146

START TO FINISH **30 min.**

- 2 fresh plums, pitted and halved
- 2 fresh nectarines, pitted and halved
- ¼ cup olive oil
- 1½ cups chicken or vegetable broth
- 1 cup couscous
- 2 green onions, thinly sliced
- 3 Tbsp. lime juice
- 1 Tbsp. honey
- ¼ tsp. salt
- ¼ tsp. black pepper
- 2 Tbsp. snipped fresh cilantro
- 1 Tbsp. snipped fresh mint
  Roasted, salted pepitas

1. Brush cut sides of fruit with 1 Tbsp. of the oil. Grill, covered, on the rack of a charcoal or gas grill directly over medium heat for 3 to 5 minutes or until charred. Remove; cut into wedges.
2. In a medium saucepan bring broth to boiling. Stir in couscous and green onions; remove from heat. Cover; let stand 5 minutes. Fluff with a fork.
3. For dressing, in a screw-top jar combine remaining oil, lime juice, honey, salt, and pepper. Cover and shake until combined. In a large bowl combine fruit, couscous, cilantro, and mint; drizzle with dressing and toss to coat. Top with pepitas. Makes 6 to 8 servings.

EACH SERVING *297 cal, 14 g fat, 1 mg chol, 341 mg sodium, 37 g carb, 3 g fiber, 8 g pro.*

Grilled Cherry Flatbread

Photo on page 147

START TO FINISH **40 min.**

- 1 lb. ready-to-use pizza dough
- 2 Tbsp. olive oil
- 3 oz. thinly sliced prosciutto, cut into strips
- 3 cups fresh sweet cherries, pitted
- 1 Tbsp. snipped fresh rosemary
- 4 oz. mixed baby greens
- 6 oz. smoked Gouda cheese, shredded (1½ cups)

1. Divide pizza dough in half. Roll each half to a 10-inch circle. Brush with 1 Tbsp. of the oil; set aside.
2. In a 12-inch cast-iron skillet heat remaining oil on the rack of a charcoal or gas grill directly over medium heat. Add prosciutto. Cover; cook 2 minutes, stirring once. Add cherries and rosemary. Cover; cook 2 minutes more or until softened, stirring once. Remove from heat. Stir in greens.
3. Place pizza dough directly on grill rack. Cover; grill 2 minutes. Turn dough over; grill 2 minutes. Top with cheese then prosciutto-cherry-greens. Grill 1 to 2 minutes more or until cheese is melted and crust is crisp. Makes 8 servings.

EACH SERVING *308 cal, 12 g fat, 35 mg chol, 654 mg sodium, 36 g carb, 2 g fiber, 14 g pro.*

FAST KID FRIENDLY

Grilled Blackberries and Ice Cream

START TO FINISH **20 min.**

- 2 cups blackberries
- 2 Tbsp. granulated sugar
- 1 tsp. finely shredded orange peel
  Ice cream or gelato
  Shaved orange peel (optional)

1. In a medium bowl stir together berries, sugar, and orange peel. Thread berries on 10- to 12-inch skewers. Grill, covered, on the rack of a charcoal or gas grill directly over medium heat 3 minutes or until slightly softened, turning occasionally. Serve warm berries over ice cream or gelato. Serve with shaved orange peel, if desired. Makes 6 servings.

EACH SERVING *186 cal, 8 g fat, 32 mg chol, 58 mg sodium, 26 g carb, 3 g fiber, 3 g pro.*

HALVE Large stone fruits—peaches, plums, nectarines—take well to direct grilling. Halve and pit first so the cut surface area comes in contact with the grill.

SKILLET Use a cast-iron skillet to grill small fruits or pieces (to contain all the juices). Cook other foods simultaneously.

KABOBS Smaller fruits, such as berries, are easy to skewer. Remember to soak wooden skewers in water for 30 minutes before grilling to prevent burning.

weeknight delicious

Fast and fresh solutions for dinner tonight.

SOY-SAUCE-MARINATED PORK CHOPS

LOW FAT KID FRIENDLY

Soy-Sauce-Marinated Pork Chops

Even with short marinade time, these chops pick up flavor. Once on the grill, the marinade ensures the chops stay moist and develop a perfect sear.
START TO FINISH **40 min.**

- 4 6- to 7-oz. bone-in pork chops, trimmed (about ½ inch thick)
- ¼ cup reduced-sodium soy sauce
- 3 Tbsp. lime juice
- 2 Tbsp. sugar
- 1 Tbsp. canola oil
- 1 Tbsp. cider vinegar
- 2 to 3 tsp. grated fresh ginger
- ¼ tsp. crushed red pepper
- 4 cups mixed spring greens
- ½ cup chopped fresh cilantro

1. Place chops in a 3-qt. rectangular baking dish. For marinade, in a small bowl whisk together soy sauce, lime juice, sugar, oil, vinegar, ginger, and crushed red pepper. Spoon 2 Tbsp. of the marinade over chops; turn to coat. Cover and let stand 20 minutes at room temperature, turning occasionally.
2. In a small saucepan bring remaining marinade to boiling. Reduce heat; simmer 1 to 2 minutes or until reduced to about ¼ cup.
3. For a charcoal or gas grill, place chops on grill rack. Cover; grill over medium heat for 3 minutes per side or until chops are slightly pink in the center (145°F), turning once.
4. Place greens on a serving platter. Top with chops. Drizzle with reduced marinade. Sprinkle with cilantro. Makes 4 servings.
EACH SERVING *259 cal, 8 g fat, 93 mg chol, 614 mg sodium, 11 g carb, 1 g fiber, 33 g pro.*

STEAK AND VEGGIE KABOBS

KID FRIENDLY

Steak and Veggie Kabobs

Lemons develop mellow smokiness and become a little sweet after a few minutes on the grill. Squeeze them over the finished steak and veggies.
START TO FINISH **40 min.**

- 1 lb. boneless beef sirloin, cut into sixteen 1½-inch cubes
- 1 medium zucchini (about 8 oz.), sliced
- 1 red onion, cut into wedges
- 2 lemons, cut into 4 wedges each
- 1 Tbsp. canola oil
  Salt and black pepper
- ½ cup mayonnaise
- ¼ cup sour cream
- 1 Tbsp. Dijon-style mustard
- 1½ tsp. snipped fresh tarragon leaves
- 1 clove garlic, minced

1. On eight 10-inch skewers, alternately thread beef, zucchini, and red onion. Add lemon wedges to ends of skewers. Brush with oil. Season with salt and pepper.
2. For a gas or charcoal grill, place kabobs on a grill rack directly over medium heat. Cover; grill 10 to 12 minutes or until desired doneness, turning once.
3. Meanwhile, for sauce, in a small bowl stir together mayonnaise, sour cream, mustard, tarragon, and garlic. Serve with kabobs. Makes 4 servings.
EACH SERVING *420 cal, 31 g fat, 86 mg chol, 482 mg sodium, 8 g carb, 1 g fiber, 27 g pro.*

GRILLED CHICKEN WITH BASIL CHIMICHURRI

New Potato, Avocado, and Egg Salad

Serve a hearty scoop of this creamy potato salad over a cold wedge of iceberg lettuce.

START TO FINISH 35 min.

- 1½ lb. tiny red new potatoes, quartered
- ¾ cup mayonnaise
- 2 Tbsp. cider vinegar
- 2 Tbsp. chopped fresh dill
- 1 Tbsp. yellow mustard
- 1 cup chopped red or orange sweet pepper
- 1 stalk celery, chopped
- ½ cup chopped red onion
- ½ cup chopped dill pickles
- 1 firm ripe avocado, halved, seeded, peeled, and sliced
- 4 hard-cooked eggs, peeled and sliced
  Salt and black pepper
  Iceberg lettuce

1. Place potatoes in a large saucepan; cover with water. Bring to boiling; reduce heat. Cook, covered, 8 to 10 minutes or just until tender. Drain; rinse with cold water. Drain; set aside.
2. Meanwhile, in a large bowl stir together mayonnaise, vinegar, dill, and mustard. Add sweet pepper, celery, onion, and pickles; stir to combine. Add potatoes, avocado, and eggs; gently stir until just coated. Season with salt and pepper. Serve over lettuce. Makes 4 servings.
EACH SERVING 593 cal, 42 g fat, 204 mg chol, 549 mg sodium, 44 g carb, 7 g fiber, 12 g pro.

FAST **KID FRIENDLY**
Grilled Chicken with Basil Chimichurri

Garlic-packed chimichurri is delicious over vegetables as well as meat.
START TO FINISH 30 min.

- 4 skinless, boneless chicken breast halves (about 6 oz. each)
- 3 Tbsp. extra-virgin olive oil
  Salt and black pepper
  Nonstick cooking spray
- ½ cup chopped fresh basil
- 2 Tbsp. finely chopped red onion
- 2 cloves garlic, minced
- 2 tsp. red wine vinegar
- 2 tsp. lemon juice
  Cooked green beans (optional)

1. Place each chicken breast half between plastic wrap. Using the flat side of a meat mallet, pound chicken to ½-inch thickness. Brush 1 Tbsp. oil on both sides of chicken; sprinkle lightly with salt and pepper. Heat a grill or grill pan coated with cooking spray over medium heat. Grill chicken 8 minutes or until done (165°F), turning once.
2. Meanwhile, for Basil Chimichurri, in a bowl combine remaining oil, basil, onion, garlic, vinegar, and lemon juice. Season with salt and pepper.
3. Serve chicken and, if desired, green beans, with chimichurri. Makes 4 servings.
EACH SERVING 301 cal, 15 g fat, 124 mg chol, 514 mg sodium, 1 g carb, 39 g pro.

NEW POTATO, AVOCADO, AND EGG SALAD

good libations

The challenge: Create a big-batch cocktail that uses no more than six ingredients, comes together in less than 15 minutes, and serves a backyard crowd. Four mixologists stir together their best tall pitchers of summer.

Sandia Spritz

Justin Elliott, Qui, Austin

1. In a blender combine 2 cups watermelon cubes, ¼ cup lime juice, ¼ cup honey, and 10 dashes aromatic bitters. Blend until smooth. Transfer to a pitcher. Add one 750-ml. bottle sweet white vermouth and 24 oz. chilled sparkling mineral water. Stir; serve over ice. Garnish with watermelon slices. Makes 10 servings.

Apposta

Charles Joly, Crafthouse Cocktails, Chicago

1. In a pitcher combine one 750-ml bottle gin, 2 cups Aperol, 2 cups sweet white vermouth, ⅔ cup strained lemon juice, and ½ cup chilled grapefruit soda. Garnish with thyme and orange peel. Serve over ice. Makes 10 to 12 servings.

Brown Derby

Eric Johnson, Bar Agricole, San Francisco

1. In a pitcher combine one 750-ml bottle bourbon, 1¼ cups lemon juice, 1¼ cups ruby grapefruit juice, ⅔ cup honey, ⅔ cup water, and 10 dashes bitters. Garnish with grapefruit slices. Serve over ice. Makes 8 to 10 servings.

Lime Fizz

Jon Palmer, The Bachelor Farmer, Minneapolis

1. In a large pitcher combine one 750-ml bottle dry vermouth, one 750-ml bottle chilled dry sparkling wine, 1½ cups lime juice, and ¾ cup simple syrup. Stir to combine. Garnish with fresh mint leaves. Serve over ice. Makes 10 to 12 servings.

OVEN-TO-GRILL BABY
BACK RIBS

july

dish up summer Revel in the simplicity of fruit cobblers, succulent ribs, pickled veggies, and flavorful weeknight meals.

159

170

173

**FIRECRACKER
CHOCOLATE CHERRY
COBBLER**

158 BETTER HOMES AND GARDENS ANNUAL RECIPES

American Cobbler

What better way to highlight the flavor of seasonal fruits than cobbler—America's sweetheart dessert.

KID FRIENDLY

Firecracker Chocolate Cherry Cobbler

The chocolate star topping has a hint of chipotle chile pepper—a nice flavor contrast to sweet-tart cherries and cooling ice cream.

PREP **40 min.** BAKE **30 min.**
STAND **30 min.**

Topping

- 1 cup all-purpose flour
- ⅓ cup granulated sugar
- 2 Tbsp. unsweetened cocoa powder
- 1 tsp. baking powder
- ¼ tsp. baking soda
- ¼ tsp. ground cinnamon
- ¼ tsp. ground chipotle chile pepper
- ¼ tsp. salt
- ¼ cup unsalted butter, cut into small pieces and chilled
- 1½ oz. semisweet chocolate, finely chopped
- ¼ cup milk
- 1 Tbsp. coarse sugar
  Vanilla ice cream (optional)

Filling

- ¾ cup granulated sugar
- ⅓ cup all-purpose flour
- 7 cups fresh or frozen pitted cherries, such as tart red, dark sweet, or Rainier

1. Preheat oven to 375°F. Grease a 2-qt. round baking dish.
2. For topping, in a medium bowl combine 1 cup flour, ⅓ cup sugar, cocoa powder, baking powder, baking soda, cinnamon, ground chipotle, and salt. Using a pastry blender or two forks, cut butter into the flour mixture until it resembles coarse crumbs. Stir in chocolate. Add milk; stir just until moistened. Knead dough three to four times in bowl until it holds together. Transfer to a floured surface. Form dough into a disk. Set aside.
3. For filling, in a large saucepan combine ¾ cup sugar and ⅓ cup flour; stir in cherries. Cook and stir until thickened and bubbly. Keep warm.
4. On a floured surface roll out dough to ¾-inch thickness. Using 2- to 3-inch star-shape cutters, cut out enough stars to cover filling, rerolling as necessary. Transfer hot filling to prepared dish. Arrange stars over filling. Brush with milk. Sprinkle tops with coarse sugar. (Place a baking sheet below the dish to catch drips during baking.)
5. Bake 30 minutes or until topping is baked through and filling is thick and bubbly. Let stand 30 minutes before serving. If desired, serve with vanilla ice cream and sprinkle with additional cinnamon. Makes 8 servings.
EACH SERVING *340 cal, 8 g fat, 16 mg chol, 183 mg sodium, 66 g carb, 4 g fiber, 4 g pro.*

HONEY-ROSÉ PLUM COBBLER

FIRECRACKER CHOCOLATE CHERRY COBBLER
Recipe on page 159

Combine fragrant fresh plums, crisp rosé wine, a crumble of goat cheese, and a drizzle of honey for a deliciously sweet and tangy cobbler.

Honey-Rosé Plum Cobbler

Sparkling or still rosé gives the honey-sweet sauce a crisp edge.

PREP 30 min. BAKE 25 min.
STAND 30 min.

Dough

1¾ cups all-purpose flour
¼ cup sugar
2 tsp. baking powder
¼ tsp. salt
½ cup milk
⅓ cup olive oil

Filling

⅔ cup rosé wine
⅓ cup honey
2 Tbsp. all-purpose flour
2½ lb. assorted plums, pitted and cut into 8 wedges each
2 oz. goat cheese (chèvre)

1. Preheat oven to 400°F. Grease a 2-qt. round baking dish.
2. For dough, in a medium bowl combine 1¾ cups flour, sugar, baking powder, and salt. Add milk and olive oil; stir to combine. Cover with plastic wrap. Set aside.
3. For filling, in an extra-large skillet stir together wine, honey, and the 2 Tbsp. flour until combined. Add plums. Cook and stir 8 minutes over medium-high heat until thickened and bubbly. Remove from heat; keep warm.
4. Transfer dough to a floured surface; roll out to ½-inch thickness. Using a 2-inch round cutter, cut rounds, rerolling as necessary. Transfer filling to prepared baking dish. Arrange rounds over filling. Sprinkle tops with sugar, if desired. (Place a baking sheet below the dish to catch drips during baking.)
5. Bake 25 minutes or until topping is golden. Top cobbler with crumbled goat cheese. Let stand 30 minutes before serving. If desired, top with additional sliced plums and drizzle with honey before serving. Makes 8 servings.
EACH SERVING *367 cal, 12 g fat, 7 mg chol, 234 mg sodium, 58 g carb, 3 g fiber, 6 g pro.*

GET STARTED

Select the ripest, juiciest, most in-season fruits you can find. Fruits at peak sweetness produce the best-tasting sauce.

Fruit filling thoroughly mixed with flour and cooked until thickened, is the spoon-scoopable supporting layer for cobbler toppings.

Heat the filling before baking to intensify flavors and ensure the biscuit topping bakes thoroughly.

A foil-lined tray under the baking dish will catch any bubbling over.

Peek at the cobbler toward the end of baking. If the filling is still cloudy, bake longer. When filling sauce becomes glossy, it's done.

The summer trio of graham crackers, chocolate, and marshmallows meets strawberries and a citrusy burst of orange for a campfire-inspired treat.

KID FRIENDLY

Strawberry S'mores Cobbler

Serve extra graham crackers to scoop up the last bits of cobbler.
PREP 30 min. BAKE 10 min.

- 1 sleeve whole graham crackers (9 to 10 rectangles)
- 3 oranges
- ¼ cup sugar
- 2 Tbsp. cornstarch
- 2 lb. fresh strawberries, hulled and quartered
- 16 to 18 large marshmallows
- 2 oz. milk or dark chocolate, broken into small pieces

1. Preheat oven to 400°F. Coarsely crush crackers into a 2-qt. round baking dish. Set aside. Finely shred 1 tsp. peel from orange. Juice oranges for ¾ cup.
2. In a large saucepan stir together orange peel, juice, sugar, and cornstarch; cook and stir until thickened and bubbly. Stir in strawberries. Spoon filling into dish, covering crackers. Top with marshmallows and chocolate, lightly pressing marshmallows into filling. (Place a baking sheet below the dish to catch drips during baking.)
3. Bake 10 minutes or until marshmallows are golden. Serve warm. Makes 8 servings.
Tip To cook this cobbler on a grill, prepare as above except use an 8×8×2-inch disposable foil baking pan. Grill, covered, over medium heat for 10 minutes.
EACH SERVING *237 cal, 4 g fat, 2 mg chol, 99 mg sodium, 49 g carb, 3 g fiber, 3 g pro.*

KID FRIENDLY

Blackberry-Sage Cobbler

Sage adds an earthy element to the deep purple blackberry filling in this cobbler. Try a different variety, such as pineapple sage, for slightly tropical flavor.
PREP 30 min. BAKE 55 min. STAND 30 min.

Topping
- 5 Tbsp. unsalted butter
- ¼ cup fresh sage leaves
- ¾ cup all-purpose flour
- ¼ cup sugar
- ¾ tsp. baking powder
- ¼ tsp. baking soda
- ¼ tsp. salt
- ⅔ cup buttermilk, room temperature
- 1 egg, lightly beaten

Filling
- 8 cups fresh blackberries
- 3 Tbsp. all-purpose flour
- 1 cup sugar
- ⅓ cup water
- 3 Tbsp. chopped fresh sage
- 1 tsp. finely shredded lemon peel

1. Preheat oven to 350°F. Grease a 2-qt. round baking dish; set aside.
2. For topping, in a skillet melt butter over medium heat. Add sage leaves; cook 4 minutes or until just starting to crisp and butter is browned. Transfer sage to paper towels. Set sage and butter aside to cool.
3. For cobbler batter, in a bowl combine flour, the ¼ cup sugar, baking powder, baking soda, and salt. In a 2-cup measure combine buttermilk, cooled butter, and egg. Add to flour mixture; stir until just combined.
4. For filling, in a large heatproof bowl toss together blackberries and flour. In a medium saucepan combine the 1 cup sugar, the water, the chopped sage, and lemon peel over medium heat. Bring to boiling. Cook 1 minute, stirring to dissolve sugar. Remove from heat. Immediately pour over berries; toss to coat. Transfer filling to prepared dish. Pour batter over filling. (Place a baking sheet below the dish to catch drips during baking.)
5. Bake 55 to 60 minutes or until topping is golden and filling is thick and bubbly. Let stand 30 minutes before serving. Top with reserved sage leaves. Makes 8 servings.
EACH SERVING *320 cal, 9 g fat, 44 mg chol, 193 mg sodium, 58 g carb, 8 g fiber, 5 g pro.*

Bring flavor from the herb garden to the quintessential blackberry cobbler with sage-infused brown butter topping.

STRAWBERRY S'MORES COBBLER

BLACKBERRY-SAGE COBBLER

**OVEN-TO-GRILL BABY
BACK RIBS**
Recipe on page 167

simple-crazy ribs

Charlie McKenna of Lillie's Q in Chicago shares his easy oven-to-grill method for quick and delicious baby back ribs.

CHARLIE McKENNA KNOWS BARBECUE. Charlie grew up in Greenville, South Carolina, where his grandmother instilled his deep love for Southern cooking. (She's the inspiration behind the name of his Chicago restaurant, Lillie's Q.) Although he's hailed as a world champion of barbecue with dozens of awards to his name, Charlie also delights in bringing small-scale 'cue to the backyard. Take his method for quick ribs: "I love all-day, slow-smoked baby back ribs, but we don't always have the time," Charlie says. "Starting the ribs in a foil pouch in the oven makes them ultra tender. Finishing them on the grill adds that smoky flavor and delicious crust."

"Good ribs start with good pork. Get to know your butcher and who they are buying their meat from."

Oven-to-Grill Baby Back Ribs

PREP 20 min. BAKE 1½ hr.
GRILL 15 min.

- ¼ cup yellow mustard
- 1 3½-lb. rack pork loin back ribs
- 1 cup Basic Barbecue Rub
- ½ cup Basic Barbecue Sauce

1. Preheat oven to 375°F. With a pastry brush, spread mustard all over both sides of ribs. Sprinkle Basic Barbecue Rub all over both sides of ribs.
2. Place ribs in the center of a double thickness of heavy foil cut 6 inches longer than ribs; wrap ribs. Bake 1½ to 2 hours or until tender (the two center bones of the rack should start to pull apart easily).
3. Transfer ribs to a baking pan (discard liquid). Spread Basic Barbecue Sauce all over both sides of ribs. Grill, covered, directly over medium heat for 15 minutes, brushing with additional sauce every 5 minutes. Adjust heat as necessary to prevent burning. Makes 4 servings.

Basic Barbecue Rub Place 1½ tsp. each celery seeds, cumin seeds, yellow mustard seeds, and coriander seeds in a spice grinder; grind until fine. Transfer to a bowl. Add ¾ cup turbinado sugar, ¾ cup dark brown sugar, ½ cup paprika, 3 Tbsp. kosher salt, 1 Tbsp. chili powder, 4 tsp. onion powder, 4 tsp. garlic powder, 1½ tsp. dried oregano, and 1½ tsp. ground black pepper. Mix well to combine.

Basic Barbecue Sauce In a large saucepan whisk together 2½ cups packed dark brown sugar, 2½ cups ketchup, ½ cup yellow mustard, ½ cup cider vinegar, ¼ cup Worcestershire sauce, juice of 1 lime, 1 Tbsp. salt, 1 Tbsp. onion powder, 1 Tbsp. garlic powder, 1½ tsp. paprika, 1½ tsp. black pepper, pinch of cayenne pepper, and dash of liquid smoke. Bring to a boil. Reduce heat and simmer, covered, for 10 minutes, stirring occasionally. Cool to room temperature. Cover; chill up to 2 weeks.

EACH SERVING *530 cal, 21 g fat, 131 mg chol, 2,337 mg sodium, 46 g carb, 3 g fiber, 43 g pro.*

RUB "A rub with a decent amount of sugar pulls out pork's natural sweetness. It's important to season well, so don't be afraid to coat generously."

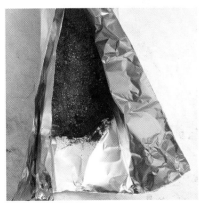

WRAP "Typically ribs cook low and slow—about 5 to 6 hours in a smoker. To speed up the process, I steam the ribs first in a foil pouch, which also makes the ribs super tender."

BUY "Look for uniform size to ensure ribs cook evenly," Charlie says. "You want both a decent thickness of meat and intermuscular fat for big-time flavor."

SLATHER "Mustard gives the rub something to adhere to. Its vinegar content goes well with pork and penetrates all layers of the meat as it cooks."

GRILL "Finish ribs on the grill to create smoky flavor plus the char, or bark, on the outside of the meat. Brushed-on sauce caramelizes to add to that outside crust."

weeknight delicious

Fast and fresh solutions for dinner tonight.

SWEET HOT CORIANDER CHICKEN

YELLOW SQUASH AND FETA GRILLED TOAST

LOW FAT

Sweet Hot Coriander Chicken

Nutty, citrusy coriander bridges orange juice, brown sugar, and a kick of chili in this flavor-packed dish. Toss roasted baby red potatoes in the remaining sauce for an easy side.

PREP **15 min.** MARINATE **15 min.** COOK **12 min.**

- 1 Tbsp. extra-virgin olive oil
- 2 tsp. packed dark brown sugar
- 2 tsp. Sriracha sauce
- 1 tsp. ground coriander
- 1 tsp. chili powder
- 4 6-oz. skinless, boneless chicken breast halves, flattened to ½-inch thickness
- ⅓ cup orange juice
  Salt and black pepper
  Snipped fresh cilantro

1. For marinade, in a small bowl stir together oil, sugar, Sriracha sauce, coriander, and chili powder. Place chicken in a shallow dish. Spoon marinade over chicken; turn to coat. Let stand 15 minutes.
2. Heat an extra-large skillet over medium-high heat. Add chicken; cook 10 minutes or until done (165°F), turning once halfway through. Transfer to a plate. Cover to keep warm.
3. Add orange juice to pan; cook 2 minutes or until reduced to about 2 Tbsp., stirring to scrape up browned bits. Spoon sauce over chicken. Season to taste with salt and pepper. Top with cilantro. Makes 4 servings.

EACH SERVING *257 cal, 8 g fat, 124 mg chol, 272 mg sodium, 5 g carb, 0 g fiber, 39 g pro.*

LOW FAT

Yellow Squash and Feta Grilled Toast

Toast is the base for a hearty dinner layered with grilled vegetables, greens, and cheese. Look for squash with smooth, unblemished skin. Skip the giants—they tend to be bitter.

PREP **25 min.** GRILL **14 min.**

- Olive oil
- 2 medium yellow summer squash, halved lengthwise
- 1 medium yellow onion, cut into ½-inch-thick slices
  Salt and black pepper
- 4 oz. cream cheese
- 1 clove garlic, minced
- 4 tsp. chopped fresh oregano
- 8 oz. sourdough or multigrain Italian bread, cut into 8 slices
- 1 cup arugula
- 2 oz. feta cheese, crumbled

1. Heat a grill to medium-high. Brush rack with olive oil. Grill squash and onion 12 minutes or just until tender, turning frequently. Season with salt and pepper. Cool slightly; coarsely chop.
2. Meanwhile, in a small bowl combine cream cheese, garlic, and oregano.
3. Grill bread for 2 minutes or until golden brown, turning frequently. To assemble, spread cream cheese mixture on each slice. Top with vegetables, arugula, and feta. Makes 4 servings.

EACH SERVING *286 cal, 11 g fat, 31 mg chol, 735 mg sodium, 36 g carb, 2 g fiber, 11 g pro.*

**BROCCOLINI AND
SWEET PEPPER
PASTA SALAD**

LOW FAT
Grilled Pork in Blackberry Sauce

With a dusting of cumin and a few turns on the grill, this pork gets a smoky edge. The balsamic-infused blackberry sauce is a deliciously tangy counterpoint. Don't miss an opportunity to grill halved or quartered peaches or nectarines for a smoky-sweet side.

PREP **20 min.** STAND **18 min.**
GRILL **23 min.**

- 1 lb. pork tenderloin
- 2 tsp. ground cumin
   Salt and black pepper
- ⅓ cup blackberry preserves
- 2 Tbsp. balsamic vinegar
- 1 Tbsp. Worcestershire sauce
- ⅛ tsp. crushed red pepper (optional)
- 2 Tbsp. chopped green onion

1. Sprinkle all sides of pork with cumin, salt, and pepper. Let stand 15 minutes.
2. Grill on a greased rack of a covered grill 23 to 25 minutes or until 145°F, turning occasionally. Remove to a cutting board; let stand 3 minutes before slicing.
3. Meanwhile, for sauce, in a small skillet combine preserves, vinegar, Worcestershire sauce, and, if desired, a pinch of crushed red pepper. Bring to boiling; boil gently, uncovered, 2 minutes or until slightly thickened. Serve sauce over pork and sprinkle with green onion. Makes 4 servings.
EACH SERVING *213 cal, 3 g fat, 74 mg chol, 114 mg sodium, 21 g carb, 0 g fiber, 24 g pro.*

FAST
Broccolini and Sweet Pepper Pasta Salad

The refreshing honey-balsamic vinaigrette is the star of this veggie-packed pasta toss. Finish it with creamy goat cheese.
START TO FINISH **25 min.**

- 5 oz. dried rotini
- 3 cups chopped Broccolini or small broccoli florets
- 3 Tbsp. white balsamic vinegar
- 2 Tbsp. canola oil
- 2 Tbsp. honey
- 2 cloves garlic, minced
- ⅛ tsp. crushed red pepper (optional)
- 1 large red sweet pepper, cut up
- ½ cup chopped red onion
- ¼ cup sliced almonds, toasted (tip, page 106)
- ¼ cup chopped fresh basil
- 2 oz. goat cheese, crumbled
   Salt and freshly ground black pepper

1. In a large pot cook pasta in lightly salted boiling water 5 minutes. Add Broccolini; cook 3 minutes more or until pasta is done. Drain; rinse with cold water to cool.
2. Meanwhile, in a large bowl whisk together vinegar, oil, honey, garlic, and, if desired, crushed red pepper. Add pasta mixture, sweet pepper, onion, almonds, and basil. Toss to combine. Gently stir in cheese. Season to taste with salt and black pepper. Makes 4 servings.
EACH SERVING *378 cal, 15 g fat, 11 mg chol, 232 mg sodium, 51 g carb, 5 g fiber, 12 g pro.*

**GRILLED PORK
IN BLACKBERRY
SAUCE**

summer in a jar

This colorful blend of veggies is a delicious way to enjoy one season's bounty long after the gardens are resting.

LOW FAT

Garlicky Pickled Mixed Veggies

PREP 45 min. COOK 10 min.

- 2 ears corn
- 3 cups cauliflower florets
- 3 medium red sweet peppers, seeded and cut into 1-inch pieces
- 12 oz. green beans, trimmed and cut into 1-inch pieces
- 3 medium carrots, cut into ½-inch slices
- 2 medium onions, cut into small thin wedges
- 3 cups water
- 3 cups white vinegar
- 1 cup sugar
- 1 Tbsp. kosher salt
- 18 cloves garlic, smashed
- 1½ tsp. crushed red pepper

1. Remove husks from ears of corn. Scrub with a stiff brush to remove silks; rinse. Cut cobs into 1- to 1½-inch pieces. In an 8-qt. pot combine corn, cauliflower, sweet peppers, green beans, carrots, and onions. Add enough water to cover. Bring to boiling. Cook, uncovered, 3 minutes; drain. Cut corn lengthwise into halves or quarters.
2. In a 4- to 5-qt. stainless-steel, enamel, or nonstick heavy pot combine 3 cups water, vinegar, sugar, and salt. Bring to boiling; stir to dissolve sugar.
3. Pack vegetables into six hot-sterilized pint canning jars, leaving ½-inch headspace. Add 3 cloves garlic and ¼ tsp. crushed red pepper to each jar. Pour hot vinegar mixture over vegetables, maintaining the ½-inch headspace. Wipe jar rims; screw on lids.
4. Process filled jars in a boiling-water canner for 10 minutes (start timing when water returns to boiling). Remove jars from canner; cool on wire racks. Makes six pint-size jars.

EACH ¼-CUP SERVING 45 cal, 0 g fat, 0 mg chol, 164 mg sodium, 9 g carb, 1 g fiber, 1 g pro.

COOK THE VEGGIES Precooking before canning removes air and preserves vegetables' color and flavor. Three minutes will do it.

PREPARE PICKLING LIQUID Clear and neutral-tasting white vinegar will not discolor vegetables or alter their flavor.

PACK AND POUR Vegetables and seasoning go into sterilized jars with ½-inch headspace. Add the hot pickling liquid, maintaining the same headspace to ensure the jar seals properly.

PROCESS Submerge jars in a boiling-water canner then start timing when water returns to boiling. Cool on a wire rack or kitchen towel—a quick change in temperature can crack jars.

For refrigerator pickles prepare through Step 3. Cool 30 minutes then chill at least 1 week before serving.

NEAPOLITAN POPS

august

dine alfresco Warm summer evenings are the ideal excuse to dine on the patio. Show off summer produce in fresh and simple recipes that leave room for dessert.

188

197

201

CLASSIC GARLIC-DILL SANDWICH PICKLES

pickling picnic

It's the season for sharing and preserving. Foodie (and canning pro) Aimée Wimbush-Bourque shows how to make a party out of all the slicing and dicing.

LOW FAT   KID FRIENDLY

Classic Garlic-Dill Sandwich Pickles

An assembly line makes light work of classic garlic dill pickles. "One person measures ingredients, while others wash, slice, or pack jars," Aimée says.

PREP **25 min.**   STAND **6 hr.**
CHILL **4 days**

- ¼ cup pickling salt
- 6 cups filtered water
- 1 Tbsp. yellow mustard seeds
- 1 Tbsp. coriander seeds
- ½ tsp. celery seeds
- 1 Tbsp. black peppercorns
- 2 fresh dill heads or 1 tablespoon dill seeds
- 2½ lb. medium pickling cucumbers
- 1½ cups apple cider vinegar
- 8 cloves garlic

1. In a large bowl or gallon bucket stir salt into the water until dissolved. Add the seeds, peppercorns, and dill heads.
2. Wash cucumbers and trim ends. Set a mandoline to ¼ inch then slice cucumbers into flat sandwich-style lengths.
3. Submerge all the sliced cucumbers in the spiced brine and weight them to completely submerge. Let cucumbers stand at room temperature for 6 to 8 hours.
4. Using tongs, divide pickles among four clean pint jars. Measure out 2 cups of the brine and combine it in a saucepan with the vinegar. Bring to boiling. Strain the remaining brine, reserving the seeds and aromatics. Divide them among the jars. Tuck 2 garlic cloves in each jar. Pour the boiling brine over the cucumber slices to cover. Cover with lids then cool to room temperature. Chill at least 4 days before serving. Makes 64 servings.
EACH SERVING *4 cal, 0 g fat, 0 mg chol, 82 mg sodium, 1 g carb, 0 g fiber, 0 g pro.*

THE HOST
Aimée Wimbush-Bourque is a Montréal-based cookbook author and food blogger (simplebites.net). Aimée's new cookbook, *Brown Eggs and Jam Jars* (Pintail; $25), inspires garden-to-table cooking with recipes for every season.

Homemade lemonade steeped with lemon balm and lemon wedges is as pretty as it is flavorful.

THE EXCUSE

Summer produce is at its peak, and gardens are overflowing. Now's the time to pickle, preserve, and freeze to savor and enjoy the bounty until next summer.

THE METHOD

Pick produce or stop by farmers markets. At home, set up assembly-line workstations.

THE DRINK

Prepared homemade lemonade to quench thirst.

THE NIBBLES

Serve fresh veggies, cheeses, salami, and crackers on platters to keep snacking simple.

THE DETAILS

"I send guests home with a little something to remember our time together," Aimée says of her fresh herb wreaths. Once dry, the herbs (rosemary and thyme among the mix) can be snipped and used in recipes.

LOW FAT   KID FRIENDLY

Lemon Balm Lemonade Concentrate

Mildly minty lemon balm lemonade is Aimée's signature summer cooler. She makes a batch of concentrate and freezes it in ice cube trays for quick prep on party day.

PREP 20 min.   COOL 2 hr.
CHILL 2 hr.

- 2 cups water
- 2 cups sugar
- 3 cups lightly packed fresh lemon balm leaves
- 2½ cups freshly squeezed lemon juice, strained (about 13 large lemons)
  Filtered water
  Ice cubes, lemon slices, and lemon balm leaves

1. In a medium saucepan combine 2 cups water and the sugar. Bring to boiling, stirring to dissolve sugar. Remove from heat.
2. Stir in 3 cups lemon balm leaves to the hot syrup. Muddle the leaves slightly to release the oils. Allow to stand, covered, about 2 hours or until completely cooled.
3. Strain the syrup through a fine-mesh sieve into a pitcher. Discard lemon balm. Add lemon juice to the syrup and stir. Chill thoroughly. Cover and store in the refrigerator up to 1 week or freeze in ice cube trays.
4. To serve, stir together 1 part lemon syrup to 1 part filtered water (still or sparkling). Serve over ice with lemon slices and fresh lemon balm leaves. Makes 10 servings.

EACH SERVING *159 cal, 0 g fat, 0 mg chol, 3 mg sodium, 43 g carb, 0 g fiber, 0 g pro.*

KID FRIENDLY

Whipped Blueberry Butter

Whipped berry butter—a blueberry topping for toast, scones, and crepes—looks yummy (and ready for gift-giving) in cute jars.

PREP 20 min.   COOL 45 min.

- 2 tablespoons honey
- 1 cup fresh blueberries
- 1 cup unsalted butter, room temperature
- ½ teaspoon sea salt

1. In a small saucepan warm honey; add the blueberries. Bring to boiling. Turn off heat and mash the berries with a fork. Set aside to cool completely, about 45 minutes.
2. Place the berry mixture and butter in a food processor or mixing bowl; pulse or beat with a mixer to combine. Add salt and process or beat for 2 to 3 minutes or until fluffy and smooth and berries are thoroughly incorporated, scraping sides occasionally.
3. Transfer to a 1-pint canning jar. Cover and chill up to 1 week or freeze up to 2 months. Serve with warm bread. Makes 26 servings.

EACH SERVING *71 cal, 7 g fat, 19 mg chol, 43 mg sodium, 2 g carb, 0 g fiber, 0 g pro.*

LEMON BALM
LEMONADE

WHIPPED
BERRY
BUTTER

girls' night outside

When Nashville stylist Ruthie Lindsey invites friends for dinner, it's a potluck of creativity. Guests bring their talents to the table in a hip Music City enclave.

Just before sunset on a warm summer day, Ruthie Lindsey hosts a handful of girlfriends for cocktails and a family-style meal. She sets the scene with foraged flowers, rustic linens, and her grandmother's tableware. With the artsy East Nashville neighborhood buzzing with talent, there's no shortage of creativity. Guests pitch in with hand-drawn menus, Southern-inspired food, handmade favors, and live music (this is Nashville, after all).

Laid-back collaboration is how Ruthie entertains, and outdoors is her favorite venue. "I'm happiest when I'm in nature," the Louisiana-raised farm girl says of her preference for alfresco dining. About five years ago, Ruthie started decorating her home as an outlet to deal with the trauma and chronic pain stemming from a car accident. Now, her design talent is both her therapy and her job, parties being her specialty and

passion. "I love to give people the chance to connect with one another," Ruthie says. "Anything I can do to foster community and connection makes me happy."

JESSIE

TO SIP:
MINT STRAWBERRY BOURBON SHRUBS

TO START:
BEET DYED DEVILED EGGS
PIMENTO CHEESE WITH SWEET PEPPER JELLY

TO SAVOR:
FETA BRINED GRILLED CHICKEN
CHICKPEA AND PARSLEY SALAD
GRILLED ROMAINE HEARTS WITH PIQUILLO DRESSING

TO SCARF:
LEMON ICE BOX PIES

"It's more than a pretty party.
I want to create an environment where
everyone feels welcome," says Ruthie.

**BOURBON
STRAWBERRY
SMASH**
Recipe on page 184

NASHVILLE

BEET-DYED DEVILED EGGS

1. In a medium saucepan combine beet, the water, and vinegar; bring to boiling. Reduce heat. Simmer, covered, 15 minutes. Remove from heat. Cool completely. Do not drain.
2. Place eggs in saucepan with beet liquid. Let stand 10 to 15 minutes. Remove eggs and discard beets and liquid. Slice eggs in half and transfer yolks to a bowl; set whites aside.
3. For filling, mash yolks with mayonnaise, relish, and mustard. Pipe or scoop filling into egg white halves. Sprinkle with watercress and coarse salt. Makes 24 halves.

EACH SERVING *61 cal, 5 g fat, 95 mg chol, 69 mg sodium, 1 g carb, 3 g pro.*

Pimiento Cheese

Ruthie Lindsey welcomes guests with this easy appetizer. The mild heat comes from banana peppers.
PREP **20 min.** CHILL **4 hr.**

- 16 oz. aged sharp white cheddar cheese, shredded
- 1 8-oz. jar diced pimiento, drained
- ½ cup mayonnaise
- 2 Tbsp. shredded or finely chopped sweet onion
- 2 mild or hot bottled banana peppers, drained and finely chopped (2 Tbsp.)
  Pinch cayenne pepper
  Toasted baguette slices or crackers
  Red jalapeño pepper jelly

1. In a large bowl stir together cheddar cheese, pimiento, mayonnaise, onion, banana peppers, and cayenne pepper. Cover; chill 4 hours or up to 3 days. Serve with toasted baguette slices or crackers and pepper jelly. Makes 3½ cups.
Note: For smoother consistency, beat with an electric mixer.

EACH 2-TBSP. SERVING *157 cal, 8 g fat, 18 mg chol, 256 mg sodium, 14 g carb, 1 g fiber, 6 g pro.*

FAST

Bourbon Strawberry Smash

Photo on page 183
START TO FINISH **30 min.**

- 2 cups fresh strawberries, hulled and cut up
- ¼ cup Simple Syrup
- 9 Tbsp. fresh lemon juice
- ¼ cup fresh mint leaves
- 18 oz. bourbon (2¼ cups)
- 2 cups club soda, chilled
  Crushed ice

1. In a 2-qt. glass pitcher combine strawberries, Simple Syrup, lemon juice, and mint leaves. Using a muddler or wooden spoon, mash together. Stir in bourbon and club soda. Add ice to fill pitcher. Top each drink with additional mint sprigs. Makes 6 servings.

EACH SERVING *262 cal, 0 g fat, 0 mg chol, 20 mg sodium, 17 g carb, 1 g fiber, 1 g pro.*

Simple Syrup In a small saucepan heat and stir ⅓ cup sugar and ⅓ cup water until sugar is dissolved. Remove from heat; cool. Cover. Chill up to 2 weeks. Makes ½ cup.

KID FRIENDLY

Beet-Dyed Deviled Eggs

A tint of pink turns a summer classic into a pretty appetizer.
PREP **50 min.** COOL **1 hr.**
STAND **15 min.**

- 1 large beet, peeled and cubed
- 2 cups water
- 1 cup white vinegar
- 12 hard-cooked eggs, peeled
- ⅓ cup mayonnaise
- 2 Tbsp. sweet pickle relish
- 1 Tbsp. whole grain mustard
  Watercress
  Coarse salt

PIMIENTO CHEESE

**BEET-DYED
DEVILED EGGS**
Recipe on page 184

**GRILLED ROMAINE
SALAD WITH
PIQUILLO PEPPER
DRESSING**
Recipe on page 188

**GARBANZO BEAN
AND PARSLEY SALAD**
Recipe on page 188

**GRILLED FETA-
BRINED CHICKEN**
Recipe on page 188

"The second the weather is warm enough, I eat outdoors as often as possible," Ruthie says.

Garbanzo Bean and Parsley Salad

Photo on page 187

This make-ahead dish is a refreshing summer side with pleasing crunch and bright flavors.

PREP 30 min. COOK 15 min.
STAND 30 min. CHILL up to 24 hr.

- 2 tsp. olive oil
- 2 16-oz. cans garbanzo beans (chickpeas), rinsed and drained
- 2 cups finely chopped celery stalks
- ¼ cup finely chopped sweet onion
- ½ cup fresh lemon juice
- 1 bunch Italian parsley, stems removed and leaves chopped (2 cups)
- ¼ cup olive oil
- 2 tsp. ground cumin
  Feta cheese, crumbled (optional)

1. In a large cast-iron skillet heat the 2 tsp. oil over medium heat. Add beans; cook and stir until crisp, about 15 minutes. Cool.
2. In a medium bowl combine celery, onion, and lemon juice. Let stand 30 minutes.
3. Add cooled beans to celery mixture. Fold in parsley. Add the ¼ cup oil and cumin; toss to coat. Season to taste with salt and pepper. Cover; chill up to 24 hours. Stir before serving. Top with feta cheese, if desired. Makes 6 servings.
EACH SERVING *219 cal, 13 g fat, 0 mg chol, 583 mg sodium, 22 g carb, 6 g fiber, 6 g pro.*

KID FRIENDLY
Grilled Feta-Brined Chicken

Photo on page 186

Salty feta and zesty citrus give this picnic staple a twist. Serve warm or at room temperature.

PREP 30 min. MARINATE 8 hr.
STAND 30 min. GRILL 12 min.

- 4 cups water
- 4 oz. feta cheese, crumbled
- 2 Tbsp. dried oregano
- 2½ tsp. kosher salt
- 2 tsp. cracked black pepper
- 2 to 3 lb. skinless, boneless chicken thighs
- 1 large lemon, halved
- ¼ cup olive oil
  Salt and black pepper
  Crumbled feta cheese (optional)
  Assorted fresh herbs (optional)

1. In a blender combine the water, the 4 oz. feta, oregano, salt, and cracked black pepper. Cover; blend until smooth. Place chicken in an extra-large resealable plastic bag or container. Pour feta brine over chicken; seal or cover. Chill 8 hours or overnight.
2. Remove chicken from brine; transfer to a towel-lined tray. Discard brine. Pat chicken dry. Let stand at room temperature 30 minutes.
3. Grill chicken on the rack of a covered grill over medium heat 12 to 15 minutes or until done (170°F), turning once.
4. Transfer chicken to a platter. Squeeze lemon over. Drizzle with oil. Season to taste with salt and pepper. If desired, top with additional feta and herbs. Makes 6 servings.
EACH SERVING *314 cal, 19 g fat, 158 mg chol, 558 mg sodium, 2 g carb, 0 g fiber, 32 g pro.*

LOW FAT   FAST
Grilled Romaine Salad with Piquillo Pepper Dressing

Photo on page 186

A quick stint on the grill sweetens romaine lettuce, making it a good match for bold pepper dressing.

PREP 20 min. GRILL 1 min.

- 1 12-oz. jar piquillo peppers or roasted red sweet peppers, drained (about 1⅓ cups)
- 1 cup sour cream
- 2 Tbsp. lemon juice
  Salt and black pepper
- 1 head romaine lettuce, cut into quarters
- 1 Tbsp. drained capers

1. For dressing, combine peppers, sour cream, and lemon juice in a blender. Cover; blend until smooth. Season to taste with salt and pepper. Chill until ready to serve.
2. Place romaine on the rack of a covered grill directly over medium heat. Grill 1 to 3 minutes or until charred and slightly wilted, turning occasionally.
3. Drizzle dressing over grilled romaine; store remaining dressing in the refrigerator up to 1 week. Sprinkle salad with capers. Makes 4 servings.
EACH SERVING *53 cal, 3 g fat, 6 mg chol, 265 mg sodium, 6 g carb, 3 g fiber, 2 g pro.*

LEMON MERINGUE TARTS

Dessert is Lemon Meringue Tarts made by Rebekah Turshen, Ruthie's friend and dessert maven at Nashville's popular City House restaurant.

KID FRIENDLY

Lemon Meringue Tarts

PREP 1 hr. CHILL 1½ hr.
BAKE 22 min.

Tart Shells
1⅓ cups all-purpose flour
⅓ cup granulated sugar
2 tsp. finely shredded lemon peel
½ cup cold butter
2 egg yolks, beaten
2 Tbsp. cold water

Lemon Cream Filling
1 egg yolk
½ cup sweetened condensed milk
¼ cup lemon juice
⅛ tsp. salt

Lemon Curd
3 egg yolks
½ cup granulated sugar
2 tsp. cornstarch
1 tsp. finely shredded lemon peel
⅓ cup lemon juice
3 Tbsp. water
2 Tbsp. butter

Meringue
4 egg whites
1 tsp. vanilla
½ tsp. cream of tartar
½ cup granulated sugar
1 Tbsp. powdered sugar

1. For Tart Shells, in a large bowl stir together flour, ⅓ cup sugar, and the 2 tsp. shredded lemon peel. Using a pastry blender, cut in the ½ cup cold butter until mixture is crumbly. Add 2 egg yolks and 2 Tbsp. water to flour mixture; stir with a fork to combine. Gently knead dough just until a ball forms. Cover with plastic wrap. Chill 30 to 60 minutes or until easy to handle.

2. Preheat oven to 375°F. Divide chilled dough into 12 equal pieces. Press each piece onto bottom and halfway up sides of twelve 3-inch muffin cups. Bake for 10 minutes or until golden. Cool in muffin cups for 10 minutes. Transfer shells to a 15×10×1-inch baking pan. Reduce oven temperature to 350°F.

3. For Lemon Cream Filling, in a small bowl whisk together 1 egg yolk, condensed milk, ¼ cup lemon juice, and salt; set aside.

4. For Lemon Curd, place 3 egg yolks in a bowl; set aside. In a small saucepan stir together ½ cup sugar and cornstarch. Stir in 1 tsp. shredded lemon peel, ⅓ cup lemon juice, 3 Tbsp. water, and 2 Tbsp. butter. Cook and stir over medium heat until thickened and bubbly. Remove from heat. Stir about half the lemon-sugar mixture into egg yolks; add to saucepan. Return to heat. Cook and stir 2 minutes more. Cover to keep warm.

5. For Meringue, in a medium bowl beat egg whites, vanilla, and cream of tartar with electric mixer on medium speed until soft peaks form. Gradually add ½ cup sugar; beat on high until stiff peaks form.

6. To assemble, spoon about 1 Tbsp. Lemon Cream Filling into each baked crust; top with 1 Tbsp. Lemon Curd. Top each with Meringue, spreading to edges of crusts. Sift powdered sugar over tarts. Bake for 12 minutes or until golden. Cool on a wire rack. Cover; chill 1 hour. If desired, serve with additional finely shredded lemon peel and honey. Makes 12 servings.

EACH SERVING *304 cal, 13 g fat, 122 mg chol, 140 mg sodium, 42 g carb, 0 g fiber, 5 g pro.*

have your cakes...

Crab, that is. No travel necessary. Charleston natives Matt and Ted Lee share their secrets for making deliciously rich crab cakes at home.

Growing up in Charleston, South Carolina, Matt and Ted Lee were never far from fresh crab. "We lived on blue crabs—those iconic American crabs of the east coast," Matt says. "As kids we were often just a few blocks from luring a fresh crab or two, and we ate them every which way."

Even if you aren't close enough to net fresh crab, you're in luck. "You can get good crab nationwide," Matt says. "Look for refrigerated tubs or cans of pasteurized crabmeat, available at most grocery stores year-round. In a pinch, use shelf-stable canned crab and mix it with pasteurized crabmeat, but we don't recommend using it 100% in this crab-forward version of crab cakes. It tends to be drier and have a tinny flavor."

BEFORE YOU SHOP, KNOW WHICH TYPE OF CRABMEAT TO PURCHASE.

CLAW Dark meat adds sweetness and flavor—plus, it's less expensive than lump.

LUMP Whole lumps of white meat from the body of the crab taste tender and rich.

CLASSIC CRAB CAKES
Recipe on page 197

MORE FROM THE LEE BROS.
Watch Matt and Ted explore food and culture in cities throughout the South on their new TV series, *Southern Uncovered with the Lee Bros.* (Sundays on Ovation). They also have three cookbooks, including the most recent, *The Lee Bros. Charleston Kitchen.*

"A crab cake should celebrate the sweet, succulent flavor of the meat. Less filler and simple ingredients allow it to shine," says Matt.

CHOOSE THE CRAB Matt and Ted recommend a mix of lump and/or backfin and claw meat. "It's what the savviest Low Country cooks do to approximate the yield from an actual crab," Ted says.

Classic Crab Cakes

A little squeeze of lemon before serving brightens the cakes and brings out even more flavor. Matt and Ted also recommend serving with tartar or hollandaise sauce.

PREP 50 min. CHILL 30 min.
COOK 2 min. per batch BAKE 5 min.

1½ lb. cooked crabmeat
6 Tbsp. mayonnaise
1 Tbsp. Dijon-style mustard
1 cup panko bread crumbs
½ cup finely chopped Italian parsley
2 green onions, finely chopped
2 cloves garlic, minced
1 tsp. kosher salt
1 tsp. freshly ground black pepper
2 eggs, lightly beaten
1 to 2 Tbsp. peanut or canola oil
¼ cup unsalted butter
  Paprika and lemon wedges
  (optional)

1. Place crabmeat in a large mixing bowl, pinching through the pile with your fingers to find any bits of shell and to break up large pieces. Add mayonnaise, mustard, ¼ cup of the bread crumbs, parsley, green onions, garlic, salt, and pepper; fold to combine. Add eggs; fold to combine.
2. To form each cake, on a tray pat about ¼ cup mixture into a 2½-inch round cutter. Lift cutter off. Form 16 cakes. Cover with plastic wrap, pressing lightly. Chill at least 30 minutes.
3. Preheat oven to 350°F. Place remaining bread crumbs in a shallow dish.
4. In an extra-large skillet heat oil over medium-high heat. Lightly coat both sides of 4 cakes in bread crumbs; add to skillet. Press lightly with a spatula; cook 1 to 2 minutes per side or until golden brown. Transfer to a shallow baking pan. Cook remaining cakes, four at a time, adding more oil, if necessary. Top each cake with a slice of butter; warm for 5 minutes. Sprinkle with paprika. Serve with lemon wedges. Makes 16 crab cakes.

EACH CRAB CAKE *128 cal, 9 g fat, 74 mg chol, 314 mg sodium, 3 g carb, 9 g pro.*

MAKE THE MIX "The ingredients elevate crab's natural flavor without overpowering," Matt says. "Parsley and green onion keep the cakes light and bright in both texture and taste."

SHAPE INTO PATTIES "The cakes are delicate since there are minimal binders," Ted says. "A round cutter makes forming the cakes a breeze, and a 30-minute chill helps them keep the shape."

COAT THE CAKES "Panko creates a wonderful contrast of textures—moist on the inside and a little crisp on the outside," Matt says. "A light coat is all you need to create delicious browning."

COOK TO GOLDEN "Don't crowd the skillet," Matt says. "You want ample room to flip. And if you crowd the pan, you'll bring down the temperature of the skillet and the cakes won't brown as well."

FINISH IN THE OVEN "Since the cakes cook in batches, we warm them all in the oven at the end with a pat of butter," Ted says. "Butter adds just a little extra decadence and goes so well with crab."

ice cream you scream

Serve carefree desserts with these creamy (and pretty) treats for a crowd.

KID FRIENDLY

Neapolitan Pops

PREP 20 min. FREEZE 6 hr.

- 15 chocolate sandwich cookies, crushed
- 3 Tbsp. melted butter, cooled
- ½ 1.75-qt. carton chocolate ice cream, softened
- ½ 1.75-qt. carton vanilla ice cream, softened
- ½ cup chopped fresh strawberries
- ½ 1.75-qt. carton strawberry ice cream, softened
- 16 Crafts sticks

1. Line a square baking pan (9×9 or 8×8-inch) with waxed paper, extending paper edges over pan. Stir together cookies and butter; press into pan. Freeze 10 minutes.

2. Spread an even layer of chocolate ice cream over cookie layer; freeze 15 minutes. Spread vanilla ice cream and freeze 15 minutes.

3. Stir strawberries into strawberry ice cream. Spread in an even layer over vanilla layer; freeze 15 minutes. Insert 16 crafts sticks, evenly spaced. Loosely cover with plastic wrap.

4. Freeze at least 4 hours for the 9×9-inch baking pan and at least 5 hours for the 8×8 baking pan, or until firm.

5. Using edges of waxed paper, lift dessert from pan. Cut between sticks into 16 pops.

EACH POP *254 cal, 13 g fat, 38 mg chol, 132 mg sodium, 32 g carb, 1 g fiber, 3 g pro.*

Get the family in on the action: Seal the cookies in a heavy-duty plastic bag then let the kids roll with a rolling pin to make the crumbs.

weeknight delicious

Fast and fresh solutions for dinner tonight.

STEAK WITH SPICY BALSAMIC GLAZE

Steak with Spicy Balsamic Glaze

Easy enough for a weeknight and impressive enough for company—the secret is in the flavor-packed glaze. Add a simple salad of peaches and spinach.

PREP 25 min. MARINATE 20 min. COOK 20 min.

- 1 lb. boneless top sirloin steak, about 1 inch thick, trimmed of fat
- ½ cup water
- ½ cup apple cider
- ¼ cup Worcestershire sauce
- ¼ cup balsamic vinegar
- ½ tsp. crushed red pepper
  Nonstick cooking spray
  Salt and freshly ground black pepper
- ¼ cup honey

1. Place steak in a resealable plastic bag. Add the water, apple cider, Worcestershire sauce, vinegar, and crushed red pepper. Seal bag. Marinate 20 minutes, turning occasionally.
2. Heat a large skillet coated with cooking spray over medium-high heat. Remove steak from bag, reserving marinade. Season with salt and black pepper. Cook 12 minutes, turning once, or until desired doneness. Remove; keep warm.
3. For glaze, add marinade and honey to skillet; whisk to combine. Bring to boiling. Boil gently, uncovered, about 7 minutes or until reduced to ⅓ cup. Serve glaze with sliced steak. Makes 4 servings.
EACH SERVING *286 cal, 5 g fat, 68 mg chol, 384 mg sodium, 34 g carb, 1 g fiber, 26 g pro.*

BASIL HALIBUT WITH JALAPEÑO BUTTER

Basil Halibut with Jalapeño Butter

Cooking jalapeños or other chile peppers in butter leaves them tender and mellow.

START TO FINISH 25 min.

- 4 6-oz. firm whitefish fillets, such as halibut, cod, or flounder, rinsed and patted dry
  Salt and black pepper
- 1 Tbsp. canola oil
- 6 Tbsp. butter
- 2 fresh jalapeño peppers, stemmed, seeded, and cut into thin strips (tip, page 96)
- ¼ cup snipped fresh basil
- 1 lime, cut into quarters

1. Brush fish with oil. Sprinkle lightly with salt and pepper. For a gas or charcoal grill, place fillets on a greased grill rack. Cover; grill directly over medium heat for 4 to 6 minutes per ½-inch thickness or until fish flakes easily when tested with a fork, turning once halfway through grilling.
2. Meanwhile, for jalapeño butter, in a large skillet heat butter over medium heat. Add jalapeños; cook and stir 5 minutes or just until tender and beginning to brown.
3. To serve, top fish with basil and jalapeño butter. Pass lime wedges. Makes 4 servings.
EACH SERVING *419 cal, 31 g fat, 148 mg chol, 370 mg sodium, 2 g carb, 1 g fiber, 33 g pro.*

ZUCCHINI RIBBONS, PASTA, AND ARUGULA

Tarragon Blue Cheese Turkey Patties

Opt for ground turkey with a bit more fat (labeled 80/20), for the juiciest, most flavorful burgers.

PREP 20 min. GRILL 12 min.

- 2 Tbsp. Dijon mustard
- 1 tsp. honey
- 1 lb. ground turkey
- 2 oz. blue cheese, crumbled
- ¼ cup finely chopped red onion
- 1 tsp. chopped fresh tarragon
- 1 to 2 tsp. bottled hot pepper sauce
- 4 sandwich buns, split and toasted
    Lettuce
    Thinly sliced red onion
    Fresh tarragon leaves

1. In a small bowl stir together the mustard and honey; set aside.
2. In a large bowl combine turkey, half the blue cheese, chopped red onion, chopped tarragon, and hot pepper sauce. Shape mixture into four patties.
3. For a gas or charcoal grill, grill patties on the greased rack of a covered grill directly over medium heat 12 to 15 minutes or until 165°F, turning once. Serve on buns with remaining blue cheese, lettuce, and onion slices. Top with honey-mustard and tarragon leaves. Makes 4 servings.
EACH SERVING *390 cal, 19 g fat, 99 mg chol, 944 mg sodium, 26 g carb, 4 g fiber, 25 g pro.*

LOW FAT   FAST

Zucchini Ribbons, Pasta, and Arugula

Cut zucchini into long, easy-to-twirl ribbons. Soften zucchini ribbons by placing in a colander then drain the pasta over them.
START TO FINISH 30 min.

- 6 oz. dried fettuccine pasta
- 2 medium zucchini, cut into thin ribbons with a vegetable peeler, mandoline, or spiral-cutter
- 3 cups arugula
- ¼ cup sliced pepperoncini peppers (about 4 peppers)
- 2 Tbsp. extra-virgin olive oil
- 1 to 2 cloves garlic, minced
- 1 tsp. finely shredded lemon peel
- 1 Tbsp. fresh lemon juice
- 1½ tsp. chopped fresh oregano
    Salt and black pepper
    Coarsely chopped almonds, toasted (tip, page 106)

1. Cook pasta according to package directions. Place zucchini in a colander; drain pasta over zucchini. Immediately run cold water over to cool. Drain well; transfer to a bowl. Add arugula, pepperoncini peppers, oil, garlic, lemon peel, lemon juice, and oregano. Toss to combine. Season to taste with salt and pepper. Top each serving with coarsely chopped almonds. Makes 4 servings.
EACH SERVING *282 cal, 11 g fat, 381 mg sodium, 37 g carb, 4 g fiber, 8 g pro.*

TARRAGON BLUE
CHEESE TURKEY
PATTIES

new ways with cantaloupe

Take juicy, ripe cantaloupe beyond the fruit plate.

Smoky Sweet-and-Sour Cantaloupe

START TO FINISH 30 min.

5 slices thick-sliced smoked bacon
1 medium red onion, sliced
½ cup Asian sweet chili sauce
2 Tbsp. rice vinegar
1 medium cantaloupe (2½ lb.), peeled, seeded, and cubed
Hot cooked rice
¼ cup roasted, salted cashews, coarsely chopped

1. Cook bacon in an extra-large nonstick skillet until crisp. Drain on paper towels, reserving 1 tablespoon drippings in skillet. Crumble bacon.

2. Cook onion in reserved drippings over medium heat until tender. Add chili sauce, vinegar, cantaloupe, and bacon; heat through. Serve over rice and top with cashews. Makes 4 servings.

EACH SERVING *394 cal, 14 g fat, 16 mg chol, 660 mg sodium, 51 g carb, 2 g fiber, 10 g pro.*

Gnocchi Cantaloupe Feta Salad

PREP 30 min. CHILL 30 min.

- 1 16-oz. package shelf-stable gnocchi
- 12 oz. cooked Andouille sausage, sliced
- 4 oz. feta cheese, crumbled
- ¼ cup water
- 2 Tbsp. olive oil
  Salt
  Black pepper
- 1 medium cantaloupe (2½ lb.), peeled, seeded, and sliced (about 4 cups)
- 3 Tbsp. chopped fresh basil or Italian parsley

1. In a large nonstick saucepan cook gnocchi according to package directions. Drain and rinse with cold water. Transfer to a large bowl; set aside.
2. In the same saucepan cook sausage over medium-high heat until lightly browned, about 5 minutes; drain off fat. Add to bowl with gnocchi.
3. In a blender or food processor, blend or process feta, the water, and olive oil until smooth. Season to taste with salt and pepper. Toss with gnocchi, sausage, and cantaloupe. Cover and chill 30 minutes. Top with basil before serving. Makes 4 servings.
EACH SERVING *661 cal, 39 g fat, 69 mg chol, 1,690 mg sodium, 59 g carb, 4 g fiber, 20 g pro.*

Pickled Cantaloupe Salad

PREP 20 min. STAND 15 min.

½ medium cantaloupe (2½ lb.), peeled, seeded, and thinly sliced (3 cups)
1 serrano chile pepper, stemmed and sliced (seeded, if desired) (tip, page 96)
½ cup chopped tomato
½ cup chopped toasted walnuts (tip, page 106)
⅓ cup apple cider vinegar
3 Tbsp. sugar
½ tsp. salt
2 cups cooked farro*
1 large ball (8 oz.) burrata cheese, quartered

1. In a large bowl combine cantaloupe, serrano, tomato, and walnuts. In a small saucepan combine vinegar, sugar, and salt. Bring to a simmer, stirring to dissolve sugar; pour over cantaloupe salad and let stand 15 minutes, stirring occasionally. Serve over farro and cheese. Makes 4 servings.

*Tip In a medium saucepan combine ¾ cup farro and 2 cups water. Bring to boiling. Reduce heat; simmer, covered, for 25 minutes or until tender. Drain.

EACH SERVING 454 cal, 25 g fat, 0 mg chol, 381 mg sodium, 45 g carb, 6 g fiber, 15 g pro.

Cantaloupe, Prosciutto, and Arugula Club

START TO FINISH 30 min.

- 3 oz. thinly sliced prosciutto
- ½ cup mayonnaise
- ¼ cup mild harissa sauce
- 12 thin slices bread, toasted

- ½ small cantaloupe (1½ to 2 lb.), peeled and thinly sliced (about 1½ cups)
- 1 cup baby arugula

1. Preheat oven to 350°F. Line a shallow baking pan with parchment paper. Arrange prosciutto in a single layer on parchment; bake 10 minutes or until crisp. Meanwhile, in a small bowl combine mayonnaise and harissa.

Spread tops of each bread slice with mayonnaise mixture. Top 4 slices with prosciutto. Top another 4 slices with cantaloupe. Top cantaloupe and prosciutto with arugula.

2. Assemble sandwiches. Secure with picks. Makes 4 servings.

EACH SERVING *371 cal, 25 g fat, 26 mg chol, 1,075 mg sodium, 26 g carb, 2 g fiber, 10 g pro.*

ROASTED SALMON WITH HERBS AND YOGURT

september

in sync Stay connected to friends past the dog days of summer—over brunch featuring colorful salads, fresh entrées, and sweet desserts.

223

227

235

MINTED GRAPEFRUIT
PUNCH

TOASTIES WITH
EGG SALAD

cooking to connect

It's an open invitation at Sara Forte's house. The Sprouted Kitchen blogger promises fun for family and friends—and always something seasonal.

Sara Forte bridges the gap between eating well and entertaining.

"Seasonal food inspires me, and I love to turn that food into something that nourishes people," she says. Along with her husband, Hugh, Sara shares this philosophy through every thoughtful, produce-focused recipe and beautiful photograph that appears on her widely read blog, *Sprouted Kitchen*. She's found a cookbook audience that is just as hungry for the food she creates. "It's healthful, colorful food that tastes good," Sara says. "I found a community of readers and friends who feel similarly." For Sara, entertaining takes its cue from food. "Keeping food close to its natural state captures its freshness and flavor—people are attracted to that," she says. "It makes bridging the gap between eating well and entertaining a breeze."

FAST
Toasties with Egg Salad

START TO FINISH **30 min.**

- 1 16-oz. loaf French or Italian bread, 4 inches wide, sliced ¾ inch thick
- 6 extra-large hard-cooked eggs, peeled and chopped
- ¼ cup chopped Italian parsley
- ¼ cup chopped chives
- 2 Tbsp. minced shallot
- 2 Tbsp. capers, drained and chopped
- 2 Tbsp. fresh lemon juice
- 2 Tbsp. extra-virgin olive oil
- 1 Tbsp. Dijon-style mustard

1. Preheat oven to 400°F. Brush one side of bread slices with olive oil. Arrange on a baking sheet. Bake 8 to 10 minutes or until toasted. (Or grill bread on the rack of a covered grill directly over medium heat for 1 to 2 minutes.)
2. Meanwhile, in a bowl stir together remaining ingredients. Season to taste with sea salt and freshly cracked black pepper. Serve on toasted bread. Top with additional minced shallot and parsley. Makes 10 to 12 servings.
EACH SERVING *233 cal, 11 g fat, 112 mg chol, 503 mg sodium, 11 g carb, 1 g fiber, 9 g pro.*

FAST
Minted Grapefruit Punch

If you use freshly squeezed grapefruit juice, prepare it ahead of time—juicing is the most time-consuming part of the recipe.

START TO FINISH **20 min.**

- ½ cup loosely packed mint leaves
- 2 Tbsp. organic cane sugar
- 6 cups freshly squeezed or refrigerated grapefruit juice
- 3 cups vodka
  Club soda, chilled

1. In the bottom of a large pitcher, muddle mint leaves and cane sugar. Stir in grapefruit juice and vodka. Cover; chill until serving. Serve punch over crushed ice with a splash of club soda and grapefruit slices. Makes 9 cups.
EACH 6-OZ. SERVING *195 cal, 0 g fat, 0 mg chol, 7 mg sodium, 16 g carb, 0 g fiber, 0 g pro.*

Easy Brunch the
Sprouted Kitchen Way

SERVE FOOD MADE FOR MINGLING
A never-ending salad, a bowl of dressed
tomatoes—anything that doesn't need tending
helps create a casual atmosphere.

FINISH WITH FRESH HERBS
Sara keeps parsley, mint, chives, and radish
sprouts on hand to add final fresh flavors
to dishes.

STREAMLINE SERVEWARE
Keep decor minimal and let the food lead.
When food is bright, colorful, and incredibly
fresh, it's beautiful.

KEEP DRINKS SIMPLE
A big batch of one amazing cocktail and really,
really good coffee are all you need to keep
guests happy and relaxed.

SUMMER TOMATO
SALAD

Sara's favorite entertaining tip: Do what you do well. Every dish, every forkful, and every sip will show it.

Summer Tomato Salad

PREP 25 min.   CHILL 30 min.

 1 medium red onion, very thinly sliced (1 cup)
 ⅓ cup white wine vinegar
 1 Tbsp. organic cane sugar
   Salt
 2 tsp. Dijon-style mustard
 2 Tbsp. white balsamic vinegar
 ½ tsp. freshly ground black pepper
 ¼ cup extra-virgin olive oil
 2½ lb. ripe red, yellow, green, and/or orange tomatoes, cut into wedges
   Radish sprouts

1. For pickled onions, place onion slices in a medium heatproof bowl; set aside. In a small saucepan warm white wine vinegar, sugar, and ½ tsp. salt over medium heat, stirring to dissolve sugar. Pour over onion slices; toss to coat. Cover; chill at least 30 minutes or up to 24 hours, stirring occasionally.
2. For dressing, in a small bowl whisk together mustard, white balsamic vinegar, pepper, and ¼ tsp. salt. Gradually whisk in olive oil.
3. Place tomatoes in a large serving bowl. Add dressing; toss to coat. Top with drained pickled onions and radish sprouts. Makes 10 to 12 servings.
EACH SERVING *83 cal, 6 g fat, 0 mg chol, 117 mg sodium, 8 g carb, 2 g fiber, 1 g pro.*

FAST

Green Salad with Grapefruit and Avocado

Photo on page 216
START TO FINISH 30 min.

 1 extra-large ruby red grapefruit, peeled and seeded
 2 5-oz. pkg. mixed baby greens (about 10 cups)
 2 avocados, halved, seeded, peeled, and sliced
 2 green onions, thinly sliced
 ¼ cup fresh lemon juice
 1 Tbsp. Dijon-style mustard
 ½ tsp. sea salt
 ½ tsp. black pepper
 ⅔ cup extra-virgin olive oil
 ½ cup roasted, salted pistachios, coarsely chopped

1. Segment grapefruit over a small bowl. Reserve 2 Tbsp. juice for dressing.
2. In a large bowl toss together greens, avocados, grapefruit, and green onions.
3. For dressing, in a small bowl whisk together lemon juice, reserved grapefruit juice, mustard, salt, and pepper. Drizzle oil in a thin steady stream, whisking constantly.
4. Lightly drizzle salad with dressing; pass remaining dressing. Top salad with pistachios just before serving. Makes 6 servings.
EACH SERVING *374 cal, 36 g fat, 0 mg chol, 311 mg sodium, 13 g carb, 6 g fiber, 4 g pro.*
Make ahead Segment grapefruit and prepare dressing up to 1 day ahead. Chill until serving.

LOW FAT

Roasted Salmon with Herbs and Yogurt

Photo on page 217
PREP 25 min.   ROAST 25 min.

 2½ lb. wild salmon fillet
   Salt and black pepper
 1 Tbsp. extra-virgin olive oil
 2 tsp. dried oregano, crushed
 1 lemon
 1 cup plain Greek yogurt (not fat-free)
 ½ English cucumber, finely chopped
 3 Tbsp. minced shallots
 2 Tbsp. chopped Italian parsley
 2 Tbsp. chopped mint leaves
 2 Tbsp. chopped fresh dillweed
 2 Tbsp. chopped fresh basil
 ½ tsp. sea salt
 ¼ tsp. freshly cracked black pepper
   Pinch crushed red pepper

1. Preheat oven to 325°F. Line a shallow baking pan with parchment. Place salmon in prepared pan. Sprinkle with salt and black pepper. Drizzle with olive oil; rub into salmon. Sprinkle with oregano. Roast 25 to 30 minutes or until fish flakes easily when tested in the center with a fork.
2. Meanwhile, remove zest from lemon; set zest aside. Halve lemon; squeeze over salmon. Top salmon with some of the yogurt; sprinkle with lemon zest and remaining ingredients. Drizzle with olive oil and pass remaining yogurt. Makes 10 servings.
EACH SERVING *201 cal, 10 g fat, 65 mg chol, 293 mg sodium, 3 g carb, 0 g fiber, 25 g pro.*
Make ahead After roasting salmon, cover and chill up to 24 hours. Serve chilled or at room temperature.

**GREEN SALAD WITH
GRAPEFRUIT AND
AVOCADO**
Recipe on page 215

ROASTED SALMON WITH HERBS AND YOGURT
Recipe on page 215

Sara loves the comforting experience of a wholesome meal that's served in a bowl. This savory breakfast bowl combines quinoa, cinnamon-roasted butternut squash, and kale. For more protein, top it with a poached egg.

Quinoa and Butternut Bowl

PREP 40 min. BAKE 25 min.

Herb Oil
- ¼ cup chopped fresh parsley
- ¼ cup chopped fresh chives
- ⅔ cup extra-virgin olive oil
- 2 lemons, zested (about 4 tsp.)
  Sea salt

Quinoa Bowl
- 1 large butternut squash (2½ lb.), peeled, seeded, and cut into ¾-inch cubes (about 7 cups)
- ¼ cup extra-virgin olive oil or coconut oil
- ½ tsp. ground cinnamon
- ½ tsp. freshly grated nutmeg
  Sea salt and black pepper
- 4 cloves garlic, minced
- ½ cup finely chopped yellow onion
- 4 cups cooked quinoa*
- 2 Tbsp. maple syrup
  Pinch cayenne pepper
- 4 cups baby kale, coarsely chopped
- 2 Tbsp. lemon juice
- 3 oz. Manchego cheese, shaved
  Radish sprouts (optional)
- 10 to 12 poached eggs (optional)

1. Preheat oven to 425°F. For Herb Oil, in blender combine parsley, chives, the ⅔ cup olive oil, lemon zest, and a few pinches of sea salt. Process or blend until nearly smooth; set aside.

2. For Quinoa Bowl, spread squash cubes in a shallow baking pan. Drizzle with 2 Tbsp. of the oil. Sprinkle with cinnamon, nutmeg, and a few pinches of salt and pepper. Toss to coat; spread in a single layer. Bake 25 minutes or until fork tender and lightly browned, turning once. Cool in pan on a wire rack.

3. In a very large skillet heat remaining 2 Tbsp. oil over medium heat. Add garlic, onion, and a pinch of salt; cook and stir 1 minute. Stir in cooked quinoa, syrup, and cayenne; cook 6 to 8 minutes or until quinoa is crispy, stirring occasionally. Transfer to a large bowl. Stir in kale until wilted. Stir in squash, lemon juice, and 2 Tbsp. of the Herb Oil. To serve, top with additional Herb Oil and Manchego cheese. Sprinkle with radish sprouts and, if desired, top with a poached egg. Makes 10 to 12 servings.

*Place 2 cups rinsed and drained quinoa in a medium-size pan. Add 4 cups water. Bring to boiling; reduce heat. Cover. Simmer 15 to 20 minutes or until tender. Drain off any excess liquid.

EACH SERVING *378 cal, 25 g fat, 8 mg chol, 327 mg sodium, 34 g carb, 5 g fiber, 8 g pro.*

Make ahead Make poached eggs then transfer to a plate or storage container. Cover; chill up to 24 hours. To reheat, bring water to simmering in a skillet. Remove from heat; add eggs. Cover; let stand until warmed through.

A staple in the Forte household, this lemony quick bread is a just-sweet-enough finish to a relaxing brunch or lunch. Top with syrupy berries and a dollop of whipped cream.

KID FRIENDLY

Lemon Loaf with Berries and Cream

Organic cane and turbinado sugar are unbleached and minimally refined sugars that retain some trace minerals usually lost during processing. The larger grains and complex flavor adds texture and richness to baked goods. Turbinado sugar's taste is similar to brown sugar and is often labeled as raw sugar.

PREP 30 min. BAKE 45 min.
COOL 10 min.

- 3 lemons
- 2 eggs
- ⅔ cup buttermilk
- ⅔ cup extra-virgin olive oil
- ½ tsp. lemon extract
- 1 cup regular rolled oats, coarsely ground*
- 1 cup all-purpose flour
- ½ cup organic cane sugar
- ⅓ cup turbinado sugar
- 1 tsp. baking powder
- ¼ tsp. baking soda
- ¼ tsp. sea salt
- ¼ cup organic cane sugar
- 5 cups fresh mixed berries
  Whipped cream

1. Preheat oven to 350°F. Grease an 8-inch loaf pan. Line pan with parchment; set aside. Finely zest 1 lemon. Remove peel from one of the remaining lemons; cut into narrow strips. Set aside. Juice lemons (about 9 Tbsp.). In a large bowl whisk together eggs, buttermilk, oil, lemon extract, zest, and 2 Tbsp. of the lemon juice. Add oats, flour, the ½ cup cane sugar, turbinado sugar, baking powder, baking soda, and sea salt. Stir gently to combine. Pour batter into prepared pan; sprinkle with additional turbinado sugar. Bake 45 to 50 minutes or until a toothpick inserted near center comes out clean. Cool in pan on a wire rack 10 minutes.
2. Meanwhile, in a small saucepan combine remaining lemon juice and the ¼ cup cane sugar. Bring to boiling over medium heat. Boil, gently stirring to dissolve sugar. Remove from heat. Pour half the syrup into a 2-cup measure; stir in lemon peel. Remove loaf from pan. Place on a wire rack set over a shallow baking pan. Gently poke top of loaf all over with a fork. Pour syrup and peel mixture over loaf. Cool completely.
3. Return remaining syrup to heat; bring just to boiling. Stir in berries. Simmer 1 to 2 minutes until berries just start to soften. Slice loaf with a serrated knife. Serve with berries and whipped cream. Makes 10 servings.
*Place oats in a blender or food processor; pulse until coarsely ground.
EACH SERVING *369 cal, 19 g fat, 48 mg chol, 171 mg sodium, 46 g carb, 4 g fiber, 5 g pro.*

Tip For the cake you can substitute ¾ cup granulated sugar for the ½ cup organic cane sugar and the ⅓ cup turbinado sugar. For the syrup, substitute ¼ cup granulated sugar for the ¼ cup organic cane sugar.

MORE FROM SARA
Sara Forte shares her passion for seasonal food on her blog, *Sprouted Kitchen*. The newer of her two cookbooks, *The Sprouted Kitchen Bowl + Spoon* (Ten Speed Press, $25), is an ode to bowl food—combinations of grains, vegetables, and lean protein in one nutritious meal.

butter up

Butter is just one of the simple steps to this utterly delicious bread pudding created by Irish chef, cookbook author, and PBS host Clodagh McKenna.

Bread and Butter Pudding with Salted Caramel Whiskey Butter Sauce

PREP 35 min.   STAND 1 hr. + 30 min.
BAKE 45 min.

Bread and Butter Pudding

- ½ cup raisins
- ½ cup Irish whiskey
- 5 eggs
- 2 cups whipping cream
- 1 cup sugar
- 1 tsp. vanilla
- ½ tsp. ground cinnamon
- ¼ tsp. ground nutmeg
- 8 slices firm white bread (12 to 14 oz.)
- ¾ cup unsalted butter, room temperature

Salted Caramel Whiskey Butter Sauce

- ¼ cup unsalted butter, cubed
- ½ cup sugar
- ½ tsp. sea salt
- 1¼ cups whipping cream

1. In a medium bowl combine raisins and whiskey; let soak 1 hour. Butter a 2-qt. rectangular baking dish; set aside.

2. For custard, in a large bowl whisk together eggs, cream, sugar, vanilla, cinnamon, and nutmeg. Generously spread one side of each bread slice with butter; cut each in half diagonally. Arrange in prepared baking dish, overlapping slices. Drain raisins, reserving whiskey. Sprinkle raisins over bread, tucking some between slices. Pour custard over bread; cover. Soak in refrigerator for 30 minutes.

3. Preheat oven to 375°F. Place uncovered baking dish in a large baking pan. Add hot water to rise halfway up sides of dish. Bake 45 minutes or until pudding is set and top is golden. Carefully remove baking dish from water bath; cool slightly on a wire rack.

4. Meanwhile, for the sauce, in a 2-qt. saucepan melt butter over medium heat. Whisk in sugar, salt, whipping cream, and 3 Tbsp. of the reserved whiskey. Bring to boiling; reduce heat. Simmer, uncovered, for 10 to 15 minutes or until slightly thickened, stirring frequently. Serve pudding warm with sauce. Makes 12 servings.

EACH SERVING 585 cal, 42 g fat, 207 mg chol, 242 mg sodium, 43 g carb, 1 g fiber, 6 g pro.

SOAK THE RAISINS "Raisins get delightfully plump when soaked," Clodagh says. "Irish whiskey gives them an extra kick and boosts the sweetness so they're bursting with deliciousness."

MAKE THE CUSTARD "The ingredients are simple, so look for the purest, high-quality butter and cream you can find. Freshly ground cinnamon and nutmeg would be all the better too."

SPREAD THE CREAMY BUTTER "I coat each crusted slice with a generous layer of Irish butter for added richness. It's the secret to my take on bread pudding."

POUR THE CUSTARD "Once you've poured the custard over, gently press the bread down so it's completely covered in liquid. This step will ensure the pudding doesn't have a dry top."

PREPARE A WATER BATH "Baking this way insulates the custard from direct heat, which can cause the eggs to cook too fast and separate. The steam also keeps the surface from drying out."

MAKE THE SAUCE The sauce has a thin consistency and thickens just a bit as it simmers. "The sauce is addictive," Clodagh says. "Pour extra over ice cream to make an Irish sundae!"

"The key to this bread pudding is to use bread that is at least 24 hours old. The drier the bread, the more rich custard it absorbs," says Clodagh.

KID FRIENDLY

Chocolate Bread Pudding

Butter, cream, and chocolate share the spotlight in this decadent bread pudding. Clodagh uses butter from grass-fed cows for the sweetest, richest taste.

PREP **30 min.** STAND **1 hr.**
BAKE **45 min.** COOL **15 min.**

5	eggs
2	cups whipping cream
1	cup sugar
½	tsp. ground cinnamon
¼	tsp. ground nutmeg
1	teaspoon vanilla
8	1-inch slices firm white bread (about 10 oz.)
¾	cup butter, at room temperature
4	oz. semisweet and/or milk chocolate, chopped (1 cup)
1	recipe Ganache

1. Butter a 2-qt. rectangular baking dish; set aside. For custard, in a large bowl whisk together the eggs, cream, sugar, cinnamon, nutmeg, and vanilla. Generously spread one side of each slice of bread with the butter. Cut the slices in half diagonally and arrange in the prepared baking dish, overlapping slices. Sprinkle the chocolate over the bread, tucking some between the bread slices. Pour the custard over the bread; cover. Soak in the refrigerator for 30 minutes.

2. Preheat oven to 375°F. Place the baking dish in a large roasting pan. Add hot water to rise halfway up the sides of the dish. Bake for 45 minutes or until the pudding is set and the top is golden. Carefully remove baking dish from water bath; cool slightly on a wire rack. Serve warm bread pudding with Ganache spooned over the top. Makes 12 servings.

Ganache In a medium saucepan bring 1 cup whipping cream just to boiling over medium heat. Remove from heat. Add 12 oz. semisweet chocolate, chopped (do not stir). Let stand 5 minutes. Stir until smooth. Cool for 15 minutes.

EACH SERVING *786 cal, 61 g fat, 238 mg chol, 249 mg sodium, 61 g carb, 3 g fiber, 8 g pro.*

MORE FROM CLODAGH
Clodagh shares seasonal menus at her two Dublin restaurants that feature fresh, local Irish produce. She is also the star of the PBS TV series *Clodagh's Irish Food Trails*, and she collaborates on projects with Kerrygold Irish butter and cheese. *Clodagh's Irish Kitchen* ($29.95; Kyle Books) is the latest of her five cookbooks.

weeknight delicious

Fast and fresh solutions for dinner tonight.

**WILD RICE AND
ROASTED CORN SALAD**

Wild Rice and Roasted Corn Salad

This recipe calls for multitasking. While the rice cooks, there is time to grill the corn and slice the avocado. Once the rice is done, toss it with the remaining ingredients, and dinner is served. Try it over a bed of spinach or other greens.

PREP **20 min.** COOK **40 min.**
GRILL **7 min.**

- ½ cup wild rice, rinsed and drained
- 4 medium ears corn, husks and silks removed
  Nonstick cooking spray
- 1 15-oz. can chickpeas (garbanzo beans), rinsed and drained
- ½ cup chopped toasted walnuts (tip, page 106)
- ⅓ cup chopped fresh basil
- 3 Tbsp. olive oil
- 1 large lime, juiced (3 Tbsp.)
- ½ tsp. salt
- ¼ tsp. black pepper
- 1 avocado, halved, seeded, peeled, and quartered

1. In a large saucepan bring 1½ cups water to boiling; stir in rice. Reduce heat; simmer, covered, 40 minutes or until kernels open. Meanwhile, coat corn with cooking spray. Grill directly over medium-high heat for 7 to 8 minutes or until charred, turning frequently. Remove; cool slightly. Cut corn from cob.
2. Drain rice, if necessary; return to pan. Stir in corn, chickpeas, walnuts, basil, oil, lime juice, salt, and pepper. Stir to heat through. Remove from heat. Serve with avocado. Makes 4 servings.
EACH SERVING *474 cal, 28 g fat, 0 mg chol, 430 mg sodium, 51 g carb, 10 g fiber, 13 g pro.*

HONEY-SRIRACHA GRILLED CHICKEN THIGHS

LOW FAT
Honey-Sriracha Grilled Chicken Thighs

The heat from sriracha sauce is balanced by sweet honey—a delicious combination!

PREP **10 min.** GRILL **30 min.**
STAND **20 min.**

- 6 Tbsp. sriracha sauce
- 2 Tbsp. honey
- 8 bone-in chicken thighs, skinned
- 2 Tbsp. fresh lime juice
- 2 Tbsp. chopped fresh cilantro

1. Whisk together 2 Tbsp. of the sriracha sauce and the honey; set aside. Place chicken in a resealable plastic bag; add remaining sriracha sauce and lime juice. Seal bag; turn to coat chicken. Let stand 15 minutes.
2. Grill chicken on greased rack of a covered gas or charcoal grill directly over medium heat for 30 to 35 minutes or until done (170°F), turning several times.
3. Transfer chicken to a platter; brush with sriracha-honey mixture. Cover; let stand 5 minutes. Top with cilantro. Makes 4 servings.
EACH SERVING *300 cal, 8 g fat, 191 mg chol, 426 mg sodium, 14 g carb, 0 g fiber, 40 g pro.*

OVERGROWN GARDEN TURKEY MELT

Charred Sweet Pepper Potato Chowder

For the best smoky flavor, wait until sweet pepper skins are blistered and blackened before adding onions.
START TO FINISH **35 min.**

Nonstick cooking spray
1 lb. red sweet peppers, chopped (3 cups)
2 large yellow onions, chopped (2 cups)
1 large russet potato, peeled and chopped
½ cup vegetable broth
2 cups milk
⅛ tsp. cayenne pepper
1 Tbsp. butter
¼ cup chopped fresh Italian parsley
Salt and black pepper
Bacon (optional)
Greek yogurt (optional)

1. Coat a 4-qt. Dutch oven with nonstick cooking spray; heat over medium-high heat. Add peppers; coat with cooking spray. Cook, uncovered, 15 minutes or until charred, stirring frequently.
2. Add onions; cook 5 to 6 minutes or until soft and golden brown, stirring occasionally. Stir in chopped potatoes and broth. Bring to boiling; reduce heat. Simmer, covered, 12 minutes or until potatoes are very tender.
3. Coarsely mash soup with a potato masher. Add milk and cayenne pepper. Heat through.
4. Remove from heat; stir in butter and parsley. Season to taste with salt and pepper. Top with bacon and Greek yogurt, if desired. Makes 4 servings.
EACH SERVING *255 cal, 11 g fat, 32 mg chol, 284 mg sodium, 30 g carb, 5 g fiber, 11 g pro.*

Overgrown Garden Turkey Melt

This sandwich is stacked with fresh veggies and herbs. For a different, take swap the turkey for ham, salami, or grilled zucchini.
START TO FINISH **30 min.**

3 Tbsp. mayonnaise
2 tsp. chopped fresh rosemary
2 cloves garlic, minced
2 cups fresh spinach, chopped
1 14-oz. can artichoke hearts, drained, chopped, and dried
2 8-oz. rounds ciabatta loaves, halved crosswise
6 oz. sliced mozzarella cheese
1 medium tomato, thinly sliced
4 oz. sliced smoked turkey

1. Preheat oven to 400°F. In a medium bowl combine mayonnaise, rosemary, and garlic. Add spinach and artichokes; stir to combine. Set aside.
2. Remove soft bread from each half to create 1-inch shells. Lay each bread half on a baking sheet. Line each with mozzarella. Spoon vegetable mixture onto each bottom bread shell. Top with tomato and turkey.
3. Bake 10 minutes or until toasted and heated through. Assemble sandwiches; cut each in half. Makes 4 servings.
EACH SERVING *495 cal, 19 g fat, 40 mg chol, 1,275 mg sodium, 55 g carb, 4 g fiber, 28 g pro.*

**CHARRED SWEET
PEPPER POTATO
CHOWDER**

Roasted Grape and Arugula Pizza

PREP 20 min. BAKE 12 min.

Olive oil
¼ cup coarse or regular cornmeal
1 lb. purchased or homemade pizza dough
6 oz. Brie cheese, thinly sliced
2 oz. blue cheese, crumbled
3 cups whole seedless red grapes
1 tsp. chopped fresh rosemary
2 cups arugula
Crushed red pepper and/or sea salt (optional)

1. Preheat oven to 450°F. Brush olive oil on two large baking sheets then sprinkle with cornmeal; set aside.
2. Divide dough into four pieces. Stretch or roll each piece into an 8×6-inch oval. Press pieces into cornmeal on baking sheets, turning to coat both sides. Top dough evenly with cheeses, grapes, and rosemary. Bake 12 to 15 minutes or until edges are golden and grapes start to shrivel. Rotate baking sheets halfway through baking.
3. To serve, top hot pizzas with arugula and sprinkle with crushed red pepper and/or sea salt. Makes 4 servings.

EACH SERVING *613 cal, 23 g fat, 53 mg chol, 893 mg sodium, 80 g carb, 4 g fiber, 24 g pro.*

Juicy Grape Pulled Pork

PREP 30 min.

SLOW COOK 10 hr. (low) or 5 hr. (high)

- 3 lb. pork shoulder roast, trimmed of fat
- 2 tsp. dried thyme, crushed
- 1 tsp. each salt and pepper
- 3 cups purple or red seedless grapes
- 1 red onion, cut into wedges (1 cup)
- 1 cup water
- ⅓ cup balsamic vinegar
- ¼ cup tomato paste
- 8 biscuits or buns, split and toasted
   Lettuce leaves, sliced tomatoes, and/or fresh thyme (optional)

1. Coat pork with dried thyme, salt, and pepper. Place roast, grapes, onion, the water, and vinegar in a 4- to 5-quart slow cooker. Cover; cook on low for 10 hours or on high for 5 hours.

2. Transfer roast to a cutting board; let rest. Using a slotted spoon, remove onions and grapes to a large bowl; cover to keep warm. Skim fat from cooking liquid; transfer to a medium saucepan. Whisk in tomato paste. Bring to boiling. Boil gently, uncovered, for 15 minutes or until slightly thickened.

3. Shred meat and add to the bowl with onions and grapes; stir to combine. Serve pulled pork on buns with sauce, and, if desired, lettuce, tomatoes, and fresh thyme. Makes 8 servings.

EACH SERVING *402 cal, 13 g fat, 102 mg chol, 800 mg sodium, 34 g carb, 2 g fiber, 35 g pro.*

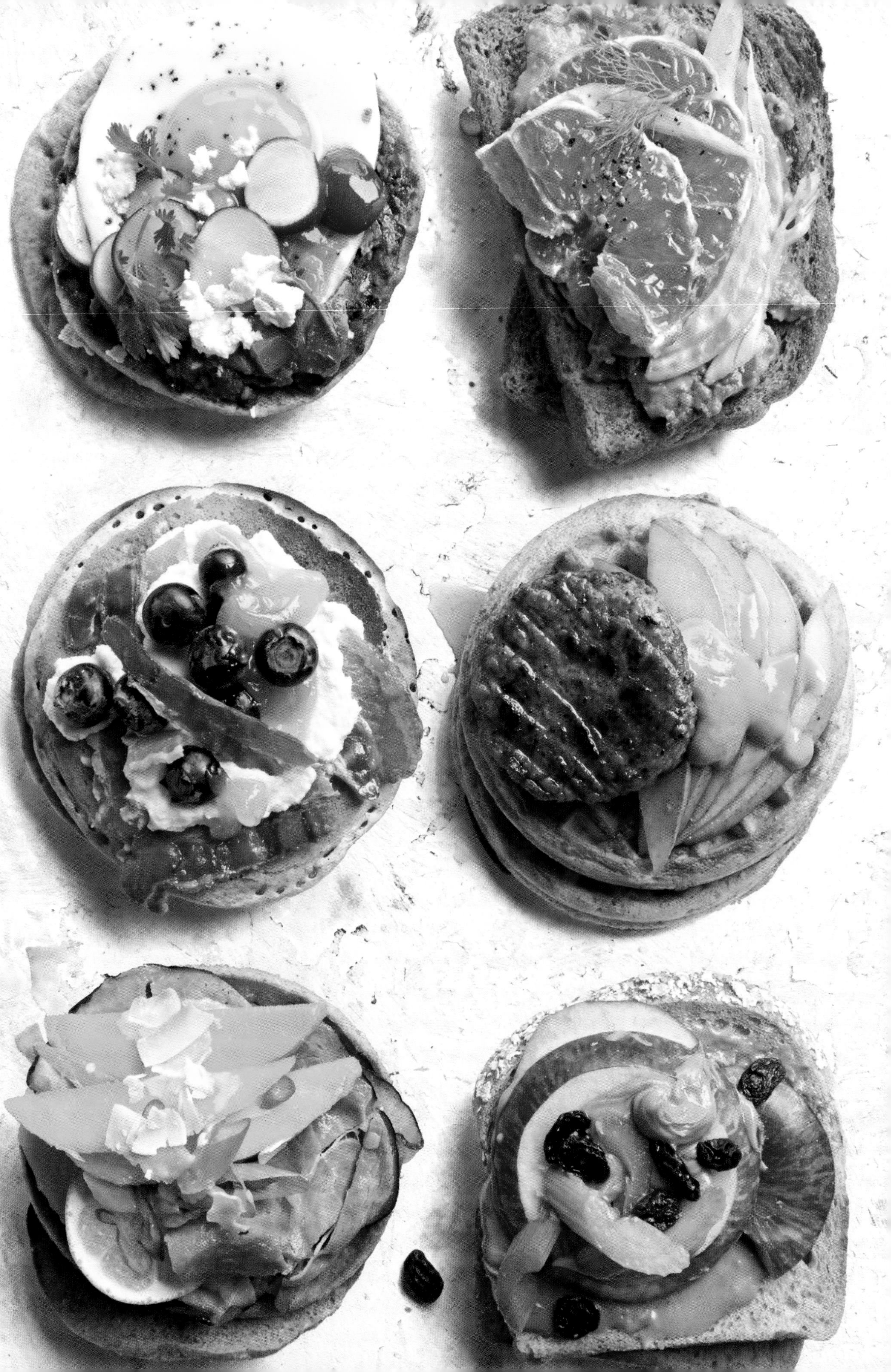

good to go

Start the day with a delicious and satisfying breakfast sandwich. Whole grains, protein, and healthful fats provide energy to stave off midmorning hunger.

LOW FAT FAST
Southwest Sunrise
START TO FINISH 15 min.

- 1 egg
- 1 whole grain sandwich thin, split, and toasted
- ¼ cup canned black beans, rinsed, drained, and mashed
- 1 Tbsp. salsa verde
- 2 to 3 thinly sliced small radishes
- 1 Tbsp. crumbled feta cheese
  Cilantro (optional)

1. Cook egg over medium heat in a small skillet coated with nonstick cooking spray until desired doneness, turning once. Spread bread with mashed beans, add egg, and top with salsa, radishes, cheese and if desired, a sprinkling of cilantro. Makes 1 serving.
EACH SERVING *258 cal, 8 g fat, 194 mg chol, 705 mg sodium, 36 g carb, 9 g fiber, 16 g pro.*

LOW FAT FAST KID FRIENDLY
Chicken and Waffles
START TO FINISH 10 min.

- 1 Tbsp. Dijon-style mustard
- ½ tsp. maple syrup
- 2 frozen whole grain waffles, toasted
- 1 to 2 chicken-maple sausage patties
- ¼ cup thinly sliced pear

1. Stir together the mustard and maple syrup. Spread over waffles. Add sausage and pear. Try it open-faced. Makes 1 serving.
EACH SERVING *292 cal, 11 g fat, 50 mg chol, 1,196 mg sodium, 39 g carb, 4 g fiber, 15 g pro.*

FAST
Avocado Grapefruit
START TO FINISH 10 min.

- 2 slices whole wheat bread, toasted
- ½ avocado, pitted, peeled, and mashed
- ¼ cup very thinly sliced trimmed, cored fennel bulb
- 2 slices peeled, seeded grapefruit
  Honey
  Pinch sea salt

1. Top one slice of bread with avocado, fennel, grapefruit, a drizzle of honey, and salt. Top with remaining bread slice. Makes 1 serving.
EACH SERVING *432 cal, 15 g fat, 0 mg chol, 476 mg sodium, 70 g carb, 12 g fiber, 10 g pro.*

FAST
Tropical Treat
START TO FINISH 10 min.

- 1 whole wheat bagel thin, split and lightly toasted
- 1 Tbsp. coconut butter
- 3 thin slices cooked ham
- ⅓ mango, seeded, peeled, and thinly sliced (⅓ cup)
- 1 Tbsp. thinly sliced green onion
- 1 Tbsp. raw coconut chips, toasted (tip, page 106)
- 1 lime wedge

1. Spread one half of the bagel thin with coconut butter and top with ham, mango, green onion, and coconut chips. Squeeze lime wedge over fillings; top with remaining bagel thin half. Makes 1 serving.
EACH SERVING *354 cal, 18 g fat, 24 mg chol, 684 mg sodium, 42 g carb, 10 g fiber, 15 g pro.*

LOW FAT FAST
Blueberries and Bacon
START TO FINISH 10 min.

- 2 slices precooked bacon, halved
- 2 frozen whole grain pancakes, toasted
- 2 Tbsp. ricotta cheese
- 1 Tbsp. lemon curd
- 2 Tbsp. fresh blueberries

1. Heat bacon according to package directions. Top a pancake with ricotta, lemon curd, blueberries, bacon, and remaining pancake. Makes 1 serving.
EACH SERVING *324 cal, 11 g fat, 38 mg chol, 561 mg sodium, 54 g carb, 7 g fiber, 10 g pro.*

FAST KID FRIENDLY
Peanut Butter Crunch
START TO FINISH 10 min.

- 2 slices 7-grain bread, toasted
- 2 Tbsp. peanut butter
- ¼ apple, cored and sliced
- 1 Tbsp. thinly sliced celery
- 1 Tbsp. raisins

1. Spread one bread slice with peanut butter and top with apple, celery, raisins; add remaining bread slice. Makes 1 serving.
EACH SERVING *403 cal, 19 g fat, 0 mg chol, 483 mg sodium, 57 g carb, 9 g fiber, 16 g pro.*

KALE CAESAR
SALAD

school days It's back to class in the kitchen. Delicious lessons about dried beans, cauliflower, and kale, plus updated flavors for everyday meals.

243

249

257

you don't know beans

You thought you did, but wait until you see how versatile beans are. From dried to canned, pinto to chickpea, you can put them in every pot, pan, and Dutch oven.

Chicken and Sausage White Bean Pot

Flageolet beans (pronounced fla-zhoh-LAY), French in origin, are prized for light flavor and creamy texture.

PREP **1 hr.** STAND **1 hr.**
COOK **1 hr., 15 min.**
BAKE **1 hr. + 20 min.**

- 1 lb. (2¼ cups) dried navy, cannellini, great Northern, or flageolet beans
- 6 oz. thick-sliced bacon or pancetta, chopped
- 12 oz. Andouille sausage
- 2 lb. bone-in chicken thighs and/or drumsticks (about 6)
- ½ tsp. salt
- ½ tsp. black pepper
- 2 cups chopped onions
- 1½ cups peeled and chopped carrots
- 1½ cups chopped celery
- 3 cloves garlic, minced
- 8 cups reduced-sodium chicken broth
- 3 Tbsp. tomato paste
- 8 sprigs Italian parsley and/or thyme
- 2 bay leaves
- ¼ cup panko bread crumbs
- 1 Tbsp. butter, melted
  Fresh Italian parsley

1. Rinse beans. In an 8-qt. Dutch oven combine beans and 8 cups water. Bring to boiling; reduce heat. Simmer, covered, 2 minutes. Remove from heat. Let stand 1 hour. (Or place beans and water in a large pot; cover and let soak in refrigerator 8 hours or overnight.) Drain and rinse.
2. In a large Dutch oven cook bacon over medium heat for 8 minutes or until crisp. Using a slotted spoon, transfer to a large bowl. Add sausage to pot; cook 6 minutes or until browned, turning occasionally. Transfer to bowl with bacon. Sprinkle chicken all over with salt and pepper; then add to pot. Cook 8 minutes over medium-high heat until well-browned all over. Transfer to bowl with bacon and sausage. Refrigerate until called for.
3. Add onions, carrots, and celery to pot; cook 8 minutes. Add garlic; cook 1 minute. Stir in drained beans, broth, tomato paste, herbs, and bay leaves. Bring to a simmer over high heat. Reduce heat. Simmer, uncovered, 40 to 45 minutes or until beans are almost tender, stirring occasionally.
4. Preheat oven to 350°F. Cut sausage into 1-inch pieces; add to stew with pancetta. Place chicken on top of stew, skin exposed. Bake, uncovered, 1 hour.
5. In a small bowl combine bread crumbs and butter; sprinkle on stew. Bake 20 minutes until bread crumbs are crisp. Remove herbs before serving. Top with chopped parsley. Makes 10 servings.
EACH SERVING *486 cal, 24 g fat, 92 mg chol, 1,092 mg sodium, 37 g carb, 9 g fiber, 30 g pro.*
For canned beans: Skip Step 1. Rinse and drain four 15-oz. cans navy, cannellini, or great Northern beans. In Step 4 stir beans into pot before adding cooked meats to stew.

Canned versus dry The long cooking for dried beans infuses them with flavor and, for many cooks, is worth the time. Canned beans are the king of convenience. Be sure to drain the liquid and rinse them well. The extra salt and starch can affect the overall texture of a dish. Plus, rinsing eliminates the canned taste.

The silky texture of lima beans has earned them the name butter beans. Neutral in flavor, they won't dominate most dishes.

Spanish-Style Gigante Beans

PREP 30 min. STAND 1 hr.
COOK 1 hr., 5 min. BAKE 45 min.

- 1 lb. dried gigante or large butter beans (lima beans)
- ¼ cup olive oil
- ½ cup finely chopped onion
- 8 cloves garlic, minced
- 2 pints grape tomatoes
- 1 cup roasted sweet peppers, chopped
- 2 tsp. smoked paprika
- ¼ tsp. saffron threads, crushed
- 2 bay leaves
- 1 cup finely chopped Italian parsley
- ½ cup marcona almonds or roasted salted almonds, chopped

1. Rinse beans. In a 4-qt. Dutch oven combine beans and 8 cups water. Bring to boiling; reduce heat. Simmer, covered, 2 minutes. Remove from heat. Let stand 1 hour. (Or place beans and water in a large pot. Cover and let soak in refrigerator 8 hours or overnight.) Drain beans and rinse. Return to Dutch oven. Add fresh water to cover by 1 inch. Cover; bring to boiling. Reduce heat to low. Simmer, covered, 45 minutes or until beans are tender, stirring occasionally. Drain, reserving 2 cups cooking liquid.
2. Preheat oven to 350°F. In the same Dutch oven heat 2 Tbsp. of the oil over medium heat. Add onion; cook 4 minutes. Add 6 cloves of the garlic, tomatoes, peppers, paprika, saffron, and bay leaves. Bring to a simmer. Reduce heat to medium-low. Simmer, uncovered, 15 minutes or until tomatoes break down. Stir in beans, reserved liquid, and 2 tsp. salt. Bring to boiling. Place Dutch oven in oven. Bake, uncovered, 45 minutes. Remove bay leaves.
3. In a small bowl combine remaining 2 Tbsp. olive oil, remaining 2 cloves garlic, parsley, and a pinch of salt. Mash with a spoon. Spoon over beans. Top with almonds. Makes 8 servings.
For canned beans Skip Step 1. Rinse and drain four 16-oz. cans gigante or butter beans. Add as directed in Step 2. Use 2 cups water for cooking liquid.
EACH SERVING *283 cal, 16 g fat, 0 mg chol, 898 mg sodium, 28 g carb, 8 g fiber, 10 g pro.*

Turkey-Farro Salad with Candied Chickpeas

Chickpeas (garbanzo beans) are a favorite in Mediterranean dishes. Call on this pantry staple as a main ingredient for falafel and hummus.
PREP 1 hr. STAND 1 hr.
COOK 2½ hr. ROAST 45 min.

- 1 cup dried chickpeas (garbanzo beans)
- ¼ cup packed brown sugar
- ½ cup olive oil
  Salt and black pepper
- 1 tsp. poultry seasoning
- 2 turkey tenderloins (1 lb. total)
- ½ cup uncooked farro
- 1½ cups reduced-sodium chicken broth
- 3 Tbsp. sherry vinegar
- 1 6-oz. package mixed salad greens
- 2 romaine hearts, chopped (8 cups)
- 1 large Gala or Honeycrisp apple, thinly sliced
- 3 seedless clementines, peeled and cut up
- 2 Tbsp. dried cranberries
- 1 oz. high-quality blue cheese, crumbled (¼ cup)

1. Rinse chickpeas. In a large saucepan or Dutch oven combine chickpeas and 4 cups water. Bring to boiling; reduce heat. Simmer, covered, 2 minutes. Let stand 1 hour. (Or place chickpeas and water in pan. Let soak in refrigerator 8 hours or overnight.) Drain and rinse beans; return to pan. Add fresh water to cover by 1 inch. Cover; bring to boiling. Reduce heat. Cover; simmer 1½ hours or until beans are very tender, stirring occasionally.
2. Preheat oven to 325°F. Drain and rinse beans; spread out on a kitchen towel to dry thoroughly. Line a shallow baking pan with parchment; spread beans in a single layer in pan. Sprinkle with brown sugar, 1 Tbsp. of the olive oil, ½ tsp. salt, and ¼ tsp. black pepper, stirring to coat. Roast 50 minutes or until amber, stirring occasionally. Remove from oven and cool in pan.
3. Sprinkle poultry seasoning and ½ tsp. salt over turkey. Heat a large nonstick skillet over medium-high heat. Add 1 Tbsp. of the olive oil and turkey. Cook 30 to 35 minutes or until done (165°F), turning to brown evenly.
4. Meanwhile, in a medium saucepan over medium-high heat, bring farro and broth to boiling. Reduce heat. Cover; simmer 30 minutes or until tender yet chewy. Drain off any liquid; cool.
5. For dressing, place vinegar in a large bowl. Whisk in remaining 6 Tbsp. olive oil in a thin, steady stream until blended. Whisk in ½ tsp. salt and ¼ tsp. black pepper. Transfer turkey to dressing in bowl; toss to coat. Cool 5 minutes. Reserving dressing, transfer turkey to cutting board to slice.
6. Add greens and apple to dressing; toss to coat. Transfer to a large serving bowl. Arrange turkey, farro, and chickpeas on greens. Top with clementines, cranberries, and cheese. Makes 8 to 10 servings.
For canned beans Skip Step 1. Rinse and drain two 15-oz. can chickpeas; dry as directed in Step 2.
EACH SERVING *407 cal, 17 g fat, 28 mg chol, 642 mg sodium, 42 g carb, 6 g fiber, 23 g pro.*

**TURKEY FARRO SALAD
WITH CANDIED
CHICKPEAS**

**SPANISH-STYLE
GIGANTE BEANS**

**STEWED FAVAS
WITH FENNEL &
SWEET POTATOES**
Recipe on page 243

ROAST BEEF AND
BEER-BRAISED
PINTO BEANS

Beans are fully cooked when they are easily smashed against the side of the pot or between two fingers. Occasionally stirring dried beans during cooking ensures even doneness.

Roast Beef and Beer-Braised Pinto Beans

PREP 45 min. STAND 1 hr. + 15 min. COOK 45 min. ROAST 40 min.

- ½ lb. dried pinto beans or small red beans
- 2 Tbsp. olive oil
- 1 1½ lb. beef top sirloin
  Salt and black pepper
- ½ tsp. dried thyme
- 1 lb. parsnips, peeled and chopped (2½ cups)
- 1 lb. butternut squash, peeled, seeded, and chopped (2½ cups)
- 6 oz. thick-sliced pancetta or bacon, chopped
- ½ cup chopped onion
- 3 cloves garlic, minced
- 1 Tbsp. chopped fresh rosemary
- ¾ cup beer, such as wheat beer or amber ale
- ¾ cup reduced-sodium chicken broth

1. Rinse beans. In a large pot combine beans and 4 cups water. Bring to boiling; reduce heat. Simmer, covered, 2 minutes. Remove from heat. Let stand 1 hour. (Or place beans and water in pan. Cover and let soak in refrigerator 8 hours or overnight.) Drain and rinse beans; return to pot. Add fresh water to cover by 1 inch. Cover; bring to boiling. Reduce heat. Simmer 45 to 60 minutes or just until beans are tender, stirring occasionally. Drain.
2. Preheat oven to 500°F. Rub 1 Tbsp. of the oil into meat. Combine 1½ tsp. salt, ½ tsp. pepper, and thyme; sprinkle 1 tsp. of the salt mixture on meat. Place parsnips and squash in a 13×9-inch roasting pan. Add remaining oil and salt mixture; toss to coat. Place meat on vegetables. Roast 20 minutes.

3. Meanwhile, in a 4-qt. Dutch oven cook pancetta over medium heat for 8 minutes or until crisp. Transfer to paper towels to drain, reserving 1 Tbsp. drippings in the pot. Add onion; cook 4 minutes or until tender. Add drained beans, garlic, rosemary, beer, and broth. Stir in reserved pancetta. Bring to a simmer over high heat. Place uncovered pot in oven alongside roasting pan.
4. Reduce oven to 300°F. Roast 20 to 30 minutes or until beans are tender and meat is done (135°F to 140°F).
5. Cover; let stand 15 minutes. Remove and slice roast. Stir roasted vegetables into bean mixture; serve with meat. Makes 6 to 8 servings.
EACH SERVING *576 cal, 27 g fat, 103 mg chol, 1,175 mg sodium, 44 g carb, 10 g fiber, 37 g pro.*
For canned beans Skip Step 1. Rinse and drain two 15-oz. cans pinto beans or small red beans. Add as directed in Step 3.

Stewed Favas with Fennel and Sweet Potatoes

Photo on page 241
Fava beans are known for meaty texture and nutty taste. Lemon juice brings out the distinctive flavor of the beans.
PREP 20 min. STAND 1 hr. COOK 1 hr., 5 min.

- 1 lb. dried fava beans or kidney beans
- ¼ cup olive oil
- 1 cup chopped large onion
- 1 small fennel bulb, trimmed, cored, and chopped
- 6 cloves garlic, minced
- 1 tsp. ground cumin
- 1 tsp. ground coriander

- 1 tsp. caraway seeds, crushed
- ¼ tsp. ground turmeric
- 2 bay leaves
- 2 lb. sweet potatoes, peeled and cut into ¾-inch pieces
- 3 cups reduced-sodium chicken broth or vegetable broth
  Salt
- ¼ cup butter, softened
  Zest of 1 orange
- ⅓ cup crumbled feta cheese

1. Rinse beans. In a 6- to 8-qt. Dutch oven combine beans and 8 cups water. Bring to boiling; reduce heat. Simmer, covered, 2 minutes. Remove from heat. Let stand 1 hour. (Or place beans and water in pan. Cover and let soak in refrigerator 8 hours or overnight.) Drain and rinse beans; return to pot. Add fresh water to cover by 1 inch; bring to boiling. Reduce heat. Cover; simmer 45 to 50 minutes or just until beans are tender, stirring occasionally. Drain.
2. In the same Dutch oven heat oil over medium heat. Add onion and fennel; cook 6 minutes or until tender. Add garlic, cumin, coriander, caraway, turmeric, and bay leaves; cook 1 minute. Add drained beans, sweet potatoes, broth, and 1 tsp. salt; bring to a simmer over high heat. Reduce heat. Cover; simmer 12 to 15 minutes or until beans and sweet potatoes are tender. Remove bay leaves. Stir in butter and orange zest. Top with feta before serving. Makes 8 servings.
EACH SERVING *462 cal, 15 g fat, 21 mg chol, 694 mg sodium, 65 g carb, 19 g fiber, 20 g pro.*
For canned beans Skip Step 1. Rinse and drain three 15-oz. cans fava or kidney beans. Add as directed in Step 2.

kale, caesar!

Still haven't jumped on the kale bandwagon? This updated version of the classic Caesar salad will get you on board.

Kale Caesar Salad

Traditional Caesar salad dressing uses raw egg yolks to create silky texture. This version calls for hard-cooked yolks for food safety and the result is a delicious, creamy dressing that marries perfectly with slightly bitter kale.

PREP 30 min. BAKE 20 min.
STAND 30 min.

8 cloves garlic, peeled
¾ cup extra-virgin olive oil
6 oz. ciabatta bread, cut or torn into 1-inch pieces (4 cups)
Salt
6 anchovy fillets
¼ cup lemon juice
1 Tbsp. Dijon-style mustard
2 hard-cooked eggs, yolks and whites separated
Black pepper
3 bunches Tuscan kale (also called dinosaur, black, or Lacinato kale), stems removed and leaves thinly sliced (about 18 cups)
⅓ cup freshly grated Parmigiano-Reggiano

1. Preheat oven to 300°F. For croutons, mince two of the garlic cloves. In a medium saucepan warm ¼ cup of the oil and the minced garlic over low heat; remove. Add bread pieces. Sprinkle with ¼ tsp. salt. Stir to coat. Spread bread pieces in a single layer on a shallow baking pan. Bake 20 minutes or until crisp and golden brown, stirring once. Cool completely. Store in an airtight container at room temperature up to 24 hours.
2. For dressing, in a blender combine the remaining garlic and oil, anchovy fillets, lemon juice, mustard, and egg yolks. Blend until smooth. Season to taste with salt and pepper. (Dressing can be chilled up to 24 hours; let stand at room temperature 30 minutes before using.)
3. Place kale in a very large bowl; add dressing. Using your hands, work dressing into kale. Let stand at room temperature 30 minutes or up to 2 hours. To serve, sprinkle with cheese and top with chopped egg whites and croutons. Makes 8 servings.
EACH SERVING *456 cal, 33 g fat, 70 mg chol, 485 mg sodium, 34 g carb, 8 g fiber, 15 g pro.*

Tuscan kale wins for this salad. Its puckered dark green leaves are tender and mild-tasting.

STEM AND SLICE Kale stems are really tough and need to be removed. Slide your thumb and forefinger along the rib to separate. Stack leaves and slice crosswise for thin, bite-size pieces.

USE YOUR HANDS Quickly work the dressing into the kale—not for long, just 30 seconds. Then let it rest to soften and relax the kale leaves.

Looking for a change? Try these inventive variations based on Kale Caesar Salad.

Chicken-Kale Caesar Salad

Prepare as directed on page 245 except replace Parmigiano-Reggiano with Asiago cheese. Top with 1½ lb. skinless, boneless chicken breast, cooked and sliced; and 1½ cups cherry tomatoes, halved.

PER SERVING *609 cal, 37 g fat, 142 mg chol, 537 mg sodium, 35 g carb, 8 g fiber, 41 g pro.*

Salmon-Kale Caesar Salad

Prepare as directed on page 245 except omit cheese. Top with 4 skinless, boneless salmon fillets (1½ lb. total), cooked and broken into chunks; ⅓ cup drained capers; and 1 medium red onion, cut into thin wedges.

PER SERVING *610 cal, 38 g fat, 128 mg chol, 636 mg sodium, 36 g carb, 9 g fiber, 36 g pro.*

Fennel and Pistachio Kale Caesar Salad

Prepare as directed on page 245. Top with 1 fennel bulb, trimmed, cored, and thinly sliced; and ½ cup roasted, salted pistachios, chopped.

PER SERVING *528 cal, 37 g fat, 70 mg chol, 551 mg sodium, 40 g carb, 10 g fiber, 17 g pro.*

CHICKEN-KALE CAESAR SALAD

SALMON-KALE CAESAR SALAD

FENNEL AND PISTACHIO KALE CAESAR SALAD

"Kale is a nutritional powerhouse—low in calories, high in fiber, and chock-full of vitamins, minerals, and antioxidants.

weeknight delicious

Fast and fresh solutions for dinner tonight.

GRILLED PORK AND VEGGIE SALAD

Grilled Pork and Veggie Salad

Autumn is the ideal time to fire up the grill for this flavorful dinner of tender pork, smoky green beans, and charred lettuce.

START TO FINISH **30 min.**

- 1 lb. boneless pork loin chops
  Salt and black pepper
- 8 oz. whole green beans, trimmed
- 1 small red onion, cut into ½-inch-thick slices
- ¼ cup olive oil
- 2 hearts of romaine, quartered lengthwise
- 2 Tbsp. cider vinegar
- ½ cup chopped fresh basil
  Crumbled cheese (such as blue or feta)

1. Line half a gas or charcoal grill with heavy-duty foil. Season pork with salt and pepper. Grill on rack of a covered grill directly over medium heat. Toss beans and onion with 1 Tbsp. of the oil; place on foil. Grill pork and vegetables 10 minutes or until pork is done (145°F) and vegetables are tender, turning once.
2. Transfer pork to a cutting board. Cover; set aside. Coarsely chop vegetables. Transfer to a large bowl.
3. Brush romaine with 1 Tbsp. of the oil. Grill 1 minute per side or until lightly charred. Chop the romaine and arrange on plates.
4. Slice pork and add to bean mixture. Add remaining oil and vinegar; toss to coat. Season with salt and pepper. Serve over charred and chopped romaine; top with basil and cheese. Makes 4 servings.
EACH SERVING *436 cal, 32 g fat, 80 mg chol, 381 mg sodium, 11 g carb, 4 g fiber, 28 g pro.*

ONE-PAN
SAUSAGE AND
ROASTED ROOTS

One-Pan Sausage and Roasted Roots

Simple and seasonal: Roasted beets, sweets, and savory sausage with horseradish-yogurt sauce.

START TO FINISH **40 min.**

- 12 oz. fresh beets, peeled and coarsely chopped
- 12 oz. sweet potatoes, peeled and coarsely chopped
- 4 shallots, peeled and quartered
- 2 Tbsp. canola oil
- 4 cooked chicken apple sausage links, scored and halved lengthwise
- 1 tsp. chopped fresh rosemary
  Salt and black pepper
- ½ cup plain Greek yogurt
- 1 Tbsp. mayonnaise
- 1 Tbsp. prepared horseradish
- ½ tsp. Worcestershire sauce

1. Preheat oven to 425°F. Place beets, potatoes, and shallots in a shallow foil-lined baking pan. Drizzle with oil; toss to coat. Arrange in a single layer. Roast 15 minutes.
2. Stir vegetables; push to one side of the pan. Place sausage, cut sides down, on the opposite side of the pan. Roast 10 minutes or until sausage begins to brown and vegetables are tender. Season with rosemary, salt, and pepper.
3. For sauce, stir together yogurt, mayonnaise, horseradish, and Worcestershire. Serve with vegetables and sausage. Makes 4 servings.
EACH SERVING *413 cal, 22 g fat, 87 mg chol, 968 mg sodium, 33 g carb, 6 g fiber, 18 g pro.*

SALMON PATTIES WITH PARSLEY MAYO

Opt for full-fat feta in this soup. Use just a bit for a big boost of flavor.

LOW FAT

Lemon Potato Soup with Feta

This hearty warming soup owes its rich flavor to creamy Yukon gold potatoes and feta cheese.

START TO FINISH **40 min.**

- 2 Tbsp. extra-virgin olive oil
- 1 cup chopped onion
- 2 cloves garlic, minced
- 4 cups reduced-sodium or homemade chicken broth
- 1½ lb. Yukon gold potatoes, chopped (4 cups)
- 2 cups chopped kale or spinach
- 1 tsp. chopped fresh oregano
- 1 lemon, zested and juiced Salt and black pepper
- 2 oz. feta cheese, crumbled

1. In a 4-qt. Dutch oven heat 1 Tbsp. of the oil over medium-high heat. Add onion and garlic; cook and stir 3 to 4 minutes or until tender. Stir in broth and potatoes. Bring to boiling; reduce heat. Cover; cook 10 to 15 minutes or until potatoes are tender. Stir in kale and oregano. Cover; cook 2 to 3 minutes or until kale has wilted. Remove from heat. Stir in lemon zest and juice and remaining oil. Let stand 10 minutes. Season to taste with salt and pepper. Top with cheese and, if desired, additional lemon zest. Makes 4 servings.

EACH SERVING *269 cal, 10 g fat, 13 mg chol, 727 mg sodium, 36 g carb, 6 g fiber, 10 g pro.*

Salmon Patties with Parsley Mayo

The perk of salmon in pouches: Tender and moist salmon that you don't have to pick through to remove small bones.

START TO FINISH **25 min.**

- 3 5-oz. pouches skinless, boneless pink salmon
- ½ cup panko bread crumbs
- ½ cup finely chopped red sweet pepper
- ½ cup finely chopped green onions
- 1 egg, lightly beaten
- ½ cup mayonnaise
- 1 Tbsp. yellow mustard Nonstick cooking spray
- 3 Tbsp. finely chopped fresh Italian parsley
- 1 Tbsp. lemon juice or white vinegar
- 1 tsp. bottled hot pepper sauce

1. In a medium bowl combine salmon, bread crumbs, sweet pepper, green onions, egg, 2 Tbsp. of the mayonnaise, and mustard. Shape into eight 2½-inch patties (about ⅓ cup each).
2. Coat a very large nonstick skillet with nonstick cooking spray. Heat over medium heat. Add patties; cook 4 to 5 minutes or until browned. Coat patty tops with nonstick cooking spray; flip. Cook 4 to 5 minutes more or until browned and cooked through (160°F).
3. For parsley mayo, in a small bowl stir together the remaining mayonnaise, parsley, lemon juice, and hot sauce. Serve with patties. Makes 4 servings.

EACH SERVING *422 cal, 33 g fat, 99 mg chol, 852 mg sodium, 8 g carb, 1 g fiber, 22 g pro.*

**LEMON POTATO
SOUP WITH FETA**

new ways with cauliflower

Think beyond crudités to rediscover this humble vegetable. Its mild taste is perfect for dishes with bold spice and rich, creamy flavor.

BUY AND STORE
Look for clean creamy white florets surrounded by thick, green leaves. Place in a plastic bag, stems down to prevent moisture on florets. Refrigerate up to 1 week.

CHOP IT UP
Cauliflower can be cumbersome to chop. The easiest way: Pull away leaves then slice off the bottom stalk. Then stand the flat base to cut the head in quarters. Cut away stems and break florets apart with your hands.

ROAST AN EASY SIDE
Toss florets with a generous amount of olive oil and sprinkle with coarse salt and chile flakes. Roast 20 minutes at 400°F or until browned. Top with fresh chopped Italian parsley and chopped green olives, if desired.

FAST

Cauliflower-Pesto Peanut Salad

START TO FINISH 20 min.

1 medium head cauliflower (2 lb.), cut into florets (4½ cups)
1 6.3-oz. jar purchased basil pesto (¾ cup)
3 Tbsp. red wine vinegar
¼ tsp. kosher salt
⅔ cup cocktail peanuts, chopped
½ cup drained fried long hot peppers, finely chopped, or 1 fresh Fresno pepper, seeded and finely chopped (tip, page 96)
1 cup baby arugula

1. Cook cauliflower in a large amount of boiling water for 4 minutes or just until tender. Drain and transfer to a large bowl of ice water to cool. Drain well. In a large bowl stir together the pesto, vinegar, salt, peanuts, and peppers. Add cauliflower and arugula; toss to combine. Top with additional chopped peanuts, if desired. Makes 4 servings.
PER SERVING *415 cal, 34 g fat, 14 mg chol, 795 mg sodium, 18 g carb, 8 g fiber, 13 g pro.*

Cauliflower Samosa Nachos

START TO FINISH 35 min.

½ 14.1-oz. pkg. rolled refrigerated pie crust (1 crust)
3 Tbsp. olive oil
1 medium head cauliflower (2 lb.), broken into small florets (4½ cups)
8 oz. small Yukon gold potatoes, halved and thinly sliced
¼ tsp. kosher salt
2 cloves garlic, minced
1½ tsp. grated fresh ginger
1 serrano chile pepper, seeded, if desired, and sliced (tip, page 96)
1½ tsp. garam masala
1 tsp. ground cumin
   Fresh cilantro leaves
   Mango chutney
   Plain Greek yogurt (optional)

1. Preheat oven to 425°F. Unroll piecrust onto a baking sheet. Bake for 10 to 12 minutes or until golden.
2. Meanwhile, in a very large skillet heat the oil over medium heat. Add cauliflower, potatoes, and salt. Cook, stirring occasionally, for 10 minutes or until lightly browned. Add the garlic, ginger, serrano, garam masala, and cumin. Cook and stir for 2 minutes. Add 1 cup water; bring to boiling. Reduce heat. Simmer, uncovered, for 4 to 5 minutes or until cauliflower and potatoes are tender. Serve over broken piecrust pieces with cilantro, chutney, and yogurt. Makes 4 servings.

PER SERVING *424 cal, 23 g fat, 0 mg chol, 674 mg sodium, 52 g carb, 5 g fiber, 5 g pro.*

Lemon-Cauliflower Rigatoni

START TO FINISH 35 min.

8 oz. dried rigatoni pasta
1 medium head cauliflower
   (2 lb.), cut through the core into
   8 wedges
3 oz. pancetta, chopped
4 cloves garlic, minced
1 tsp. snipped fresh rosemary
2 cups whipping cream

1 tsp. grated lemon zest
½ cup shredded Parmesan cheese
   Snipped fresh rosemary (optional)

1. Cook pasta according to package directions, adding cauliflower the last 7 minutes of cooking. Drain. Place 2 cauliflower wedges on each plate. Set pasta aside.
2. Meanwhile, in a very large skillet cook pancetta over medium heat until crispy. Remove with a slotted spoon and set aside. Add garlic and 1 tsp. rosemary to

skillet; cook for 30 seconds. Add cream and zest to skillet. Bring to a simmer. Simmer, uncovered, for 3 minutes or until slightly thickened; stir in Parmesan. Add pasta to the cream sauce and stir to coat; spoon over cauliflower. Top with pancetta and, if desired, additional rosemary. Makes 4 servings.
PER SERVING *768 cal, 55 g fat, 187 mg chol, 591 mg sodium, 52 g carb, 4 g fiber, 19 g pro.*

Cauliflower-Parmesan Pizza

PREP 20 min. BAKE 39 min.

- 1 lb. purchased pizza dough
- 2½ Tbsp. olive oil
- ¾ cup panko breadcrumbs
- ⅓ cup grated Parmesan cheese
- 1 tsp. dried Italian seasoning
- ¼ tsp. kosher salt
- 1 small head cauliflower, cut into small florets (3½ cups)
- 2 eggs, lightly beaten
- 1 cup marinara sauce
- 2 cups shredded mozzarella cheese (8 oz.)
- ½ cup chopped pitted green olives
  Fresh basil leaves (optional)

1. Preheat oven to 425°F. Grease a very large baking sheet. Roll dough to a 15×10-inch rectangle. Place dough on prepared baking sheet; reshape dough as needed. Prick all over with a fork then brush dough with 4 tsp. of the oil. Bake for 12 to 15 minutes or until lightly browned and crisp. Remove from oven; set aside.

2. Grease a large baking pan; set aside. In a small bowl combine the panko, Parmesan, Italian seasoning, and salt.

In a large bowl toss cauliflower with eggs; add panko mixture and toss to coat. Spread cauliflower mixture evenly on prepared baking pan. Bake for 20 to 25 minutes or until browned and tender, turning pieces once.

3. Top baked pizza dough with marinara, mozzarella, and cauliflower. Bake for 7 to 9 minutes more or until heated through. Drizzle with remaining 1 Tbsp. olive oil. Top with olives and, if desired, fresh basil leaves. Serve immediately. Makes 4 servings.

PER SERVING *677 cal, 29 g fat, 136 mg chol, 1,697 mg sodium, 71 g carb, 6 g fiber, 32 g pro.*

Cauliflower and Chorizo Tacos

START TO FINISH 35 min.

14 to 16 oz. uncooked chorizo sausage
1 medium head cauliflower (2 lb.),
  cut into florets (about 4½ cups)
8 6-inch corn tortillas, warmed*
1 cup refried beans, warmed**
  Fresh or pickled jalapeño pepper
  slices (tip, page 96), crumbled
  queso fresco, chopped green
  onions, and/or lime wedges

1. In a very large skillet brown chorizo. Remove from skillet with a slotted spoon; drain on paper towels. Reserve 2 Tbsp. drippings in skillet. Add cauliflower to skillet. Cook over medium heat for 15 minutes or until tender and lightly browned, stirring occasionally. Return chorizo to skillet and warm through.

2. Spread each tortilla with some of the beans. Divide cauliflower mixture among tortillas. Top with jalapeño, cheese, and onions. Serve with lime wedges. Makes 4 servings.

PER SERVING *641 cal, 42 g fat, 92 mg chol, 1,539 mg sodium, 34 g carb, 8 g fiber, 33 g pro.*
*Stack tortillas and wrap in foil. Heat in a 350°F oven for 10 minutes.
**Place refried beans in a bowl. Cover with vented plastic wrap. Heat on high (100% power) for 1 minute or until heated through.

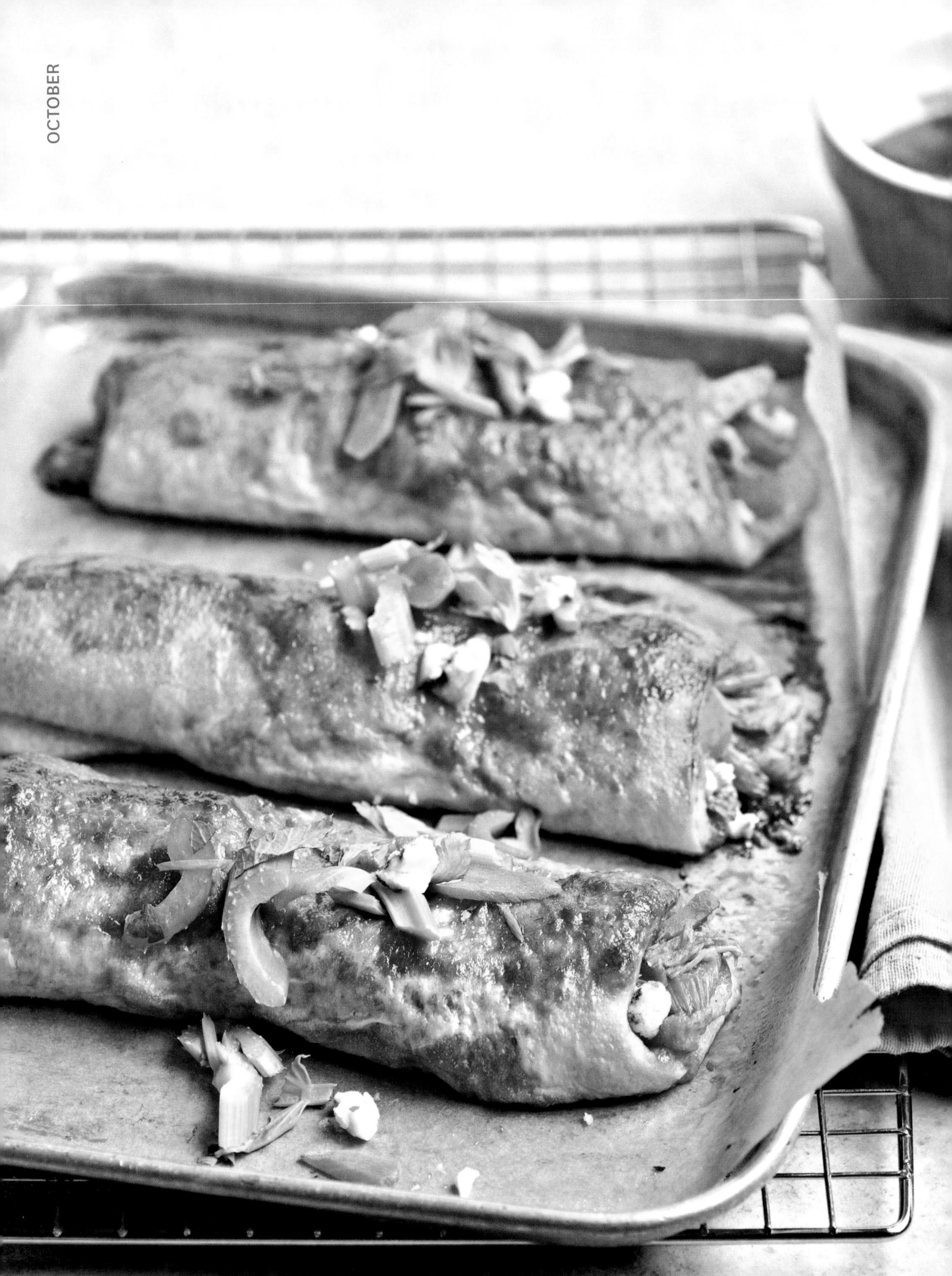

better buffalo chicken

Everything you love about zesty chicken wings is neat to eat—wrapped up in pizza dough. Less messy, but you'll still want napkins!

Buffalo Chicken Rolls

If you enjoy lots of heat, choose a spicy bottled barbecue sauce or add a bit more hot pepper sauce.

PREP **25 min.** COOK **12 min.**
BAKE **27 min.**

- 1 lb. skinless, boneless chicken breast halves
- 1 Tbsp. vegetable oil
- 3 medium carrots, thinly bias-sliced
- 3 stalks celery, thinly bias-sliced
- 4 oz. blue cheese, crumbled
- ½ cup bottled barbecue sauce
- ½ tsp. bottled hot pepper sauce
- 1 13.8-oz. pkg. refrigerated pizza dough

1. Preheat oven to 375°F. Line a 15×10×1-inch baking pan with parchment. Set aside.

2. In large skillet cook chicken in hot oil over medium heat for 6 minutes. Meanwhile, set aside a few carrot and celery slices and a small amount of cheese. Turn chicken. Add remaining carrots and celery to skillet. Cover. Cook 6 to 8 minutes more or until chicken reaches 170°F and vegetables are crisp-tender. Cool slightly, then pull chicken into shreds using two forks. In a large bowl combine shredded chicken, cooked carrots and celery, ⅓ cup of the barbecue sauce, and hot pepper sauce.

3. Unroll pizza crust and cut into four rectangles (about 4×6 inches each). Divide buffalo chicken filling among rectangles, leaving a 1-inch space on each long side. Sprinkle with remaining cheese. Bring long sides of dough up over filling, pinching to seal seam. Place rolls, seam sides down, in prepared baking pan.

4. Bake, uncovered, 27 to 30 minutes or until golden brown, brushing with barbecue sauce the last 5 minutes of baking. To serve, sprinkle with reserved carrots, celery, and cheese. Makes 4 rolls.

EACH SERVING *574 cal, 17 g fat, 87 mg chol, 1,399 mg sodium, 63 g carb, 3 g fiber, 41 g pro.*

make a toast

Sweet, savory, and totally crunchy. Come snack time, this melt-in-your mouth nibble cures every craving.

FAST   KID FRIENDLY

Apple-Cheddar Bagel Snack

For cooking, some apples are better than others. For sweetness, choose Gala, Fuji, or Golden Delicious. Want sweet plus tart? Try Braeburn, Jonagold, or Jonathan. And for extra-tart bites, pick Granny Smith.

START TO FINISH **24 min.**

- 2 cinnamon-raisin swirl bagels, split
- 2 Tbsp. butter, softened
- 8 tsp. cinnamon-sugar*
- 4 crosswise slices cooking apple, seeds removed
- 4 slices white cheddar cheese
  Fresh sage leaves (optional)

1. Preheat broiler. Toast bagels. Spread cut sides of bagels with 1 Tbsp. of the butter. Sprinkle each bagel half with 1 tsp. cinnamon-sugar.

2. In a medium skillet melt remaining 1 Tbsp. butter over medium heat. Sprinkle apple slices with remaining cinnamon-sugar. Cook apple slices 1 minute on each side or just until slices start to brown.

3. Top each bagel half with a slice of white cheddar cheese and an apple slice. Place bagels on a baking sheet. Broil 3 to 4 inches from heat for 2 to 3 minutes or until cheese begins to melt. Top with sage, if desired. Makes 4 servings.

EACH SERVING *278 cal, 13 g fat, 38 mg chol, 287 mg sodium, 31 g carb, 1 g fiber, 9 g pro.*

***Cinnamon-sugar** can be found in the spice aisle. If you prefer to make some, mix ¼ cup sugar with 1 Tbsp. cinnamon. Store in an airtight container.

CLEMENTINE-FIG
SPICE CAKES

november

Gather Add new recipes to the Thanksgiving repertoire—choose from Southern classics, scrumptious cakes, and reinvented sides.

266

273

281

bring it

Invited to contribute to a Thanksgiving dinner? Four rising food stars show their signature take-along dishes.

Salt-Roasted Beets with Tehina

Photo on page 267

Michael Solomonov is known for his landmark restaurant in Philadelphia, Zahav. His dish makes a bold statement—in both flavor and color—with his Israeli take on a grated beet salad. Nutty tehina, a sauce made with tahini, mellows the sweetness of the beets while bringing earthiness to the forefront.

PREP 25 min. BAKE 1½ hr.
COOL 1 hr. STAND 10 min.

 5 cups kosher salt
 8 medium beets (2 lb.)
 ½ cup Basic Tehina Sauce
 ½ cup olive oil
 ¼ cup lemon juice
 ¼ cup chopped fresh dill
 2 Tbsp. chopped fresh mint
 ½ tsp. salt

1. Preheat oven to 375°F. Spread 1 cup of the salt in a baking dish. Place whole unpeeled beets on salt. Cover with remaining salt. Bake until tender, about 1½ hours. Once cool enough to handle, remove beets from salt; peel. Set aside. Once completely cooled, grate beets into a bowl using coarse holes of a box grater. Add the ½ cup Basic Tehina Sauce, olive oil, lemon juice, dill, and mint. Season with salt. Mix well. Serve at room temperature or chilled. Makes 4 cups.

Basic Tehina Sauce Break up one head of garlic with your hands, letting unpeeled cloves fall into a blender. Add ¾ cup lemon juice and ½ tsp. salt. Blend on high for a few seconds to a coarse puree. Let stand 10 minutes. Pour sauce through a fine-mesh strainer set over a bowl, pressing solids to extract liquid. Discard solids. Add 2 cups jarred tahini, ½ tsp. ground cumin, and 1 tsp. salt to sauce. Whisk in 1½ cups ice water, a few tablespoons at a time, until smooth and velvety. (Sauce might separate at first, but will emulsify as you whisk and add water.) Season to taste with salt and pepper. Refrigerate up to 1 week or freeze up to 1 month. Makes 4 cups.*
*Combine leftover Tehina Sauce with fresh herbs, such as parsley, chives, dill, and mint, for a delicious veggie dip.

EACH ½-CUP SERVING *203 cal, 18 g fat, 0 mg chol, 321 mg sodium, 11 g carb, 5 g fiber, 3 g pro.*

KID FRIENDLY

Gluten-Free Harvest Rice Stuffing

Photo on page 267

Heather Christo, cookbook author and blogger, is the go-to girl for food that's delicious and allergy-free. She offers rice stuffing that brims with holiday flavors—butternut squash, cranberry, apple, and sage.

PREP 30 min. COOK 1 hr.

 1 lb. mild pork sausage, without casing
 2 large yellow onions, chopped (2 cups)
 ¼ cup olive oil
 1 medium butternut squash, peeled and chopped (about 2½ cups)
 2 cups green apples, chopped
 ¼ cup dry sherry or apple juice
 2 cups long-grain white rice
 2 tsp. kosher salt
 1 cup roughly chopped walnuts
 1 cup dried cranberries
 4 cups reduced-sodium chicken broth
 1 cup chopped Italian parsley
 ½ cup chopped sage

1. In a heavy 4-qt. pot cook sausage over medium-high heat 5 minutes or until lightly browned and cooked through, using a wooden spoon to break up pieces. Transfer to a bowl.
2. Add onions and olive oil to pot; cook and stir over medium heat 10 minutes or until tender. Add squash; cook and stir 3 minutes. Add apples; cook and stir 3 minutes. Add sherry, using a wooden spoon to scrape up any browned bits.
3. Add rice and kosher salt to pot. Return sausage to pot. Stir in walnuts and cranberries. Stir in broth. Bring to boiling; reduce heat. Cover. Simmer 40 minutes or until rice is tender. Remove from heat. Stir in parsley and sage. Makes 12 cups.

EACH ½-CUP SERVING *199 cal, 10 g fat, 13 mg chol, 329 mg sodium, 20 g carb, 1 g fiber, 6 g pro.*

Looking for something new to take to the feast? These colorful and delicious dishes complement any gathering.

Vegetarian Sprouts and Mushrooms Lasagna

Elizabeth Stein is the founder of Purely Elizabeth Foods, and her meatless lasagna is always a welcome addition for vegetarians and veggie-lovers. Loaded with Brussels sprouts, mushrooms, and kale, and with an intensely flavorful pumpkin-cashew filling and a sprinkling of mozzarella, Elizabeth's take is both healthful and delicious.

PREP 45 min. SOAK 30 min.
BAKE 55 min.

- 2 cups raw cashews
- 1 15-oz. can pumpkin puree
- 3 cloves garlic
- 1 tsp. salt
- ¼ cup water
- 2 Tbsp. olive oil
- 8 oz. cremini mushrooms, sliced
- 8 oz. shredded Brussels sprouts
- 5 oz. chopped kale
- 5 cups marinara sauce
- 12 lasagna noodles, cooked according to package directions
- 8 oz. shredded mozzarella cheese Brussels sprouts leaves (optional)

1. Preheat oven to 350ºF. Soak cashews in water 30 minutes; drain. Transfer to a food processor. Add pumpkin puree, 1 clove of the garlic, and salt. Process until nearly smooth. Add the water. Process until smooth and spreadable; set aside.
2. Meanwhile, in a large skillet heat olive oil over medium-high heat. Mince remaining 2 garlic cloves; add to skillet. Cook and stir 30 seconds or until fragrant. Add mushrooms and Brussels sprouts. Cook 5 to 7 minutes or until tender. Add kale. Cook 2 to 3 minutes until wilted. Remove from skillet.
3. To assemble, spread 1 cup marinara in a 3-qt. baking dish. Layer with 3 noodles, one-third of the cashew mixture, one-third of the vegetables, and 1 cup marinara. Repeat twice. Top with remaining 3 noodles, remaining sauce, and the mozzarella. Cover with foil. Bake 45 minutes. Uncover. Bake 10 to 15 minutes more until bubbly around edges. If desired, top with lightly sauteed Brussels sprout leaves for fresh color and crunch. Makes 12 servings.

EACH SERVING *378 cal, 18 g fat, 14 mg chol, 787 mg sodium, 41 g carb, 7 g fiber, 16 g pro.*

KID FRIENDLY

Spicy Green Bean Casserole

The cooking philosophy of Angelo Sosa, chef at Añejo in New York City: Respect tradition and be inspired by adventure. Take his green bean casserole. Familiar flavors—creamy mushroom sauce, fresh green beans, and crispy bread crumb topping—get a dose of chili powder and serrano chile.

PREP 30 min. COOK 20 min.
BAKE 12 min.

- 5 Tbsp. unsalted butter
- 1 Tbsp. vegetable oil
- 1 cup panko bread crumbs
- 2 Tbsp. slivered almonds
- 12 oz. cremini and/or shiitake mushrooms, sliced ¼ inch thick
- 1 medium onion, thinly sliced
- 4 cloves garlic, minced
- 1 tsp. minced serrano or jalapeño pepper (tip, page 96)
- 1 tsp. salt
- 2 Tbsp. all-purpose flour
- 1 tsp. chipotle chili powder
- ½ tsp. white pepper
- ¼ tsp. ground nutmeg
- 1 bay leaf
- 1 cup chicken stock or broth
- 1 cup half-and-half
- 1 lb. haricots verts, rinsed, trimmed, and halved

1. Preheat oven to 475ºF. For panko topping, in a saucepan melt 2 Tbsp. of the butter with the oil; stir in panko and almonds. Cook and stir over medium-low heat 3 to 4 minutes or until golden brown. Transfer to a paper towel-lined tray.
2. In a heavy 10-inch skillet melt remaining butter over medium heat. Add mushrooms, onion, garlic, serrano, and salt. Cook 3 to 6 minutes or until mushrooms release moisture and onions are tender, stirring occasionally. Add flour, chili powder, white pepper, nutmeg, and bay leaf. Cook and stir 2 minutes more. Add stock and half-and-half. Bring to a simmer. Reduce heat. Simmer, uncovered, 7 to 10 minutes or until thickened, stirring occasionally. Remove from heat. Remove bay leaf.
3. Meanwhile, in a large pot bring 1 gallon water and 1 Tbsp. salt to boiling. Add beans. Cook 4 to 6 minutes. Drain; submerge in a large bowl of ice water. Drain again. Stir beans into mushroom mixture. Transfer to a 2-qt. baking dish. Bake, uncovered, 12 to 15 minutes or until bubbly. Remove. Sprinkle with panko topping. Makes 5 cups.

EACH ½-CUP SERVING *151 cal, 11 g fat, 24 mg chol, 344 mg sodium, 12 g carb, 2 g fiber, 4 g pro.*

SPICY GREEN BEAN CASSEROLE

VEGETARIAN SPROUTS AND MUSHROOMS LASAGNA

SALT-ROASTED BEETS WITH TEHINA
Recipe on page 265

GLUTEN-FREE HARVEST RICE STUFFING
Recipe on page 265

little town, big thanks

Join Kimberly Schlapman, star of country stage and kitchen, as she takes family on the road to celebrate the holiday that she loves most, at the place she loves best—Blackberry Farm.

No meal is more important than Thanksgiving dinner to Kimberly Schlapman, one of the founding members of country music powerhouse Little Big Town.

While growing up in the Appalachian foothills of northeast Georgia, her family crowded around a big Thanksgiving table filled with food, talk, and laughter. "I loved hearing these stories," she says. "Even if they were repeated, I would hang on every word."

Kimberly re-creates that feeling at her own table in Tennessee. Every year, the family settles in for a holiday centered on food that is rooted in heritage yet fresh with new ideas. "My whole life has been about these gatherings," Kimberly says.

For the annual gathering, it's time to head to Blackberry Farm. Tucked into a 9,200-acre estate in the Great Smoky Mountains, it's a three-hour drive from the Nashville home that Kimberly shares with her husband, Stephen, and their daughter, Daisy Pearl.

The farm offers the perfect setting for a Thanksgiving Day hike that assures everyone will be hungry when food comes out around 4 p.m. Kimberly's recipes—many of which she shares on her Cooking Channel show, *Kimberly's Simply Southern*, and in her new book, *Oh Gussie! Cooking and Visiting in Kimberly's Southern Kitchen*—are favorites from her family.

The dressing has crumbled corn bread along with torn biscuits—a mainstay in Kimberly's kitchen. The corn casserole is a simple dish given sophistication with shallots and fried sage. "My husband brought this to the family, and everybody loves him for it," Kimberly says. The sweet potato casserole is updated this year with fresh cranberries to balance the sweetness.

Kimberly can't resist bringing a little of her Georgia roots to the Tennessee table. Even though peach season has long passed, she tucks frozen slices inside the turkey and adds a peach glaze to the crispy skin.

"Any entertainer loves an ovation," Kimberly says. "I'm waiting for the people I love to go 'mmmmm' when I feed them. It's the most beautiful ovation to me because it's from my family."

KID FRIENDLY

Maw Maw's Biscuits

Photo on page 272

Kimberly's mother taught her the family biscuit recipe, which can be traced back to Kimberly's Great-Grandma Burrell. Like most Southern baking, the recipe relies on self-rising flour. Kimberly makes small batches in a cast-iron skillet, but for holidays she bakes them by the tray and combines them with corn bread for dressing.

PREP 20 min.

BAKE 12 min. per batch

- 6 cups self-rising flour
- ¾ cup butter, cubed and chilled (1½ sticks)
- 2¼ cups cold milk
- 6 Tbsp. butter, melted

1. Preheat oven to 450°F. In a large bowl combine the flour and ¾ cup cold butter. Using your hands or a pastry blender, mix flour and butter until crumbly. Add milk; mix well with a fork just until combined. Gently knead dough a few times or just until it comes together. Transfer to a floured surface. Roll to ½-inch thickness. Using a 3-inch round cutter, cut about 20 biscuits, rerolling dough as needed.

2. Place biscuits on baking sheets. Brush with melted butter. Bake, one sheet at a time, 12 to 15 minutes, or until golden. Makes about 20 biscuits.

Make ahead Store baked biscuits in a resealable freezer bag; freeze up to 2 months. To serve, wrap frozen biscuits in foil. Warm in a 350ºF oven for 20 minutes.

EACH BISCUIT *235 cal, 11 g fat, 29 mg chol, 539 mg sodium, 29 g carb, 1 g fiber, 5 g pro.*

**KALE SALAD
WITH DATES**
Recipe on page 276

Kimberly grew up thinking every family set a beautiful table and ate homemade biscuits for every meal. Before the music, the fame, and a celebrated cookbook, there was always Thanksgiving.

MAW MAW'S
BISCUITS
Recipe on page 269

SOUTHERN DRESSING
AND GRAVY

CREAMY CORN
CASSEROLE

BUTTERMILK
MASHED POTATOES
Recipe on page 276

KALE SALAD
WITH DATES
Recipe on page 276

PEACH-GLAZED
ROAST TURKEY

Peach-Glazed Roast Turkey

PREP 20 min. ROAST 3 hr.
STAND 15 min.

- 1 14- to 16-lb. whole turkey
  Salt and black pepper
- 1 cup frozen peach slices, thawed,
  or 1 peach, peeled and quartered
- 1 lemon, quartered
- 5 fresh thyme sprigs
- 5 fresh rosemary sprigs
- 2 Tbsp. butter, melted

Peach Glaze

- 2 Tbsp. butter
- 1 large yellow onion, chopped
  (1 cup)
- 1 cup peach preserves
- 1 cup orange juice
- ½ cup cider vinegar
- 2 tsp. dry mustard
- 1 tsp. salt

1. Preheat oven to 325°F. Place turkey in a roasting pan. Generously sprinkle inside cavity of turkey with salt and pepper. Stuff with peach slices, lemon, and herbs. Tie legs together with kitchen twine. Tuck wings back and under body to prevent burning. Brush turkey with melted butter and generously season with salt and pepper. Roast turkey 2½ hours.
2. Meanwhile, for Peach Glaze, in a saucepan melt butter over medium heat. Add onion; cook 5 minutes or until translucent. Stir in preserves, orange juice, vinegar, mustard, and salt. Bring to boiling. Reduce heat. Boil gently, uncovered, 35 minutes or until thickened.
3. Cut string from turkey legs. Roast 30 to 75 minutes more or until a meat thermometer inserted into the thigh (not touching bone) registers 175°F. Brush with ½ cup of the Peach Glaze the last 20 minutes of roasting. Cover turkey loosely with foil, if necessary, to prevent overbrowning. Transfer turkey to a carving board. Let rest, covered, 15 minutes before carving. Serve with reserved Peach Glaze. Makes 14 servings.
EACH SERVING *559 cal, 19 g fat, 239 mg chol, 803 mg sodium, 19 g carb, 1 g fiber, 70 g pro.*

Southern Dressing and Gravy

PREP 25 min. COOK 8 min.
BAKE 45 min.

Dressing

- ¾ cup butter (1½ sticks)
- 1 medium red onion, chopped
  (1 cup)
- 2 medium carrots, chopped (1 cup)
- 2 stalks celery, chopped (1 cup)
- 5 cups coarsely crumbled corn
  bread
- 5 3-inch biscuits, such as Maw
  Maw's Biscuits, page 269, torn
  into large pieces
- 3 to 4 cups reduced-sodium
  chicken broth
- 2 eggs, lightly beaten
- ½ to 1 cup whole milk
- 1 Tbsp. chopped fresh sage
- 2 Tbsp. chopped celery leaves
- 1 tsp. each salt and black pepper

Gravy

- 3 Tbsp. butter
- 3 Tbsp. all-purpose flour
- 1 cup whole milk
- 1 cup reduced-sodium chicken broth

1. Preheat oven to 375°F. In a large skillet melt ½ cup of the butter over medium heat. Add onion, carrots, and celery; cook and stir 8 minutes until softened.
2. For Dressing, in a large bowl mix vegetable mixture, corn bread, biscuits, chicken broth, eggs, milk, sage, celery leaves, salt, and black pepper (mixture will be soupy). Transfer dressing to a 3-qt. baking dish. Cut remaining ¼ cup butter into cubes; scatter over dressing. Bake 45 minutes or a thermometer registers 165°F. and dressing is browned.
3. Meanwhile, for Gravy, in a small saucepan heat the 3 Tbsp. butter over low heat. Add flour; whisk constantly until well combined and foamy, about 1 minute. Slowly whisk in milk and broth until thickened and bubbly; cook and stir 1 minute more. Season to taste with salt and freshly cracked pepper. Makes 18 servings of ½ cup dressing and 2 Tbsp. gravy.
EACH SERVING *239 cal, 20 g fat, 64 mg chol, 628 mg sodium, 20 g carb, 1 g fiber, 5 g pro.*

Creamy Corn Casserole

PREP 25 min. BAKE 50 min.

- ½ cup butter (1 stick)
- 1 shallot, minced (2 Tbsp.)
- 3 Tbsp. all-purpose flour
- 2 Tbsp. chopped fresh sage
- ½ tsp. salt
- 2 cups whipping cream
- 2 16-oz. pkg. frozen whole kernel
  corn
- 1 sleeve saltines (about 40)
- 2 eggs, lightly beaten
- 2 Tbsp. sugar
  Chopped roasted red sweet
  peppers (optional)
- 1 recipe Fried Sage Leaves
  (optional)

1. Preheat oven to 350°F. In a large 4-qt. saucepan melt ¼ cup of the butter over medium heat. Add shallot; cook 1 minute. Stir in flour, sage, and salt. Whisk in cream. Cook and stir over medium heat until thickened and bubbly. Stir in corn.
2. Finely crush half the saltines. Stir into corn mixture along with eggs and sugar. Transfer to a 2-qt. baking dish. Bake, covered, 15 minutes.
3. Meanwhile, in a small saucepan melt remaining butter. Crush remaining saltines; add to butter. Toss to coat. Top casserole with crackers and continue baking, uncovered, about 35 to 40 minutes more or until heated through. If desired, top with roasted sweet peppers and Fried Sage Leaves. Makes twelve ½-cup servings.
EACH SERVING *342 cal, 25 g fat, 106 mg chol, 82 mg sodium, 28 g carb, 2 g fiber, 5 g pro.*
Fried Sage Leaves In a skillet heat 1 Tbsp. vegetable oil over medium heat. Add 12 sage leaves; cook 1 minute or until crisp. Transfer to paper towels; drain.

"Thanksgiving is when we take care of the people we love most. I am at home wherever my family is," says Kimberly.

PEACH-GLAZED ROAST TURKEY
Recipe on page 273

**SWEET POTATO
CASSEROLE**
Recipe on page 276

LOW FAT FAST KID FRIENDLY

Buttermilk Mashed Potatoes

Photo on page 272
START TO FINISH **30 min.**

    4 lb. Yukon gold potatoes, peeled
       and chopped
    1 Tbsp. salt
    1 cup buttermilk
  ½ cup milk
  ½ cup butter (1 stick)
    2 cloves garlic, minced
  ¼ cup chopped fresh chives
    1 tsp. salt
  ½ tsp. black pepper

1. In a Dutch oven combine potatoes, 1 Tbsp. salt, and enough water to cover. Bring to boiling. Reduce heat. Simmer, uncovered, 10 to 15 minutes or until potatoes are fork-tender.
2. Meanwhile, in a saucepan warm buttermilk, milk, butter, and garlic.
3. Drain potatoes; transfer to a large bowl. Using an electric mixer, beat potatoes while slowly pouring in hot buttermilk mixture. Beat until creamy and smooth. Stir in chives, 1 tsp. salt, and pepper. Makes twenty ½-cup servings.
EACH SERVING *102 cal, 5 g fat, 13 mg chol, 172 mg sodium, 13 g carb, 1 g fiber, 2 g pro.*

KID FRIENDLY

Sweet Potato Casserole

Photo on page 275
PREP **15 min.** COOK **25 min.**
BAKE **45 min.**

    6 lb. whole sweet potatoes
    1 cup self-rising flour
    1 cup packed light brown sugar
    1 cup butter (2 sticks)
    1 7-oz. jar marshmallow crème
    2 tsp. vanilla
    1 tsp. salt
    1 cup fresh cranberries

1. In an 8- to 10-qt. pot of boiling water cook whole sweet potatoes for 25 to 30 minutes or until tender. Drain. Set aside until cool enough to handle.

2. Meanwhile, for topping, in a small bowl combine flour, sugar, and ½ cup of the butter. Using your hands or a pastry blender, cut butter into flour until large clumps form. Freeze on a baking tray until ready to use.
3. Preheat oven to 350°F. Remove skins from potatoes. Return to pot. Mash with a potato masher. Melt remaining butter; add to potatoes with marshmallow crème, vanilla, and salt; stir to combine. Transfer mashed sweet potatoes to a 3-qt. rectangular baking dish.
4. Pile frozen crumb topping over sweet potatoes. Top with cranberries. Bake 45 to 50 minutes or until lightly golden. Makes twenty-six ½-cup servings.
EACH SERVING *206 cal, 7 g fat, 19 mg chol, 253 mg sodium, 34 g carb, 3 g fiber, 2 g pro.*

Kale Salad with Dates

Photo on page 271
START TO FINISH **35 min.**

  1½ lb. red or green kale, stemmed,
       chopped, rinsed, and dried
       (15 cups)
    5 Tbsp. lemon juice
  1¼ tsp. kosher salt
  ¼ cup extra-virgin olive oil
    2 Tbsp. honey
    1 shallot, minced
  ½ tsp. crushed red pepper
    1 Honeycrisp apple, cored and
       sliced
    1 cup pecan halves, toasted and
       chopped
  ½ cup pitted dates, chopped
       (10 dates)
    3 oz. Pecorino Romano cheese,
       shaved

1. In a large salad bowl combine kale, 3 Tbsp. of the lemon juice, and ¼ tsp. kosher salt. Massage kale 5 minutes to tenderize.
2. In a screw-top jar combine the remaining lemon juice, olive oil, honey, shallot, remaining salt, and crushed red pepper. Shake well.
3. Toss kale with apple, pecans, dates, and cheese. Add dressing; toss to coat. Makes twenty-four ½-cup servings.
EACH SERVING *105 cal, 7 g fat, 4 mg chol, 125 mg sodium, 10 g carb, 2 g fiber, 3 g pro.*

KID FRIENDLY

Black Walnut Cake

For the Schlapman family, it's not Thanksgiving without this black walnut cake.
PREP **45 min.** BAKE **25 min.**
COOL **30 min.**

Cake
    2 cups granulated sugar
  ½ cup butter, softened (1 stick)
  ½ cup shortening
    4 eggs
  3½ cups all-purpose flour
    2 tsp. baking soda
  ½ tsp. salt
  1½ cups buttermilk
    2 tsp. vanilla
  1½ cups black walnuts, ground

Cream Cheese Frosting
    2 8-oz. packages cream cheese,
       softened
    1 cup butter, softened (2 sticks)
    8 cups powdered sugar
    1 Tbsp. vanilla

1. Preheat oven to 350°F. Grease three 9-inch round cake pans; set aside.
2. For Cake, in a large bowl beat sugar, butter, and shortening with an electric mixer until light and fluffy. Add eggs, one at a time, beating well after each addition. In a separate bowl combine flour, baking soda, and salt. Alternately add to butter mixture with buttermilk, mixing well after each addition. Stir in the vanilla and ground walnuts.
3. Divide batter among prepared pans. Bake 25 minutes or until a toothpick inserted near center of each comes out clean. Cool in pans completely. Remove from pans; transfer to cooling rack.
4. Meanwhile, for Cream Cheese Frosting, in a large bowl beat cream cheese with an electric mixer until creamy and smooth. Beat in butter. Slowly beat in powdered sugar and vanilla until smooth.
5. To assemble, frost cake using about 1 cup frosting between layers. Makes about 16 servings.
EACH SERVING *841 cal, 42 g fat, 125 mg chol, 514 mg sodium, 107 g carb, 2 g fiber, 10 g pro.*

BLACK WALNUT
CAKE

**PUMPKIN PIE
WITH POMEGRANATE
POACHED PEARS**

save room for pie

Pumpkin pie—the quintessential of Thanksgiving dessert—is updated with flavors sure to please everyone at the table.

KID FRIENDLY

Baked Piecrust

PREP 15 min.   CHILL 30 min.
BAKE 13 min.

1¼ cups all-purpose flour
 1 tsp. sugar
 ½ tsp. salt
 ⅓ cup butter, cut into cubes
 2 Tbsp. shortening
 4 to 5 Tbsp. very cold water

1. In a bowl combine flour, sugar, and salt. Using a pastry blender, cut in butter and shortening until pea size. Sprinkle 1 Tbsp. of the water over flour mixture; toss with a fork. Repeat, using 1 Tbsp. of water at a time until flour is moistened. Gather pastry into a ball; kneading gently until it holds together. Wrap in plastic. Chill 30 minutes.
2. Preheat oven to 425°F. On a lightly floured surface use your hands to slightly flatten pastry. Roll pastry from center to edge into a 13-inch diameter. Fold into fourths and place on a 9-inch pie plate. Unfold and ease into pie plate without stretching. Trim to ½ inch beyond edge of pie plate. Fold under extra pastry, even with plate's edge. Crimp as desired.
3. Poke sides and bottom of pastry with a fork. Line with a double thickness of foil and pie weights or dried beans. Bake 10 to 12 minutes or until set. Remove foil and weights. Bake 3 to 4 minutes more or until very lightly browned. Cool completely.
EACH SERVING *169 cal, 11 g fat, 20 mg chol, 207 mg sodium, 15 g carb, 1 g fiber, 2 g pro.*

Pumpkin Pie with Pomegranate Poached Pears

Star anise and orange complement pumpkin and pears deliciously. Look for pomegranate seeds (also labeled arils) in the produce department of grocery stores.
PREP 40 min.   COOK 19 min.
BAKE 55 min.

 1 recipe Baked Piecrust
 2 small Bosc pears
 1 cup pomegranate juice
 ½ cup ruby port
 ⅓ cup granulated sugar
 1 star anise
 1 15-oz. can pumpkin
 ⅔ cup packed brown sugar
 1 tsp. ground cinnamon
 1 tsp. ground ginger
 ½ tsp. salt
 ½ tsp. orange zest
 ¼ tsp. ground allspice
 4 eggs, lightly beaten
 1 cup half-and-half or light cream
1½ tsp. cornstarch
 ½ cup pomegranate seeds
 1 clementine, peeled and sectioned

1. Prepare Baked Piecrust; set aside. Peel pears; cut in half lengthwise. Use a melon baller to remove cores.

2. Meanwhile, in a small saucepan combine pomegranate juice, port, sugar, and star anise. Bring to boiling, stirring to dissolve sugar. Add pear halves. Simmer, covered, 15 to 20 minutes or just until pears are tender. Remove from heat. Transfer pears and poaching liquid to a bowl. Chill until ready to use.
3. Preheat oven to 375°F. For filling, in a large bowl combine pumpkin, brown sugar, cinnamon, ginger, salt, orange zest, and allspice. Add eggs; stir to combine. Stir in half-and-half. Pour filling into piecrust. Cover edges with foil. Bake 55 to 60 minutes or until edges are puffed and center appears set. Cool on a wire rack. Chill within 2 hours.
4. Remove pears from poaching liquid; slice lengthwise. In a small saucepan stir together ½ cup poaching liquid and cornstarch until combined. Discard remaining liquid and anise. Cook and stir over medium heat until thickened and bubbly. Remove from heat. Cool slightly. Stir in pomegranate seeds and clementine sections. Top pie with pomegranate poached pears. Makes 8 servings.
EACH SERVING *437 cal, 17 g fat, 125 mg chol, 412 mg sodium, 62 g carb, 3 g fiber, 7 g pro.*

SALTED PECAN
BOURBON
PUMPKIN PIE

BUTTERMILK
CARDAMOM
PUMPKIN PIE

MEXICAN
CHOCOLATE
PUMPKIN PIE

Salted Pecan Bourbon Pumpkin Pie

The light texture of this pie is balanced by the intensity of molasses and bourbon.
PREP 40 min. BAKE 55 min.

- 1 recipe Baked Piecrust, page 279
- 1 15-oz. can pumpkin
- ½ cup plus 1 Tbsp. packed brown sugar
- 1 tsp. ground cinnamon
- ½ tsp. ground ginger
- ¼ tsp. salt
- 3 eggs, lightly beaten
- ¾ cup half-and-half or light cream
- 2 Tbsp. bourbon
- 1 tsp. vanilla
- 3 Tbsp. mild molasses
- 1 Tbsp. butter
- 1 cup pecan halves
- ½ tsp. flaked sea salt
- 1 recipe Bourbon Whipped Cream

1. Prepare Baked Piecrust; set aside. Preheat oven to 375°F. In a large bowl combine pumpkin, ½ cup of the brown sugar, cinnamon, ginger, and the ¼ tsp. salt. Stir in eggs until combined. Stir in half-and-half, bourbon, and vanilla until combined. Pour pumpkin filling into piecrust. Cover edges with foil. Bake 40 minutes or until edges begin to puff and center is almost set.
2. Meanwhile, in a small saucepan combine molasses, butter, and the remaining 1 Tbsp. brown sugar. Stir until sugar is dissolved and butter is melted. Stir in pecans. Spoon pecan topping over pie. Place a foil-lined baking sheet on the rack below pie. Bake 15 minutes more or until center is set. Sprinkle with sea salt. Cool completely. Chill within 2 hours. Serve with Bourbon Whipped Cream. Makes 8 servings.
Bourbon Whipped Cream In a chilled bowl beat 1 cup whipping cream, 1 Tbsp. bourbon, and 2 tsp. sugar until soft peaks form.
EACH SERVING *433 cal, 26 g fat, 102 mg chol, 482 mg sodium, 44 g carb, 3 g fiber, 7 g pro.*

KID FRIENDLY

Buttermilk Cardamom Pumpkin Pie

Silky texture. A flurry of sweet spice. One elegant update.
PREP 40 min. BAKE 45 min.

- 1 recipe Baked Piecrust, page 279
- 1 cup plus 2 Tbsp. sugar
- 1¼ tsp. ground cardamom
- 3 Tbsp. all-purpose flour
- ¼ tsp. salt
- 1 15-oz. can pumpkin
- 3 eggs, lightly beaten
- ½ cup buttermilk
- 1 tsp. vanilla bean paste
- ¼ cup butter, melted

1. Prepare Baked Piecrust; set aside. Preheat oven to 350°F. In a small bowl combine 2 Tbsp. of the sugar and 1 tsp. of the cardamom; set aside. In a large bowl combine the remaining sugar, flour, salt, and the remaining cardamom; mix well. Add pumpkin; mix well. Add eggs; stir to combine.
2. In a small bowl combine buttermilk, vanilla bean paste, and melted butter. Add to pumpkin mixture, stirring just until combined. Pour pumpkin filling into piecrust; sprinkle with half the sugar mixture. Cover edges with foil. Bake 45 to 50 minutes or until edges are puffed and center appears set. Cool on a wire rack. Chill within 2 hours. Sprinkle with remaining sugar mixture. Makes 8 servings.
EACH SERVING *395 cal, 19 g fat, 106 mg chol, 371 mg sodium, 52 g carb, 2 g fiber, 6 g pro.*

Mexican Chocolate Pumpkin Pie

This pumpkin pie satisfies chocolate cravings and sneaks in some heat.
PREP 40 min. BAKE 1 hr.

- 1 recipe Baked Piecrust, page 279
- 1 3.1-oz. disc Mexican chocolate
- 2 Tbsp. butter
- ¾ cup packed brown sugar
- 1 tsp. pumpkin pie spice
- ¼ tsp. salt
- ¼ tsp. mild chili powder
- ⅛ tsp. cayenne pepper
- 1 15-oz. can pumpkin
- 4 eggs, lightly beaten
- 1 cup half-and-half or light cream
- 1 recipe Chocolate Ganache
  Grated chocolate (optional)
  Chili powder (optional)

1. Prepare Baked Piecrust; set aside. Preheat oven to 350°F. In a small saucepan heat chocolate and butter over medium-low heat, stirring constantly, just until melted; set aside to cool. In a large bowl combine brown sugar, pumpkin pie spice, salt, chili powder, and cayenne. Stir in pumpkin and eggs until combined. Gradually stir in half-and-half until combined.
2. Stir 1½ cups of the pumpkin filling into the cooled chocolate mixture. Pour into piecrust. Pour remaining pumpkin filling over chocolate layer. Cover edges with foil. Bake 60 minutes or until edges are puffed and center appears set. Cool on a wire rack. Chill within 2 hours. Spoon Chocolate Ganache over. Sprinkle with grated chocolate and chili powder. Makes 8 servings.
Chocolate Ganache In a small bowl place 3 oz. chopped semisweet chocolate and ¼ tsp. cinnamon. In a small saucepan bring ¼ cup whipping cream to simmering; pour over chocolate. Let stand 5 minutes. Stir until smooth.
EACH SERVING *491 cal, 28 g fat, 143 mg chol, 365 mg sodium, 57 g carb, 3 g fiber, 8 g pro.*

home cooking: bake it easy

Sweeten the holidays while shortening time in the kitchen. These desserts have smart tips built in to save time and make baking fuss-free.

KID FRIENDLY

Cornmeal Butter Cake with Pomegranate Sauce

Corn bread meets pound cake in a slightly sweet bundt.

PREP 15 min. BAKE 40 min.
COOL 15 min. COOK 35 min.

      2   cups all-purpose flour
    1½   cups sugar
      ½   cup white cornmeal
      2   tsp. baking powder
      ½   tsp. baking soda
      ½   tsp. salt
      4   eggs
    1½   cups buttermilk (no substitutes)
      1   cup butter, melted (2 sticks)
      1   recipe Pomegranate Sauce

1. Preheat oven to 350°F. Grease and flour a 10-inch fluted tube pan; set aside. In a large bowl whisk together flour, sugar, cornmeal, baking powder, baking soda, and salt. Add eggs, buttermilk, and butter. Whisk to combine. Pour into prepared pan.
2. Bake 40 minutes or until a toothpick inserted near center comes out clean. Cool in pan on a wire rack 15 minutes. Remove from pan; cool completely. Spoon Pomegranate Sauce over cake. Makes 12 servings.
Pomegranate Sauce In a medium saucepan combine 2 cups pomegranate juice, ½ cup sugar, and 2 Tbsp. lemon juice. Bring to boiling; reduce heat. Simmer, uncovered, 35 to 40 minutes or until thickened, stirring occasionally. Remove from heat. Stir in 1 cup pomegranate seeds. Cool.
EACH SERVING *434 cal, 18 g fat, 105 mg chol, 412 mg sodium, 64 g carb, 0 g fiber, 6 g pro.*

why it's easy Just whisk, pour in the pan, and bake. This cake has lovely tender texture that marries well with deep red pomegranate sauce.

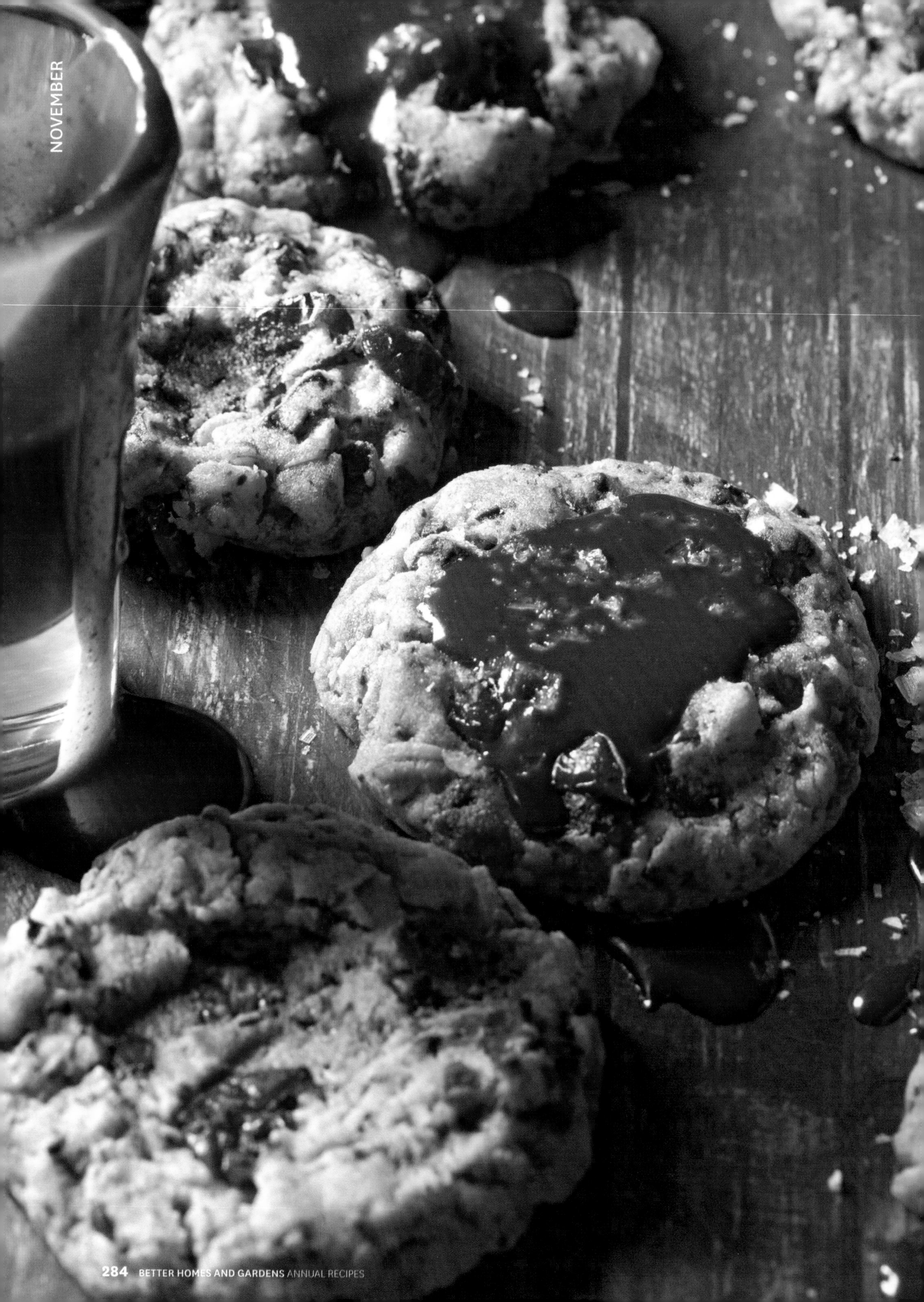

why it's easy No fancy cutting or shaping. Indent with your thumb to hold a pool of creamy ganache.

Bourbon Cranberry Chippers

A sprinkle of sea salt is a nice contrast to the sweetness of this cookie. Dried cherries would be equally delicious in place of the cranberries.

PREP **30 min.** STAND **1 hr.**
BAKE **8 min.** COOL **2 min.**

- 1 cup dried cranberries
- ¼ cup bourbon
- 1 cup butter, softened (2 sticks)
- 1 cup packed brown sugar
- ½ cup granulated sugar
- 1 egg
- 1 tsp. vanilla
- 2½ cups all-purpose flour
- 1 cup regular rolled oats
- 1 tsp. baking soda
- 8 oz. semisweet chocolate, chopped
- ½ cup macadamia nuts, chopped
- 1 recipe Bourbon Ganache
  Flaked or coarse sea salt (optional)

1. In a small bowl combine cranberries and bourbon. Cover; let stand 1 hour (do not drain).

2. Preheat oven to 375°F. Line cookie sheets with parchment; set aside. In a large bowl beat butter 30 seconds. Add sugars; beat until combined. Add egg and vanilla; beat until combined. Add flour, oats, and baking soda; beat until combined. Stir in chocolate, nuts, and cranberry-bourbon mixture.

3. Shape dough into 1½-inch balls. Arrange 2 inches apart on prepared cookie sheets. Using your thumb, indent the center of each ball. Bake 8 to 10 minutes or until lightly browned. Remove cookie sheet to a wire rack. If necessary, to reshape cookies using the rounded side of a teaspoon measure, repress indents and carefully press in edges. Cool 2 minutes. Remove cookies to wire rack; cool completely.

4. Spoon Bourbon Ganache into the indentations. Let stand until slightly firm or chill 10 to 15 minutes until firm. Sprinkle with salt, if desired. Makes 46 cookies.

Bourbon Ganache Place 1 cup semisweet chocolate pieces in a small heatproof bowl; set aside. In a small saucepan bring 1 cup whipping cream to a simmer. Pour over chocolate; let stand 5 minutes. Stir until smooth. Stir in 1 Tbsp. bourbon. Let stand 15 minutes to thicken slightly.

EACH COOKIE *176 cal, 10 g fat, 22 mg chol, 64 mg sodium, 21 g carb, 1 g fiber, 2 g pro.*

Make ahead Prepare through Step 3. Store in an airtight container in the freezer up to 3 months. To serve, prepare Bourbon Ganache. Remove cookies from freezer. Spoon ganache over. Thaw 30 to 45 minutes. (Ganache will set on chilled cookies as they thaw.)

why it's easy A crust of gingersnaps comes together fast in the food processor, and a filling bakes evenly without a water bath that is called for in most recipes.

KID FRIENDLY

Ginger-Cider Cheesecake

Creamy, thick cheesecake is brightened by a double dose of ginger—fresh and candied—in the filling. This cheesecake will get you out of the kitchen quickly, but it does take time to chill. Make it the night before so it has plenty of time to set.

PREP **45 min.** BAKE **45 min.**
COOL **45 min.** CHILL **3 hr.**

- 30 gingersnaps (7 oz.), plus more for topping
- ¼ cup butter, melted (½ stick)
- ½ cup plus 1 Tbsp. granulated sugar
- 3 8-oz. packages cream cheese, softened
- ½ cup packed brown sugar
- 3 Tbsp. all-purpose flour
- ½ cup apple cider
- 3 eggs, lightly beaten
- ¼ cup finely chopped candied ginger
- 2 Tbsp. grated fresh ginger
- 1 recipe Cranberry Glaze
  Fresh sage leaves (optional)

1. Preheat oven to 350°F. For crust, place the 30 gingersnaps in a food processor; process until fine. Add butter and the 1 Tbsp. granulated sugar; process until combined. Press mixture into bottom and 1½ inches up the side of a 9-inch springform pan; set aside.

2. For filling, in a large bowl beat cream cheese, the ½ cup granulated sugar, brown sugar, and flour with an electric mixer until smooth. Beat in cider just until combined. Stir in eggs, candied ginger, and fresh ginger. Pour into crust-lined pan. Arrange additional gingersnaps over top. Place on a rimmed baking sheet. Bake 45 to 50 minutes or until edges puff and center is nearly set.

3. Cool in pan on a wire rack 15 minutes. Use a knife to loosen cheesecake from sides of pan. Cool 30 minutes more. Remove sides of pan. Cool completely. Cover. Chill 3 to 4 hours before serving.

4. To serve, spoon Cranberry Glaze over cheesecake. Sprinkle with fresh sage leaves, if desired. Makes 12 servings.

Cranberry Glaze In a small saucepan combine 1 cup apple cider, 1 cup cranberries, and ¼ cup sugar. Bring to boiling, stirring to dissolve sugar; reduce heat. Boil gently, uncovered, 25 minutes or until syrupy. Cool.

EACH SERVING *462 cal, 27 g fat, 119 mg chol, 369 mg sodium, 51 g carb, 1 g fiber, 6 g pro.*

why it's easy Simple syrup (which you can make ahead) candies the clementines—and they make a beautiful impact. Frosting, icing, and decorating not required.

Clementine-Fig Spice Cakes

Candied clementine slices, sweet dried figs, and a hit of spice: These mini cakes are a forkful of fall flavors and a welcome gift, especially when wrapped in rum-soaked cheesecloth.

PREP 30 min. COOK 30 min.
BAKE 35 min. COOL 10 min.

- 3 clementines
- 3 cups sugar
- 1 cup dried figs, stemmed and finely chopped
- 2 cups all-purpose flour
- 2 tsp. apple pie spice
- 1 tsp. baking soda
- 1 tsp. salt
- 1 cup butter, melted (2 sticks)
- 3 eggs
- ½ cup milk
- 1 tsp. vanilla

1. Using a sharp paring knife, thinly slice clementines (do not peel). In a medium saucepan stir together 1½ cups of the sugar and ½ cup water. Bring just to boiling, stirring to dissolve sugar. Add clementine slices to syrup. Return to a simmer. Simmer, uncovered, 30 minutes, stirring occasionally. Remove slices. Set aside to cool, reserving syrup.

2. Preheat oven to 350°F. Grease six 10-oz. custard cups.* Arrange candied clementine slices in the bottom of each; set aside. In a medium microwave-safe bowl combine figs and ½ cup water. Cover with waxed paper. Microwave on high 3 minutes. Carefully remove bowl. Let stand 15 minutes (do not drain).

3. Meanwhile, in a large bowl whisk together flour, remaining sugar, spice, baking soda, and salt. Add butter, eggs, milk, and vanilla. Whisk to combine. Add figs and liquid; stir to combine. Add batter to prepared cups, filling each about three-quarters full. Place cups in a 15×10×1-inch baking pan.

4. Bake 35 minutes or until cakes spring back when lightly touched. Remove. Cool in cups on a wire rack 10 minutes. Loosen sides of cakes. Invert onto serving platter. Spoon reserved syrup over cakes. Serve warm. Makes 6 cakes.

*To use a jumbo muffin tin, grease 3-inch cups. Arrange clementine slices in bottom of each. Spoon batter over, filling cups about three-quarters full. Bake 25 minutes or until tops spring back when lightly touched. Cool in cups 10 minutes; remove. Serve as above.

For rum-soaked cakes Cool and wrap in 100%-cotton cheesecloth soaked in rum. Wrap in plastic wrap; chill up to 5 days. Unwrap and let stand 30 minutes (or wrap in paper towel and warm in microwave 30 seconds). Serve with syrup as directed.

EACH ½ CAKE *464 cal, 17 g fat, 88 mg chol, 445 mg sodium, 75 g carb, 2 g fiber, 5 g pro.*

Applelicious Sheet Cake

This anytime cake packs triple apple flavor: fresh, dried, and apple butter.
PREP 20 min. BAKE 40 min.

- 2 medium baking apples such as Honeycrisp, Braeburn, and Gala
- ⅓ cup butter, melted
- 1⅔ cups packed dark brown sugar
- 1 cup apple butter
- 2 eggs
- 2 tsp. vanilla
- 1⅔ cups all-purpose flour
- 1 tsp. baking powder
- 1 tsp. baking soda
- ¼ tsp. salt
- 1 cup finely chopped dried apples
- 1 recipe Maple Icing
  Ground cinnamon

1. Preheat oven to 350°F. Grease a 13×9×2-inch baking pan; set aside. Peel, core, and coarsely shred one apple using a box grater; thinly slice remaining apple in rounds, crosswise. Cover; set aside.

2. In a bowl whisk together butter, brown sugar, apple butter, eggs, and vanilla until smooth. Add flour, baking powder, baking soda, and salt; whisk to combine. Fold in dried and freshly shredded apple. Spread batter into prepared pan. Arrange apple slices over batter.

3. Bake 40 minutes or until golden and a toothpick inserted near center comes out clean. Remove to a wire rack. Pour Maple Icing over hot cake; spread evenly. Cool completely. Dust with cinnamon. Makes 24 servings.

Maple Icing In a small bowl stir together ½ cup powdered sugar, 1 Tbsp. melted butter, 1 Tbsp. maple syrup, 1 Tbsp. milk, and ¼ tsp. vanilla until smooth.

EACH SERVING *209 cal, 4 g fat, 24 mg chol, 141 mg sodium, 43 g carb, 1 g fiber, 2 g pro.*

why it's easy
The apple is quickly shredded with a box grater—no chopping necessary!

new ways with brussels sprouts

They're no longer a dinner sidekick. Cooked perfectly, they are the hero of the plate.

BUY AND STORE

The best sprouts are bright green with firm, compact leaves. The smaller the head, the more tender. Store in the fridge unwashed in a plastic bag up to 3 days. Before cooking, wash sprouts, trim the woody ends, and discard any with blemished leaves.

HIGH HEAT

Roast them, fry them, or eat them raw, but don't boil them. Boiling is the root of the veggies' bad rap—it saps all their natural nutty sweetness and leaves them mushy, a bit bitter, and tasting like overcooked cabbage. High heat makes them sweet!

BRUSSELS SPROUTS CHIPS

Trim ends of Brussels sprouts, then halve, and remove cores with your hands or a sharp paring knife. Place the leaves in a small bowl and toss with enough oil to lightly coat, then salt and pepper to taste. Spread on a baking sheet and roast 5 minutes at 400°F or until leaves are crispy.

Sprouts, Avocado, and Apples

START TO FINISH 40 min.

- 1 lb. Brussels sprouts
- ⅓ cup fresh lemon juice
- ⅓ cup extra-virgin olive oil
- ½ tsp. kosher salt
- ¼ tsp. black pepper
- 1 avocado, halved, seeded, peeled, and thinly sliced
- 1 Braeburn apple, cored and thinly sliced
- ½ cup roasted and salted pumpkin seeds (pepitas)
- 1 oz. Parmesan cheese, shaved

1. Trim about ¼ inch from stem ends of Brussels sprouts. Remove and discard any wilted outer leaves. Wash sprouts and pat dry. Peel away green outer leaves individually, leaving hard center cores (save cores for another use).

2. In a large bowl combine the lemon juice, olive oil, salt, and pepper, whisking to combine. Add Brussels sprouts leaves, avocado, apple, pumpkin seeds, and Parmesan cheese to the bowl; toss to combine. Makes 4 servings.

PER SERVING *450 cal, 39 g fat, 5 mg chol, 451 mg sodium, 18 g carb, 7 g fiber, 13 g pro.*

Cheesy Brussels Sprouts and Chorizo Bake

PREP 20 min. BAKE 30 min.
STAND 15 min.

- 1 lb. small Brussels sprouts, trimmed and quartered (2¾ cups)
- 8 oz. whole tiny new potatoes, thinly sliced (1¾ cups)
- 3 oz. cooked smoked chorizo sausage, thinly sliced
- 1 shallot, finely chopped
- 1 egg, lightly beaten
- 2 cups whipping cream
- ½ tsp. kosher salt
- 4 oz. Manchego cheese or Parmesan cheese, shredded (1 cup)

1. Preheat oven to 400°F. Divide sprouts, potatoes, chorizo, and shallot among four 12- to 14-oz. individual baking dishes.

2. In a medium bowl combine egg, cream, and salt; divide among dishes. Top each with cheese. Place the baking dishes in a 15×10×1-inch baking pan. Bake 30 minutes or until potatoes and sprouts are tender. Let stand 15 minutes before serving. Makes 4 servings.

PER SERVING *753 cal, 66 g fat, 258 mg chol, 963 mg sodium, 22 g carb, 5 g fiber, 21 g pro.*

Brussels Sprouts and Eggs Bucatini

Twirl up this hearty pasta for lunch or a light dinner. Toasted panko bread crumbs give the dish nice crunch.

START TO FINISH **35 min.**

- 6 oz. dried bucatini pasta
- 6 Tbsp. extra-virgin olive oil
- 1 cup panko bread crumbs
- 1 lb. Brussels sprouts, shredded (4 cups)
- ½ tsp. kosher salt
- 1 3.5-oz. jar capers, drained (⅓ cup)
- ⅓ cup snipped fresh Italian parsley
- ¼ tsp. crushed red pepper
- 6 hard-cooked eggs, peeled and coarsely chopped
  Olive oil (optional)
  Snipped fresh Italian parsley (optional)

1. Cook pasta according to package directions; drain, reserving ½ cup cooking water. Set pasta and water aside, covering to keep warm.
2. Meanwhile, heat 2 Tbsp. olive oil in an extra-large skillet over medium heat. Add panko; toast 5 to 7 minutes or until golden, stirring occasionally; remove from skillet and set aside.

3. Heat remaining olive oil in the skillet over medium-high heat. Add Brussels sprouts and salt. Cook, stirring occasionally, 4 minutes or until tender and browned. Add capers, parsley, crushed red pepper, eggs, pasta, and pasta water; stir to combine and heat through. Transfer to a serving dish. Drizzle with additional olive oil and top with toasted bread crumbs and additional parsley, if desired. Makes 4 servings.

PER SERVING *556 cal, 30 g fat, 280 mg chol, 736 mg sodium, 53 g carb, 6 g fiber, 21 g pro.*

Sprouts and Cherry Toasties

START TO FINISH 30 min.

6 oz. applewood smoked bacon, cut into 1½-inch pieces
1 lb. Brussels sprouts, trimmed and halved or quartered
½ tsp. kosher salt
4 slices rustic wheat bread, toasted
¾ cup ricotta cheese
½ cup cherry jam
   Fresh thyme (optional)

1. Cook bacon in an extra-large skillet over medium heat until crisp; remove from pan and drain on paper towels. Reserve 3 Tbsp. bacon drippings in the skillet; discard remaining drippings. Cook Brussels sprouts with kosher salt in the reserved drippings over medium heat for 7 to 8 minutes or until tender, stirring occasionally. Remove skillet from heat and stir in reserved bacon.
2. Spread each slice of bread with one-fourth of the ricotta and the cherry jam. Top each with Brussels sprouts and, if desired, thyme. Makes 4 servings.
PER SERVING *545 cal, 23 g fat, 46 mg chol, 841 mg sodium, 67 g carb, 7 g fiber, 19 g pro.*

CINNAMON-SPICE
ROLLS WITH
VANILLA ICING

december

celebrate Savor and share the aromas, tastes, and textures of foods distinctive to the season.

303

310

317

a toast to the roast

Chef Scott Peacock cooks up celebratory stunners. Roast beef and pork loin, stuffed chicken or brisket—we salute you!

KID FRIENDLY

Rosemary Olive Roast Beef

Garlic Rosemary Olives spooned over the roast just before serving add a punch of briny intensity to what Chef Scott Peacock describes as "very serious beef."

PREP **30 min.** ROAST **1 hr., 30 min.** STAND **15 min.**

- 1 3½- to 4-lb. beef sirloin tip roast
- 2 Tbsp. chopped fresh rosemary
- 1 Tbsp. kosher salt
- 2 tsp. freshly ground black pepper
- 2 Tbsp. olive oil
  Garlic Rosemary Olives

1. Preheat oven to 350°F. Season beef all over with rosemary, salt, and pepper. In a 12-inch skillet heat oil over medium-high heat. Add roast to skillet; brown well on all sides. Transfer to a rack set in a roasting pan. Roast 1 hour and 30 minutes to 1 hour and 45 minutes or until 135°F. Remove from oven. Transfer to a cutting board. Cover. Let stand 15 minutes. Serve with Garlic Rosemary Olives. Makes 8 to 10 servings.

Garlic Rosemary Olives In a large skillet warm 1½ cups pitted mixed olives; 5 cloves peeled, halved garlic; 3 Tbsp. olive oil; 3 sprigs fresh rosemary; and 3 sprigs fresh thyme over medium heat for 3 to 5 minutes until warmed through, swirling occasionally to avoid browning garlic. Season with kosher salt, black pepper, and ¼ tsp. Aleppo pepper. Cook 1 minute more. Spoon warm over roast.

EACH SERVING *483 cal, 34 g fat, 146 mg chol, 703 mg sodium, 3 g carb, 1 g fiber, 41 g pro.*

"Roasts are deeply flavorful moments on the plate, and each side dish is a refreshing complement. You take a bite of the roast, then the side, and the flavors start all over again."

ROSEMARY OLIVE
ROAST BEEF

CARROT AND PARSNIP
SWIRL
Recipe on page 300

Carrot and Parsnip Swirl

Photo on page 299

To concentrate the deep sweetness of root vegetables, Scott cooks them without adding liquid. Stirring is essential to prevent them from caramelizing, so stay nearby to give them a toss every few minutes.
PREP **30 min.** COOK **35 min.**

- ½ cup butter
- 2 lb. thin parsnips, peeled and sliced ¼ inch thick
  Kosher salt
- 2 lb. carrots, peeled and sliced ¼ inch thick
- 8 oz. russet potatoes, peeled and sliced ¼ inch thick
- 1 leek, white with very small amount of light green, cut into ½-inch slices and washed
- 1¼ cups whipping cream
- ¼ tsp. freshly grated nutmeg
  Chives

1. In a large saucepan melt 3 Tbsp. of the butter over medium heat. Add parsnips; season with kosher salt. Reduce heat to low. Cook, covered, 35 to 45 minutes, stirring occasionally to prevent browning. In a separate saucepan repeat with 3 Tbsp. of the butter, carrots, potatoes, leek, and kosher salt.
2. Using an immersion blender or a food processor, puree parsnips with ¾ cup of the cream and 1 Tbsp. of the butter until smooth. Repeat with carrot-potato-leek, the remaining ½ cup cream, and remaining butter. Add additional cream to each mixture as needed. Season to taste with kosher salt and nutmeg. To serve, swirl mixtures together in a serving dish. Top with fresh snipped chives. Makes sixteen ½-cup servings.
EACH SERVING *165 cal, 13 g fat, 41 mg chol, 148 mg sodium, 12 g carb, 3 g fiber, 1 g pro.*

KID FRIENDLY

Pineapple-Glazed Pork Roast

To ensure the most flavor out of the brown sugar brine, look for a pork loin that has not been injected with saline solution.
PREP **35 min.** MARINATE **8 hr.**
ROAST **55 min.** STAND **10 min.**

- 8 cups cold water
- ½ cup kosher salt
- 4 fresh bay leaves
- ¼ cup packed brown sugar
- 1 3½- to 4-lb. center cut pork loin
- 2 Tbsp. olive oil
- 1 Tbsp. butter
- ½ cup grainy mustard
- ½ cup packed brown sugar
- 1 large ripe pineapple, peeled, cored, and cut into chunks (5 cups)
  Aleppo pepper

1. In a large pot stir together water, salt, bay leaves, and the ¼ cup brown sugar until dissolved. Add pork. Cover and chill at least 8 hours or up to 48 hours.
2. Preheat oven to 425°F. Remove pork from brine; discard liquid and reserve bay leaves. Pat pork dry. In an extra-large skillet heat oil and butter over medium heat. Add pork; brown well on all sides. Transfer to a foil-lined roasting pan. Spread pork all over with mustard. Pat the ½ cup brown sugar evenly over pork. Spoon pineapple over. Sprinkle with Aleppo pepper.
3. Roast 15 minutes. Reduce heat to 350°F. Roast 40 to 50 minutes more or until done (145°F), basting once and adding bay leaves after 30 minutes. Transfer roast to a cutting board. Cover. Let stand 10 minutes before slicing. Spoon pan juices over. Makes 10 to 12 servings.
EACH SERVING *379 cal, 17 g fat, 112 mg chol, 517 mg sodium, 21 g carb, 1 g fiber, 33 g pro.*

FAST

Whole-Leaf Endive Salad

"The takeaway here is to use the tender inner leaves of a head of lettuce," Scott says. "It's astonishing how long they remain intact, even once they're dressed."
START TO FINISH **30 min.**

- 2 cloves garlic, halved
- 1 tsp. kosher salt
- ¼ cup red wine vinegar
- 1 tsp. honey
- 1 tsp. Dijon-style mustard
- ¼ tsp. freshly ground black pepper
- ¾ cup olive oil
- ¼ cup chopped curly parsley
- 1 head radicchio, separated into leaves (5 cups)
- 1 head Bibb lettuce, firm inner leaves only (5 cups)
- 1 to 2 heads Belgian endive, separated into leaves (2½ cups)
- 1 bunch arugula (2 cups)
- 1 bunch curly parsley, leaves and tender parts only (2 cups)

1. For dressing, place garlic on cutting board. Sprinkle with salt; coarsely chop. Rub to a paste with the side of a chef's knife. Transfer to a small bowl; whisk in vinegar. Let stand 15 minutes. Whisk in honey, mustard, and black pepper. Gradually whisk in oil. Stir in chopped parsley.
2. In a large serving bowl arrange whole leaves of radicchio, lettuce, endive, arugula, and parsley sprigs. Drizzle with dressing. Makes eight ½-cup servings.
EACH SERVING *205 cal, 21 g fat, 0 mg chol, 177 mg sodium, 5 g carb, 2 g fiber, 2 g pro.*

WHOLE-LEAF
ENDIVE SALAD

PINEAPPLE-GLAZED
PORK ROAST

**HARVEST WILD
RICE SALAD**
Recipe on page 305

**STUFFED
CHICKEN
ROAST**

Wrapped in bacon and stuffed with spicy sausage, port-soaked cherries, and spinach, ordinary chicken breasts transform into an elegant holiday roast. Serve with the fruit-strewn wild rice salad, it's a meal of familiar ingredients made extra-special.

KID FRIENDLY

Stuffed Chicken Roast

This is a get-to-know-your-butcher recipe. Ask for whole, or unsplit, chicken breasts. They tend to be large these days, so keep a close eye on total weight—about 3 pounds.

PREP **1 hr.** ROAST **1 hr., 45 min.** STAND **10 min.**

¾ cup ruby port
½ cup dried tart red cherries
¼ cup sugar
½ lb. hot Italian sausage, casing removed if present
1 Tbsp. butter
½ cup chopped onion
5 oz. fresh baby spinach
2¼ oz. provolone cheese, cut into ½-inch cubes
¼ cup soft bread crumbs
2 Tbsp. chopped curly parsley
2 whole skinless, boneless chicken breasts (about 3 lb.)
12 slices thick-cut bacon (1 lb.)
Kosher salt and black pepper

1. In a small saucepan combine port, cherries, and sugar. Bring to boiling, stirring constantly to dissolve sugar. Reduce heat. Simmer, uncovered, 10 minutes. Remove from heat. Cool completely (or cover and chill overnight). Drain cherries. Reserve port sauce. Transfer cherries to a large bowl.
2. Preheat oven to 400°F. In a large skillet cook sausage over medium heat until browned, stirring to break up pieces. Remove sausage from skillet, reserving drippings. Add to bowl with cherries. Add butter and onion to skillet; cook and stir until tender, about 5 minutes. Gradually add spinach;

cook and stir until wilted. Transfer to a colander set over a bowl. Press out liquid with the back of a spoon; discard liquid. Coarsely snip spinach mixture; add to bowl with cherries and sausage. Add cheese, bread crumbs, and parsley; stir to combine. Set aside.
3. Pound chicken between two pieces of plastic wrap to an even ½-inch thickness. Set aside. On two pieces of plastic wrap overlapped to form one large sheet, vertically lay six 18-inch pieces of kitchen string at 2-inch intervals. Weave a 24-inch piece of kitchen string crosswise, along the center. Lay bacon strips at a slight diagonal across string, overlapping slices. Evenly arrange chicken on bacon, leaving a 1½-inch bacon border at the top and bottom, overlapping chicken pieces as needed to create a rectangle. Press to make even thickness. Sprinkle with kosher salt and black pepper. Spread sausage mixture across center of chicken. Using the plastic wrap, quickly lift and fold chicken and bacon over filling. Tuck chicken and bacon under opposite side to form a roll. Using plastic wrap, turn seam side up. Pull plastic wrap away, then tie strings to form a tight roll, tying the horizontal string last. Add string and toothpicks to secure where necessary.
4. Line a roasting pan with foil; add rack. Transfer roast, seam side down, to rack. Roast 1¾ hours or until done in center (165°F). Transfer roast to a cutting board. Let stand 10 minutes before slicing. Serve with reserved port sauce. Makes 10 to 12 servings.
EACH SERVING *486 cal, 23 g fat, 139 mg chol, 692 mg sodium, 17 g carb, 1 g fiber, 39 g pro.*

FOLD, DON'T ROLL

The bacon, chicken, and filling create a lot of moving parts. Use the plastic wrap to fold the roll, then tuck and squish things as needed while tying and shaping the roast. This is a move to make without hesitation. Fold confidently! Add string and toothpicks to secure weak spots. Keep in mind the underbelly of the roast will go largely unseen. There are few things a crust of browned bacon can't hide.

"This roast can be assembled up to a day ahead, cooked before guests arrive, and served at room temperature," Scott says.

LOW FAT

Harvest Wild Rice Salad

Photo on page 302

Next to the Stuffed Chicken Roast, this refreshing wild rice salad filled with oranges, apples, and pears, plus zippy watercress, is the duo of chicken and wild rice all grown up.

PREP 30 min. COOK 45 min. CHILL 1 hr.

1½ cups uncooked wild rice, rinsed and drained
4 cups water
  Kosher salt
1 recipe Orange Cider Dressing
4 navel oranges, peeled, sectioned, and cut into 1-inch pieces (1 cup)
2 medium stalks celery, bias-sliced ¼-inch thick
1 red apple, cored and coarsely chopped
1 pear, cored and coarsely chopped
1 cup coarsely chopped roasted, salted pistachios
2 cups watercress

1. Place rice, water, and 2 tsp. kosher salt in a large saucepan. Bring to boiling; reduce heat. Cover and simmer 45 to 50 minutes or until rice is tender. Drain well. Cool. Make Orange Cider Dressing. Add rice; toss to combine. Cover and chill at least 1 hour or up to 24 hours.
2. To serve, add oranges, celery, apple, pear, and pistachios to rice; stir to coat. Add watercress; toss lightly. Makes twenty-two ½-cup servings.
Orange Cider Dressing In a large nonreactive bowl combine ¼ cup cider vinegar, 2 Tbsp. finely chopped shallot, 1 tsp. kosher salt, and ½ tsp. freshly ground black pepper. Let stand 10 minutes. Whisk in 1 tsp. orange zest, 5 Tbsp. orange juice, 1 Tbsp. honey, and 1 tsp. Dijon-style mustard. Slowly whisk in ¼ cup extra-virgin olive oil. Season to taste with kosher salt.

EACH SERVING *120 cal, 5 g fat, 0 mg chol, 190 mg sodium, 16 g carb, 2 g fiber, 3 g pro.*

COOKED JUST RIGHT
Worried about doneness? There's no better way to ensure roasts are cooked than taking a temp. There are several models to choose from—dial oven-going meat thermometers, plus dial and digital instant-read thermometers.

SCOTT'S PANTRY
The chef shares his go-to ingredients:
Kosher Salt "Each brand of salt measures differently, so a pinch of one isn't the same as another," Scott says. "Find a salt you like, and use it exclusively to understand its weight in your hands and the way it imparts flavor."
Curly Parsley Sure, flat-leaf and curly leaf parsley are interchangeable when it comes to flavor, but they perform very differently in recipes. "Curly parsley has a larger surface area—its ridges and ripples add volume and texture," Scott says.
Dijon Mustard "Dijon has body, acidity, and plenty of depth," Scott says. "But overall, the flavor is grounding. In most recipes, its job is to provide balance. It should not be the loudest flavor, but the element that brings everything to a point."
Fresh Nutmeg A few dashes are enough to bring out the inherent nuttiness in root vegetables or cheese. A word of caution from Scott: "If you can't find whole nutmeg to grate fresh, just omit it from the recipe."

Tomato and Onion Brisket

Aside from the longer cooking time, the key to a tender brisket is adding the smallest possible amount of liquid. "It's very easy for a braise to become a boil," Scott says. "When liquid levels are right, flavor concentrates in the meat and sauce."

PREP 45 min. BAKE 3 hr., 15 min. STAND 15 min.

- 1 3½- to 4-lb. fresh beef brisket, trimmed of all but ¼ inch fat
- 1 Tbsp. olive oil
- 1 Tbsp. schmaltz (rendered chicken fat)
- 4 large onions, chopped (4 cups)
- 1 head garlic, broken into cloves, peeled, and halved
- 1 14½-oz. can diced tomatoes (undrained)
- 1 cup chicken stock or reduced-sodium chicken broth
- 1 cup dry white wine
- 4 fresh bay leaves
- 1 celery heart, halved lengthwise
- 1 Tbsp. tomato paste
   Curly parsley, torn
   Finely grated fresh horseradish
- 1 recipe Ginger Pickled Onions

1. Preheat oven to 325°F. Season beef with kosher salt and pepper. In a 12-inch skillet heat oil and schmaltz over medium-high heat. Add meat; brown well on both sides. Transfer to a 3-qt. baking dish. Set aside. Add onions and garlic to skillet; cook and stir until onions are translucent, about 5 minutes. Stir in tomatoes, stock, wine, bay leaves, celery heart, and tomato paste. Bring to boiling. Boil gently, uncovered, 2 to 3 minutes. Pour mixture around meat. Cover baking dish with parchment, then tightly with a double thickness of foil. Roast 3 to 3½ hours. Transfer roast to a cutting board. Cover. Let stand 15 minutes.

2. Skim fat from tomato mixture; discard bay leaves. Return baking dish to oven. Bake 10 minutes more or until sauce is thickened. Slice meat across the grain and serve with tomato mixture. Top with parsley and horseradish. Serve with Ginger Pickled Onions. Makes 10 to 12 servings.

Ginger Pickled Onions In a nonreactive saucepan combine 1 cup cider vinegar, ¾ cup packed light brown sugar, 1 tsp. kosher salt, and a 1½-inch piece of peeled, thinly sliced ginger. Bring to a rapid simmer, stirring occasionally until sugar is dissolved. Simmer, uncovered, 5 to 7 minutes or until syrupy. Add 1 thinly sliced red onion; simmer 1 minute more. Remove from heat. Cool completely.

EACH SERVING *583 cal, 36 g fat, 107 mg chol, 514 mg sodium, 30 g carb, 3 g fiber, 29 g pro.*

Sweet Root Vegetable Kugel

Find schmaltz, aka rendered chicken fat, near the meat counter at grocery stores or at well-stocked butcher shops. Whether you keep kosher or not, this silky, nutty-tasting fat is a delicious alternative to butter.

PREP 50 min. BAKE 1 hr., 15 min. STAND 15 min.

- 2 Tbsp. schmaltz (rendered chicken fat)
- 1 lb. rutabaga, peeled and cubed
   Kosher salt and black pepper
- ½ tsp. freshly grated nutmeg
- ½ medium butternut squash, peeled, seeded, quartered, and sliced (3 cups)
- 1 sweet potato, peeled, quartered, and sliced
- 1 large onion, chopped
- 1½ lb. Swiss chard, stems removed, leaves and stems chopped, separately

- 10 eggs
- ½ cup extra-virgin olive oil
- ½ cup chopped curly parsley
- ¼ cup crushed matzo
- ½ tsp. kosher salt
- ½ cup dried prunes, coarsely chopped

1. Preheat oven to 350°F. Line an 8-inch springform pan with parchment, allowing parchment to extend about 1 inch above the edge of the pan. Wrap foil tightly around outside of pan to prevent leaks. Set inside a shallow baking pan. Set pans aside.

2. In an extra-large skillet heat 1 Tbsp. of the schmaltz over medium heat. Add rutabaga; season with kosher salt, pepper, and nutmeg. Cook and stir 7 minutes or until tender. Add squash and sweet potato; cook 10 minutes more or until vegetables are tender, stirring frequently. Remove vegetables from skillet. Add remaining schmaltz to skillet. Add onion; cook and stir 4 to 5 minutes or until tender. Add chard leaves; cook 4 minutes more. Transfer to a colander; press out and discard liquid. Add chard stems to skillet; cook and stir 5 minutes or until tender.

3. In a large bowl whisk together eggs, oil, parsley, matzo, and ½ tsp. kosher salt until well combined.

4. Place chard mixture in the prepared pan. Top with half the rutabaga mixture, then prunes. Top with remaining rutabaga mixture. Carefully pour egg mixture over layers. Sprinkle with cooked stems. Bake 1 hour and 15 minutes or until set in the center (160ºF). Remove. Cool in pan 15 minutes. Remove foil and sides of pan. Peel away parchment. Serve warm or at room temperature. Makes 12 servings.

EACH SERVING *246 cal, 15 g fat, 157 mg chol, 341 mg sodium, 21 g carb, 4 g fiber, 8 g pro.*

SWEET ROOT VEGETABLE KUGEL

TOMATO AND ONION BRISKET

baked, sealed, delivered

Baking queen Dorie Greenspan baked and tested dozens of cookies to create a break-free collection of cookies for shipping. (She even dropped packed boxes!)

"One delicious vanilla dough gets tweaked with sugars, white chocolate, and spice to create four cookies that taste and ship great together."
Dorie Greenspan

Tips for a Crumble-Free Delivery

Find a Container Choose an airtight tin or box to ensure fresh delivery.

Add Cushion Divide the tin into small compartments with pieces of cardboard, then reduce shifting by filling gaps around cookies with crinkle paper.

Pick a Box and Stuffing Find a box that allows a 2- to 3-inch buffer of packing material between box and tin. Eco-friendly plain popped popcorn or packing peanuts will minimize rattling and breakage.

Pack Right First line the bottom of the box with a thick layer of popcorn or packing peanuts, place the tin on top, then add more popcorn or peanuts to fill. (Overfill slightly for a snug fit when sealing the box.) Seal all seams with plastic packaging tape to keep out moisture.

MORE FROM DORIE
Dorie has been called a "culinary guru" by *The New York Times*, has won six *James Beard and International Association of Culinary Professionals* awards, and has 10 cookbooks to her name, including her most recent, *Baking Chez Moi.*

Vanilla Cookie Dough

Use this dough as the base for an assortment of cookies. Make sure the butter has softened to room temperature. It should have lost its chill and be spreadable—30 minutes should do the trick.

START TO FINISH 15 min.

- 1 lb. butter, cut into chunks and softened
- 1⅓ cups sugar
- 1 tsp. salt
- 2 egg whites
- 1 Tbsp. vanilla
- 4 cups all-purpose flour

1. In an extra-large mixing bowl beat butter with an electric mixer on medium to high speed for 30 seconds. Add sugar and salt; beat on medium speed 3 minutes or until smooth and creamy. Add egg whites and vanilla; beat until combined. Gradually add flour, beating until combined. Divide dough into 4 portions. Cover each dough portion with plastic wrap until ready to use.

Double-Ginger Crumb Cookies

PREP 20 min. FREEZE 1 hr.
BAKE 14 min.

- 1 portion Vanilla Cookie Dough
- 1 tsp. grated fresh ginger
- ¼ cup all-purpose flour
- 2 Tbsp. sugar
- ¼ tsp. ground ginger
- ⅛ tsp. salt
- 2 Tbsp. cold butter, cut into small pieces

1. In a large bowl stir together dough and fresh ginger. Working between sheets of parchment paper, roll dough to ¼-inch thickness. Slide onto a cookie sheet. Freeze at least 1 hour or chill at least 3 hours.
2. For topping, in a bowl combine flour, sugar, ground ginger, and salt. Cut in butter until mixture just starts to cling together. Cover. Chill at least 1 hour.
3. Preheat oven to 350°F. Line cookie sheets with parchment; set aside.
4. Remove parchment paper from dough. Place dough on a lightly floured surface. Using a 2-inch round cutter, cut circles from dough. Arrange 1½ inches apart on prepared cookie sheets. Gather scraps, roll, chill until firm, and cut as above. Sprinkle topping over cutouts.
5. Bake 14 to 16 minutes or until golden. Cool on cookie sheets 5 minutes. Transfer cookies to wire racks to cool. Makes 15 cookies.
EACH COOKIE *131 cal, 8 g fat, 20 mg chol, 128 mg sodium, 14 g carb, 0 g fiber, 1 g pro.*

Vanilla Polka Dot Cookies

PREP 15 min. BAKE 16 min.

- ⅓ cup pearl sugar (Swedish sugar)
- 1 portion Vanilla Cookie Dough

1. Preheat oven to 350°F. Line cookie sheets with parchment paper. Place sugar in a small bowl.
2. Shape rounded teaspoons of dough into 1¼-inch balls. Roll in sugar to coat. Arrange 2 inches apart on prepared cookie sheets. Gently press each ball with bottom of a small glass.
3. Bake 16 to 18 minutes or until golden around edges and bottoms. Cool on cookie sheets 5 minutes. Transfer cookies to wire racks to cool. Makes about 20 cookies.
EACH COOKIE *95 cal, 5 g fat, 13 mg chol, 75 mg sodium, 12 g carb, 0 g fiber, 1 g pro.*

VANILLA POLKA DOTS COOKIES

DOUBLE-GINGER CRUMB COOKIES

Christmas Spice Cookies

PREP 20 min. FREEZE 1 hr.
BAKE 14 min.

- ½ tsp. ground cinnamon
- ¼ tsp. ground ginger
  Pinch ground cloves
  Pinch ground allspice
- 1 portion Vanilla Cookie Dough
- 4 tsp. white sanding sugar
- 4 tsp. turbinado sugar

1. In a large bowl stir together ¼ tsp. of the cinnamon, the ginger, cloves, and allspice. Add dough; stir to combine. Working between sheets of parchment paper, roll dough to ¼-inch thickness. Slide onto a cookie sheet. Freeze at least 1 hour or chill at least 3 hours.
2. Preheat oven to 350°F. Line cookie sheets with parchment paper; set aside. In a small bowl combine sugars and remaining cinnamon.
3. Remove parchment paper from dough. Place dough on a lightly floured surface. Using a 2-inch round cutter, cut circles from dough. Arrange 1½ inches apart on prepared cookie sheets. Gather scraps, roll, chill until firm, and cut as above. Sprinkle tops with sugar-cinnamon mixture.
4. Bake 14 to 16 minutes or until golden around edges and bottoms. Cool on cookie sheets 5 minutes. Transfer cookies to wire racks to cool. Makes 15 cookies.
EACH COOKIE *112 cal, 6 g fat, 16 mg chol, 95 mg sodium, 13 g carb, 0 g fiber, 1 g pro.*

White Chocolate-Poppy Seed Cookies

PREP 20 min. FREEZE 1 hr.
BAKE 14 min.

- 1 portion Vanilla Cookie Dough
- ⅓ cup finely chopped white baking pieces
- 1 Tbsp. poppy seeds
- ½ cup white chocolate baking pieces, melted

1. Place dough in a large bowl. Add chopped white baking pieces and poppy seeds; stir to combine. Working between sheets of parchment paper, roll dough to ¼-inch thickness. Slide onto a cookie sheet. Freeze at least 1 hour or chill at least 3 hours.
2. Preheat oven to 350°F. Line cookie sheets with parchment paper; set aside.
3. Remove parchment paper from dough. Place dough on a lightly floured surface. Using a 2-inch round cutter, cut circles from dough. Arrange 1½ inches apart on cookie sheets. Gather scraps, roll, chill until firm, and cut as above.
4. Bake 14 to 16 minutes or until golden around edges and bottoms. Cool on cookie sheets 5 minutes. Transfer cookies to wire racks to cool.
5. Spread tops of cooled cookies with melted white baking pieces. Sprinkle with additional poppy seeds. Chill 30 minutes or until chocolate sets. Makes 18 cookies.
EACH COOKIE *148 cal, 8 g fat, 14 mg chol, 94 mg sodium, 16 g carb, 0 g fiber, 1 g pro.*

WHITE CHOCOLATE-POPPY SEED COOKIES

CHRISTMAS SPICE COOKIES

This simple buttery dough is easy to work with and the cookies are nicely crisp—the perfect texture to ship, ensuring cookies arrive intact.

**SALTED LEMON ROLLS WITH
CREAM CHEESE ICING**
Recipe on page 315

home cooking: on a roll

Enjoy the merriest of mornings with homemade sweet rolls. All the work is done the night before, so it's just a quick pop in the oven while you lounge in your PJs.

**CRANBERRY-CHERRY
ROLLS WITH VANILLA ICING**
Recipe on page 315

CINNAMON-SPICE ROLLS WITH VANILLA ICING

The secret to light-as-air rolls? Potato! It adds moisture and structure without developing additional gluten, which can make rolls tough.

KID FRIENDLY

Christmas Rolls Dough

PREP 45 min. RISE 45 min.
CHILL 2 hr. STAND 30 min.
BAKE 20 min.

- 4 to 4½ cups all-purpose flour
- 1 package active dry yeast
- 1 cup milk
- 1 cup cooked, mashed potato*
- ⅓ cup butter, cut up
- ⅓ cup granulated sugar
- 1 tsp. salt
- 2 eggs
- ½ cup butter, softened
- 1 recipe Cranberry-Cherry, Salted Lemon, or Cinnamon-Spice Filling
- 1 recipe Vanilla or Cream Cheese Icing

1. In a large bowl combine 1½ cups of the flour and the yeast; set aside. In a medium saucepan heat and stir milk, mashed potato, the ⅓ cup butter, sugar, and salt just until warm (120°F to 130°F) and butter is almost melted; add to flour mixture along with eggs. Beat with an electric mixer on medium-low speed for 30 seconds, scraping sides of bowl constantly. Beat on high speed 3 minutes. Stir in as much remaining flour as you can.

2. Turn out dough onto a lightly floured surface. Knead in enough remaining flour to make a moderately soft dough that is smooth and elastic (3 to 5 minutes total kneading time). Shape into a ball. Place in a lightly greased bowl; turn once to grease surface of dough. Cover; let rise in a warm place until double in size (45 to 60 minutes).

3. Punch down dough; turn out onto a lightly floured surface. Cover; let rest 10 minutes. Meanwhile, lightly grease a 13×9-inch baking dish; set aside. Prepare filling.

4. Roll dough into an 18×12-inch rectangle. Spread the ½ cup butter over dough. Spread or sprinkle filling over, leaving 1 inch uncovered along one long side. Roll rectangle, starting from long side with filling. Pinch dough to seal seams.

5. Cut dough into 12 equal pieces. Arrange pieces, cut sides down, in prepared baking dish. Cover loosely with oiled plastic wrap. Chill at least 2 hours or up to 24 hours.

6. Let chilled rolls stand, covered, 30 minutes at room temperature. Preheat oven to 350°F. Uncover. Bake 30 to 35 minutes or until golden brown and done in center (200°F). Cool in dish on a wire rack 10 minutes. Drizzle with icing. Serve warm. Makes 12 rolls.

*Prick a 10-oz. unpeeled potato with a fork. Microwave on high 5 to 7 minutes or until tender. Halve, then scoop pulp into a bowl; discard skin. Mash potato.

EACH ROLL *522 cal, 15 g fat, 67 mg chol, 327 mg sodium, 92 g carb, 2 g fiber, 7 g pro.*

Cranberry-Cherry Filling Spread ⅓ cup cherry preserves and 1½ cups fresh or frozen cranberries over buttered dough.

Salted Lemon Filling Sprinkle ⅔ cup finely chopped preserved lemon (find at Middle Eastern markets or health food stores), ⅔ cup granulated sugar, and 2 tsp. finely shredded lemon peel over buttered dough. Sprinkle tops of baked, iced rolls with 1 tsp. coarse sea salt.

Cinnamon-Spice Filling Sprinkle 1 cup brown sugar, 2 Tbsp. ground cinnamon, 2 Tbsp. finely chopped crystallized ginger, and ½ tsp. fresh cracked black pepper over buttered dough.

Vanilla Icing In a bowl stir together 3 cups powdered sugar, 1 tsp. vanilla, and 4 to 5 Tbsp. milk until thick drizzling consistency.

Cream Cheese Icing In a bowl beat 4 oz. softened cream cheese, 2 Tbsp. softened butter, and 1 tsp. vanilla with a mixer on medium speed until light and fluffy. Gradually beat in 2¼ cups powdered sugar. Beat in 2 Tbsp. honey.

WATCH THE TEMP If the milk mixture heats beyond 130°F, the yeast might fail. Use a candy thermometer to check the temp, and watch for the point when the butter is almost melted.

LESS IS BEST Too much flour creates heavy, dense rolls. Start with the smallest amount listed, then gradually work in more as you knead. (You might not need any extra flour at all.)

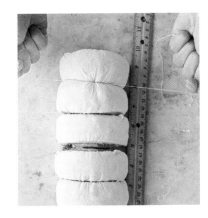

EASY CUT A ruler helps with an even cut. We slice the log using kitchen string because it doesn't squish the spiral. Place a loop of string around the log, then pull the ends in opposite directions.

new ways with pears

When the produce aisles are full of color, invite these autumn favorites to dinner.

CHECK THE NECK
The best way to check for ripeness is to gently press a thumb near the stem. If the fruit gives a little, it's ripe. Bartlett pears will change color when ripe, but for Anjou, Comice, Bosc, and Concorde, the color change is too subtle to rely on.

CHOICES, CHOICES
When you want pears that hold their shape in a recipe, choose firm varieties like Bosc, Anjou, or Concorde. Soft varieties, like Bartlett and Comice, are better for snacking, smoothies, or butters.

RIPE FOR PICKING
Under-ripe pears will begin to ripen at room temperature, and you can speed the process by putting them in a paper bag. Once ripe, store pears in the fridge up to 5 days.

Pear and Sweet Potato Soup

PREP 25 min. COOK 30 min.

- 2 Tbsp. butter
- 1 cup chopped onion
- 1 clove garlic, minced
- 4 medium pears, peeled, cored, and chopped (4 cups)
- 1 medium sweet potato, peeled and chopped (1½ cups)
- 1 medium russet potato, peeled and chopped (1 cup)
- 1 tsp. salt
- ½ tsp. chopped fresh thyme
- 4 cups reduced-sodium chicken broth
  Sautéed pear slices*, sour cream, fresh thyme sprigs, and/or cracked black pepper (optional)

1. In a large saucepan or Dutch oven melt butter over medium-low heat. Add onion and garlic; cook and stir 5 minutes or until tender. Add pears, potatoes, salt, and thyme. Cook and stir 3 minutes more. Stir in broth. Bring to boiling; reduce heat. Simmer, covered, 30 to 35 minutes or until tender. Using an immersion blender, blend until smooth. Season to taste.

Top with sauteed pear slices, a drizzle of sour cream, fresh thyme sprigs, and, if desired, cracked black pepper. Makes 6 servings.

*Sauteed Pear Slices Slice a pear vertically with the stem and core intact; remove seeds. In a large skillet cook slices in 1 Tbsp. hot butter over medium-high heat for 4 minutes or until golden brown, turning once. Drain slices on paper towels.

PER SERVING *168 cal, 4 g fat, 10 mg chol, 810 mg sodium, 31 g carb, 5 g fiber, 4 g pro.*

KID FRIENDLY

Roasted Pear Ham Melt

PREP 20 min. ROAST 45 min.

- 4 pears, cored and cut lengthwise into ½-inch slices
- 2 Tbsp. olive oil
- 8 ½-inch white bread slices
- ½ cup red pepper jelly
- 8 oz. thinly sliced ham
- 4 slices white cheddar cheese

1. Preheat oven to 425°F. In a large shallow baking pan toss pear slices with 2 Tbsp. olive oil. Roast 20 to 25 minutes or until very tender. Cool slightly.

2. Spread all bread slices with pepper jelly. Layer four of the bread slices with ham, roasted pear slices, and cheese. Top with remaining bread slices, spread sides down. Brush both sides of each sandwich with additional olive oil.

3. Heat a large skillet or griddle over medium heat. Cook sandwiches 2 to 3 minutes or until bottoms are golden and cheese is melted, turning once halfway through cooking. Makes 4 servings.

EACH SERVING *709 cal, 22 g fat, 54 mg chol, 1,286 mg sodium, 106 g carb, 9 g fiber, 24 g pro.*

FAST

Pear and Brussels Sprout Salad

START TO FINISH 30 min.

¼ cup olive oil
¼ cup balsamic vinegar
½ tsp. kosher salt
¼ tsp. cracked black pepper

2 cups baby spinach
4 oz. Brussels sprouts, trimmed and shredded (about 1 cup)
½ cup chopped pitted dates
½ cup walnuts, toasted and chopped (tip, page 106)
¼ cup shaved Parmesan cheese
4 medium pears, cored and thinly sliced
1 15-oz. can cannellini beans, rinsed and drained

1. For dressing, in a large serving bowl whisk together olive oil, vinegar, salt, and pepper.
2. Add spinach, Brussels sprouts, dates, walnuts, and Parmesan to bowl; toss to coat. Add pear slices and beans. Toss to combine. Makes 4 servings.

EACH SERVING 509 cal, 25 g fat, 4 mg chol, 485 mg sodium, 64 g carb, 14 g fiber, 12 g pro.

LOW FAT   FAST
Pear and Pork Stir-Fry
START TO FINISH 30 min.

¼ cup reduced-sodium soy sauce
 2 Tbsp. honey
 1 Tbsp. rice vinegar
¼ tsp. crushed red pepper
 1 Tbsp. vegetable oil
 3 medium pears (1 lb.), cored and
    cut into 1- to 2-inch wedges
 1 Tbsp. grated fresh ginger

 1 lb. pork tenderloin, cut into
    ¼-inch thick slices
 1 small head radicchio, cored and
    coarsely chopped (2½ cups)
    Hot cooked rice (optional)
    Green onions, sliced diagonally

1. For sauce, in a small bowl stir together soy sauce, honey, vinegar, and crushed red pepper; set aside.
2. In a very large skillet or wok heat oil over medium heat. Add pears and ginger; cook 2 to 3 minutes until

starting to soften. Remove pear mixture from skillet. Add pork; cook 2 to 3 minutes or until slightly pink in center. Push pork from center of skillet. Stir sauce; add to skillet. Bring to boiling. Cook and stir until slightly thickened. Return pears to skillet; add radicchio and stir to coat and heat through. Serve over rice and top with green onion slices. Makes 4 servings.
EACH SERVING 291 cal, 7 g fat, 74 mg chol, 605 mg sodium, 31 g carb, 4 g fiber, 25 g pro.

Recipe Index

Nutrition information.

With each recipe, we give important nutrition information you can easily apply to your own needs. You'll find the calorie count of each serving and the amount, in grams, of fat, cholesterol, sodium, carbohydrates, fiber, and protein to help keep tabs on what you eat. To stay in line with the nutrition breakdown of each recipe, follow the suggested number of servings.

How we analyze.

The Better Homes and Gardens® Test Kitchen computer analyzes each recipe for the nutritional value of a single serving.

- The analysis does not include optional ingredients.

- We use the first serving size listed when a range is given. For example, When we say a recipe "Makes 4 to 6 servings," the nutrition information is based on 4 servings.

- When ingredient choices (such as butter or margarine) appear in a recipe, we use the first one mentioned for analysis. The ingredient order does not mean we prefer one ingredient over another.

- When milk and eggs are recipe ingredients, the analysis is calculated using 2 percent (reduced-fat) milk and large eggs.

What you need.

The dietary guidelines below suggest nutrient levels that moderately active adults should strive to eat each day. There is no real harm in going over or under these guidelines in any single day, but it is a good idea to aim for a balanced diet over time.

Calories: About 2,000

Total fat: Less than 65 grams

Saturated fat: Less than 20 grams

Cholesterol: Less than 300 milligrams

Carbohydrates: About 300 grams

Sodium: Less than 2,400 milligrams

Dietary fiber: 20 to 30 grams

Low Fat icon.

Certain recipes throughout the book have an icon above the recipe title that indicates the recipe is low fat. For a recipe to earn this icon, it must meet certain nutritional requirements. For a main dish, one serving should have 12 grams or less of fat per serving, one serving of a side dish should have 5 grams or less of fat, an appetizer serving should have 2 grams or less of fat, and cookies and desserts should have 2 grams or less of fat per serving. Occasionally the fat level will slightly exceed one of the recommended numbers, but typically they remain below the listed amounts.

Metric Information

The charts on this page provide a guide for converting measurements from the U.S. customary system, which is used throughout this book, to the metric system.

Product Differences

Most of the ingredients called for in the recipes in this book are available in most countries. However, some are known by different names. Here are some common U.S. American ingredients and their possible counterparts:

- Sugar (white) is granulated, fine granulated, or castor sugar.
- Powdered sugar is icing sugar.
- All-purpose flour is enriched, bleached, or unbleached white household flour. When self-rising flour is used in place of all-purpose flour in a recipe that calls for leavening, omit the leavening agent (baking soda or baking powder) and salt.
- Light-color corn syrup is golden syrup.
- Cornstarch is cornflour.
- Baking soda is bicarbonate of soda.
- Vanilla or vanilla extract is vanilla essence.
- Green, red, or yellow sweet peppers are capsicums or bell peppers.
- Golden raisins are sultanas.

Volume and Weight

The United States traditionally uses cup measures for liquid and solid ingredients. The chart below shows the approximate imperial and metric equivalents. If you are accustomed to weighing solid ingredients, the following approximate equivalents will be helpful.

- 1 cup butter, castor sugar, or rice = 8 ounces = ½ pound = 250 grams
- 1 cup flour = 4 ounces = ¼ pound = 125 grams
- 1 cup icing sugar = 5 ounces = 150 grams

Canadian and U.S. volume for a cup measure is 8 fluid ounces (237 ml), but the standard metric equivalent is 250 ml.

1 British imperial cup is 10 fluid ounces.

In Australia, 1 tablespoon equals 20 ml, and there are 4 teaspoons in the Australian tablespoon.

Spoon measures are used for small amounts of ingredients. Although the size of the tablespoon varies slightly in different countries, for practical purposes and for recipes in this book, a straight substitution is all that's necessary. Measurements made using cups or spoons always should be level unless stated otherwise.

Common Weight Range Replacements

Imperial / U.S.	Metric
½ ounce	15 g
1 ounce	25 g or 30 g
4 ounces (¼ pound)	115 g or 125 g
8 ounces (½ pound)	225 g or 250 g
16 ounces (1 pound)	450 g or 500 g
1¼ pounds	625 g
1½ pounds	750 g
2 pounds or 2¼ pounds	1,000 g or 1 Kg

Oven Temperature Equivalents

Fahrenheit Setting	Celsius Setting*	Gas Setting
300°F	150°C	Gas Mark 2 (very low)
325°F	160°C	Gas Mark 3 (low)
350°F	180°C	Gas Mark 4 (moderate)
375°F	190°C	Gas Mark 5 (moderate)
400°F	200°C	Gas Mark 6 (hot)
425°F	220°C	Gas Mark 7 (hot)
450°F	230°C	Gas Mark 8 (very hot)
475°F	240°C	Gas Mark 9 (very hot)
500°F	260°C	Gas Mark 10 (extremely hot)
Broil	Broil	Grill

*Electric and gas ovens may be calibrated using celsius. However, for an electric oven, increase celsius setting 10 to 20 degrees when cooking above 160°C. For convection or forced air ovens (gas or electric), lower the temperature setting 25°F/10°C when cooking at all heat levels.

Baking Pan Sizes

Imperial / U.S.	Metric
9×1½-inch round cake pan	22- or 23×4-cm (1.5 L)
9×1½-inch pie plate	22- or 23×4-cm (1 L)
8×8×2-inch square cake pan	20×5-cm (2 L)
9×9×2-inch square cake pan	22- or 23×4.5-cm (2.5 L)
11×7×1½-inch baking pan	28×17×4-cm (2 L)
2-quart rectangular baking pan	30×19×4.5-cm (3 L)
13×9×2-inch baking pan	34×22×4.5-cm (3.5 L)
15×10×1-inch jelly roll pan	40×25×2-cm
9×5×3-inch loaf pan	23×13×8-cm (2 L)
2-quart casserole	2 L

U.S. / Standard Metric Equivalents

⅛ teaspoon = 0.5 ml	
¼ teaspoon = 1 ml	
½ teaspoon = 2 ml	
1 teaspoon = 5 ml	
1 tablespoon = 15 ml	
2 tablespoons = 25 ml	
¼ cup = 2 fluid ounces = 50 ml	
⅓ cup = 3 fluid ounces = 75 ml	
½ cup = 4 fluid ounces = 125 ml	
⅔ cup = 5 fluid ounces = 150 ml	
¾ cup = 6 fluid ounces = 175 ml	
1 cup = 8 fluid ounces = 250 ml	
2 cups = 1 pint = 500 ml	
1 quart = 1 litre	